RECYCLING AND EXTENDED PRODUCER RESPONSIBILITY

T0360889

Recycling and Extended Producer Responsibility
The European Experience

RUI CUNHA MARQUES
University of Lisbon, Portugal

NUNO FERREIRA DA CRUZ,
London School of Economics and Political Science, UK

Routledge
Taylor & Francis Group

LONDON AND NEW YORK

First published 2015 by Ashgate Publishing

2 Park Square, Milton Park, Abingdon, Oxfordshire OX14 4RN
711 Third Avenue, New York, NY 10017

Routledge is an imprint of the Taylor & Francis Group, an informa business

First issued in paperback 2018

Copyright © 2015 Rui Cunha Marques and Nuno Ferreira da Cruz

Rui Cunha Marques and Nuno Ferreira da Cruz have asserted their right under the Copyright, Designs and Patents Act, 1988, to be identified as the authors of this work.

All rights reserved. No part of this book may be reprinted or reproduced or utilised in any form or by any electronic, mechanical, or other means, now known or hereafter invented, including photocopying and recording, or in any information storage or retrieval system, without permission in writing from the publishers.

Notice:
Product or corporate names may be trademarks or registered trademarks, and are used only for identification and explanation without intent to infringe.

British Library Cataloguing in Publication Data
A catalogue record for this book is available from the British Library

The Library of Congress has cataloged the printed edition as follows:
Marques, Rui Cunha.
  Recycling and extended producer responsibility : the European experience / by Rui Cunha Marques and Nuno Ferreira da Cruz.
    pages cm
  Includes bibliographical references and index.
  ISBN 978-1-4724-5081-4 (hardcover)
  1. Manufacturing processes–Waste minimization–
Europe. 2. Lean manufacturing–Europe. 3. Factory and trade waste–Europe.
4. Recycling (Waste, etc.)–Europe. I. Da Cruz, Nuno Ferreira. II. Title.
  TS169.M37 2015
  670–dc23

                                                                          2014049111

ISBN 978-1-4724-5081-4 (hbk)
ISBN 978-1-138-54687-5 (pbk)

Contents

List of Figures   *vii*
List of Tables   *xi*
Foreword by João Simão Pires   *xv*
Preface   *xvii*
Acknowledgements   *xxi*
Acronyms   *xxiii*

1	Introduction to Recycling	1
	The Waste Management Problem	1
	The European Approach to the Problem	3
	Waste Hierarchy	6
	Preliminary Remarks	9
2	The European Directive 94/62/EC on Packaging and Packaging Waste	13
	Recovery and Recycling Targets	13
	Extended Producer Responsibility	15
	Current European Panorama	19
3	Packaging Waste Recycling Systems	25
	Belgium	25
	France	33
	Germany	43
	Italy	54
	Portugal	63
	Romania	73
	United Kingdom	82
4	The Costs and Benefits of Recycling	97
	Financial Flows	97
	Environmental Impacts	103
	All Costs and Benefits	116

5   The Value-For-Money of Recycling   119
          Belgium   119
          France   130
          Italy   132
          Portugal   143
          Romania   154
          United Kingdom   157
          Summary of Findings   160

6   Conclusions   169
          Final Remarks   169
          Implications for European Policies   173
          Lessons-learned for Other Countries   175
          Future Avenues of Research   176

References   *179*
Index   *191*

List of Figures

1.1   Municipal waste generation and treatment in the EU-27   2
1.2   Waste hierarchy   7

2.1   Simplified illustration of the life-cycle of packaging waste   16
2.2   Example of an EPR scheme (household flow)   17
2.3   Municipal waste generation of European countries in 1996, 2004
      and 2012 (kg per capita)   19
2.4   Packaging waste recovery and recycling rates in 2011 and PPW
      Directive targets   21
2.5   Packaging waste generation in 2010 for the country case-studies
      (kg per capita)   22

3.1   Generation of municipal waste in Belgium (kg per capita)   32
3.2   Recycling rate of packaging waste by material in Belgium   33
3.3   Generation of municipal waste in France (kg per capita)   42
3.4   Recycling rate of packaging waste by material in France   43
3.5   Generation of municipal waste in Germany (kg per capita)   53
3.6   Recycling rate of packaging waste by material in Germany   54
3.7   Generation of municipal waste in Italy (kg per capita)   62
3.8   Recycling rate of packaging waste by material in Italy   63
3.9   Generation of municipal waste in Portugal (kg per capita)   72
3.10 Recycling rate of packaging waste by material in Portugal   73
3.11 Generation of municipal waste in Romania (kg per capita)   81
3.12 Recycling rate of packaging waste by material in Romania   82
3.13 Generation of municipal waste in the UK (kg per capita)   95
3.14 Recycling rate of packaging waste by material in the UK   96

4.1   System boundary defined for economic-financial and
      environmental analyses   98
4.2   The economic-financial benefits and costs of recycling   103
4.3   Comparison of benefits and costs of recycling   117

5.1   Cost coverage in Belgium considering the tons of packaging waste
      collected in 2010   119
5.2   Costs of the service per packaging waste stream in Belgium   121
5.3   LCIA contribution results of the "Recycling scenario" and the
      "Incineration scenario" in Belgium   124

5.4   Economic and environmental results achieved for Belgium
       with the Eco-costs2012 method per ton of packaging waste
       collected: a) with and b) without the economic and environmental
       opportunity costs   127
5.5   Economic and environmental results achieved for Belgium with the
       Stepwise2006 method per ton of packaging waste collected: a) with
       and b) without the economic and environmental opportunity costs   128
5.6   Economic and environmental results achieved for Belgium with the
       Ecovalue08 method per ton of packaging waste collected: a) with
       and b) without the economic and environmental opportunity costs   129
5.7   Cost coverage in France considering the tons of packaging waste
       collected in 2010   131
5.8   Costs of selective collection and sorting in France   132
5.9   Cost coverage in Italy considering the tons of packaging waste
       collected in 2010   133
5.10   Costs of the service per packaging waste stream in Italy   134
5.11   Economic and environmental results achieved for the Lombardia
       region with the Eco-costs2012 method per ton of packaging waste
       collected: a) with and b) without the economic and environmental
       opportunity costs   140
5.12   Economic and environmental results achieved for Lombardia
       region with the Stepwise2006 method per ton of packaging waste
       collected: a) with and b) without the economic and environmental
       opportunity costs   141
5.13   Economic and environmental results achieved for Lombardia
       region with the Ecovalue08 method per ton of packaging waste
       collected: a) with and b) without the economic and environmental
       opportunity costs   142
5.14   Cost coverage in Portugal considering the tons of packaging waste
       collected in 2010   143
5.15   Costs of the service per packaging waste stream in Portugal   144
5.16   LCIA contribution results of the "Recycling scenario" and the
       "Incineration scenario" in Portugal   148
5.17   Economic and environmental results achieved for Portugal
       with the Eco-costs2012 method per ton of packaging waste
       collected: a) with and b) without the economic and environmental
       opportunity costs   152
5.18   Economic and environmental results achieved for Portugal
       with the Stepwise2006 method per ton of packaging waste
       collected: a) with and b) without the economic and environmental
       opportunity costs   153

5.19   Economic and environmental results achieved for Portugal with
        the Ecovalue08 method per ton of packaging waste collected:
        a) with and b) without the economic and environmental
        opportunity costs   154
5.20   Cost coverage in Romania considering the tons of packaging waste
        collected in 2010   155
5.21   Costs of the service per packaging waste stream in Romania   156
5.22   Cost coverage for the curbside sort collection case-study (England)
        considering the tons of packaging waste collected in 2010   157
5.23   Cost coverage for the two-streams co-mingled collection case-
        study (England) considering the tons of packaging waste collected
        in 2010   158
5.24   Cost coverage for the single-stream co-mingled collection case-
        study (England) considering the tons of packaging waste collected
        in 2010   159

6.1   Cost coverage of the packaging waste management service per ton
        selectively collected in 2010 for Portugal, France, Belgium   170
6.2   Economic and environmental results achieved with the
        Ecocosts2012 method per ton of packaging waste selectively
        collected in each country   172

List of Tables

1.1   Examples of EU legislation on waste management and recovery   4

2.1   EU recycling and recovery targets by weight of packaging waste   14
2.2   Municipal waste generation and treatment in 2010 for the country
       case-studies (thousands of tons)   20
2.3   Packaging waste generation in 2010 for the country case-studies
       (thousands of tons)   22
2.4   Packaging waste recycling in 2010 for the country case-studies
       (thousands of tons)   23

3.1   Green Dot fees for 2010 in Belgium   28
3.2   Fixed contributions from 2010 in Belgium   29
3.3   FSLA in 2010 in Belgium   31
3.4   Generation of packaging waste by material in Belgium (thousands
       of tons)   32
3.5   Green Dot fees for 2010 in France   38
3.6   FSLA in 2010 in France   39
3.7   Values of the variables to calculate the 2010 FSLA per material
       in France   40
3.8   Additional support to French local authorities in 2010 (metals from
       incineration and composting)   40
3.9   Take-back prices in France according to the take-back scheme
       option and material (€/ton)   41
3.10   Generation of packaging waste by material in France (thousands
       of tons)   42
3.11   Operators of dual systems and market shares in the last quarter of
       2010 (%)   48
3.12   Green Dot fees for 2007 in Germany   51
3.13   Trademark fees *Der Grune Punkt* by material   51
3.14   Generation of packaging waste by material in Germany (thousands
       of tons)   53
3.15   Direct management by CONAI   56
3.16   License fees for 2010 in Italy   57
3.17   FSLA for steel in 2010 in Italy   59
3.18   FSLA for aluminum in 2010 in Italy   59
3.19   FSLA for glass in 2010 in Italy   59
3.20   FSLA for plastics in 2010 in Italy   60

3.21   FSLA for paper in 2010 in Italy   61
3.22   FSLA for aluminum recovered in MBT plants or from bottom ash
       of combustion plants in 2010 in Italy   61
3.23   Generation of packaging waste by material in Italy (thousands
       of tons)   62
3.24   Green Dot fees for 2010 in Portugal   69
3.25   FSLA in 2010 in Portugal   70
3.26   Complementary Report fee for 2010 in Portugal   71
3.27   Information and motivation fee for 2010 in Portugal   71
3.28   Generation of packaging waste by material in Portugal (thousands
       of tons)   72
3.29   Recycling/recovery objectives of packaging waste for required
       companies in Romania   75
3.30   National recycling/recovery objectives of packaging waste
       in Romania   75
3.31   Green Dot fees for 2010 in Romania   79
3.32   SLA in 2010 in Romania   80
3.33   Average take-back prices in Romania in 2010   80
3.34   Generation of packaging waste by material in Romania (thousands
       of tons)   81
3.35   Packaging recovery/recycling targets according to the Producer
       Responsibility Obligations Regulations   85
3.36   Recycling obligations of the economic operators in 2011   92
3.37   Annual registration fees in 2011   92
3.38   Annual membership fee bandings   94
3.39   Average PRN prices predicted for 2011   94
3.40   Generation of packaging waste by material in the UK (thousands
       of tons)   96

4.1   Variables used in the economic and financial analysis   102
4.2   Energy mix in 2010 for Belgium, Italy and Portugal   107
4.3   Inputs of waste sorting (weighted averages) for the year 2010   110
4.4   Recycling process and avoided product considered for Portugal
       and Belgium   112
4.5   Recycling process and avoided product considered for Italy   113
4.6   LCIA methods used for each valuation method   114

5.1   Environmental impacts incurred by the different packaging waste
       management operations per ton of packaging waste managed in
       2010 in Belgium   122
5.2   Total environmental impacts allocated to the "Recycling scenario"
       in Belgium   122
5.3   Total environmental impacts allocated to the "Incineration
       scenario" in Belgium   123

5.4   Environmental valuation for the "Recycling scenario" in
        Belgium (Eco-costs2012)   125
5.5   Environmental valuation for the "Incineration scenario" in
        Belgium (Eco-costs2012)   125
5.6   Environmental valuation for the "Recycling scenario" in
        Belgium (Stepwise2006)   126
5.7   Environmental valuation for the "Incineration scenario" in
        Belgium (Stepwise2006)   126
5.8   Environmental valuation for the "Recycling scenario" in
        Belgium (Ecovalue08)   126
5.9   Environmental valuation for the "Incineration scenario" in
        Belgium (Ecovalue08)   127
5.10   Environmental assessment of the management of one ton of
        selectively collected material in the Lombardia region
        (Eco-costs2012)   135
5.11   Environmental assessment of the management of one ton of
        selectively collected material in the Lombardia region (Stepwise2006)   135
5.12   Environmental assessment of the management of one ton of
        selectively collected material in the Lombardia region (Ecovalue08)   136
5.13   Environmental assessment of the avoided management of one ton of
        selectively collected material in the Lombardia region
        (Eco-costs2012)   136
5.14   Environmental assessment of the avoided management of one ton
        of selectively collected material in the Lombardia region
        (Stepwise2006)   137
5.15   Environmental assessment of the avoided management of one ton
        of selectively collected material in the Lombardia region
        (Ecovalue08)   137
5.16   Environmental assessment of the recovery activity for one ton of
        selectively collected material in the Lombardia region
        (Eco-costs2012)   138
5.17   Environmental assessment of the recovery activity for one ton of
        selectively collected material in the Lombardia region
        (Stepwise2006)   138
5.18   Environmental assessment of the recovery activity for one ton of
        selectively collected material in the Lombardia region (Ecovalue08)   138
5.19   Environmental impacts incurred by the different packaging waste
        management operations per ton of packaging waste managed in
        2010 in Portugal   146
5.20   Total environmental impacts allocated to the "Recycling scenario"
        in Portugal   147
5.21   Total environmental impacts allocated to the "Non-recycling
        scenario" in Portugal   147

5.22   Environmental valuation for the "Recycling scenario" in
       Portugal (Eco-costs2012)   149
5.23   Environmental valuation for the "Incineration scenario" in
       Portugal (Eco-costs2012)   149
5.24   Environmental valuation for the "Recycling scenario" in
       Portugal (Stepwise2006)   150
5.25   Environmental valuation for the "Incineration scenario" in
       Portugal (Stepwise2006)   150
5.26   Environmental valuation for the "Recycling scenario" in
       Portugal (Ecovalue08)   151
5.27   Environmental valuation for the "Incineration scenario" in
       Portugal (Ecovalue08)   151
5.28   The global and unit economic-financial costs and benefits of the
       Belgian packaging waste recycling system in 2010   161
5.29   The global and unit economic-financial costs and benefits of the
       French packaging waste recycling system in 2010 (this information
       refers to 20% of the French population)   161
5.30   The global and unit economic-financial costs and benefits of the
       Italian (Lombardia region) packaging waste recycling system
       in 2010   162
5.31   The global and unit economic-financial costs and benefits of the
       Portuguese packaging waste recycling system in 2010   162
5.32   Amendments to the FSLA for packaging waste management 100%
       costs coverage   163
5.33   Percentage of public money used to achieve break-even   163
5.34   Total environmental costs and benefits obtained with the
       Ecocosts2012 method   165
5.35   Total environmental costs and benefits obtained with the
       Stepwise2006 method   165
5.36   Total environmental costs and benefits obtained with the
       Ecovalue08 method   166

Foreword

The Municipal Solid Waste management sector has been facing several challenges and opportunities at a global scale: accelerated economic growth across emerging economies, increased concentration of a growing population in urban settings; increased environmental costs associated with traditional disposal methods; greater social concern and stakeholders' engagement in a society's environmental choices and policies; while in parallel, price pressures on primary non-renewable raw materials and new breakthroughs on waste management methods, technologies, institutions and regulatory frameworks have led to a renewed emphasis on recycling and overall resource efficiency.

In the case of packaging material, traditional market mechanisms, with few exceptions, have faced the obvious constraint of the market price of recyclables typically falling short of the costs of the necessary systems for selective collection and sorting. This has left policy makers worldwide with the notion that other economic and environmental benefits, such as the avoided costs of traditional collection and landfilling, are being left out of the overall cost-benefit analysis that should underpin waste management policy.

Against this background, *Recycling and Extended Producer Responsibility: The European Experience*, represents a very significant contribution to this field: for practitioners; researchers and policy makers.

In effect, the European Union, under the drive of its 1994 Directive on "Packaging and Packaging Waste," has been at the forefront internationally of the implementation of the "Extended Producer Responsibility Principle." Still, the way this has been implemented across different member states has presented significant variation. The comparative analysis of the experience in seven different European countries (Belgium, France, Germany, Italy, Portugal, Romania and the United Kingdom) provides great perspective and insight on some of the key common elements and possible distinctive features in the approaches adopted at the national level. These can be highly valuable to countries that are at an earlier stage of the implementation cycle.

Over a three year period the two leading authors of this book were deeply involved in the Project sponsored by the European Investment Bank under the acronym EIMPack ('Economic Impact of the Packaging and Packaging Waste Directive'). During that period, I enjoyed the personal privilege of exchanging views with the authors on both methodological aspects and on some of the key findings as they emerged from their extensive field work and quantitative analysis. I equally had the pleasure of being an avid consumer of the multiple working papers and articles that stemmed from this substantive research endeavor.

The book examines in detail the legal and institutional frameworks in these seven countries, describing sector structures, the existing logistic and financial flows in each system and the performance levels exhibited in each case. It equally introduces an overarching framework for an analysis and discussion of the costs and benefits of recycling, their nature (financial and non-financial) and how they are allocated in each instance across consumers, producers, waste management operators, local authorities and taxpayers.

This constitutes the stepping stone for an empirical "Value-for-Money" analysis of recycling across the European continent, one that will, hopefully, both inform future EU policy and inspire readers across other geographies who face similar challenges.

JOÃO SIMÃO PIRES

Economist, Católica Lisbon School of Business and Economics
Former Executive Board member at ERSAR—The Portuguese Water and Waste
Services Regulation Authority

Preface

The rise in the rate of waste generation over the last decades has had strong implications for the European waste management policy. Most of the changes regarding waste management operations were rule-driven (triggered by EU legislation). Concerning the specific case of waste from consumer goods, the Packaging and Packaging Waste (PPW) Directive (94/62/EC) stands out among the many rules and strategies. This EU law fixed challenging targets for the recovery and recycling rates of packaging waste to be attained by all member states. The particular case of packaging waste has been emphasized due to the escalating tipping fees, the environmental impacts of landfilling this type of material (e.g. a significant portion of packaging waste is non-biodegradable) and the possibility of using this waste as a resource (avoiding the consumption of raw materials).

An overriding value of the PPW Directive is the Extended Producer Responsibility (EPR) principle. According to it, all economic operators placing packaging onto the EU market are responsible for its proper management and recovery. However, in general, the collection and treatment of urban waste (from households and small businesses) is the responsibility of local authorities. Therefore, it is necessary to establish a system of financial compensations between the producers (i.e. the industry) and the waste management operators (i.e. the local authorities). In many EU member states, this EPR system is managed by the so called 'green dot' companies. Note that to pursue an 'enhanced environmental protection' and operationalize the recycling policy, EU local authorities had to undertake large investments in equipment, facilities and infrastructure (particularly the ones required to carry out the selective collection and sorting activities).

The purpose of this book is twofold. Firstly, by analyzing the legal and institutional schemas of several member states (for which the recycling systems are currently at different maturity stages) and accounting for all the costs and benefits of their local authorities due to selective collection and sorting, the book will provide an accurate illustration of how the EPR principle has been translated into practice. To accomplish this, the book attempts to provide answers to the following empirical questions: is the industry paying for the net financial cost of 'preparation for recycling' activities? If not, are at least the extra-costs arising from the recycling being recovered via the sale of sorted materials (i.e. by the market), or are they being supported by the consumer (i.e. by the industry which reflects its costs on the price of the products) or by citizens in general (i.e. through higher waste management fees or local taxes)?

Secondly, by monetizing the net environmental benefits attained with the recycling system in some of the member states under analysis and comparing the results with the financial-economic balance mentioned above, the book discusses the success and Value-for-Money (VfM) of the EU recycling policy. Therefore, the book also seeks to answer the following research question: what is the economic rate of return of the enhanced environmental protection achieved due to the fulfilment of the recovery and recycling targets?

Although the ultimate objective (the recovery and recycling targets prescribed in the PPW Directive) is similar for all member states, the institutional and operational strategies adopted to achieve the targets vary considerably from country to country. Considering this, the book looks into the institutional frameworks and recycling systems of seven member states, namely, Belgium, France, Germany, Italy, Portugal, Romania and the UK. As mentioned earlier, while these countries are currently at different stages of maturity, they are representative of the overall reality in Europe.

There are three main factors that sustain the relevance of this book. First, there were legal and institutional impacts resulting from the structuring of the recycling systems. Entities from the public and the private sectors had to develop and coordinate their efforts in order to create the proper legal framework and monitoring systems. The waste market structure in each member state was necessarily impacted by the new Waste Hierarchy (prevention, reuse, recycling, other types of recovery and disposal) imposed by EU Directives since new activities had to be carried out. Moreover, national and EU decision-makers had to address the potential conflicts among the legal and economic mechanisms devised by each country to respect both the operation of the single market and the environmental protection objectives. This dimension is addressed in the third chapter.

Second, there were financial impacts arising from the extra costs that were incurred by waste management operators (e.g. the costs involved with the selective collection and sorting of waste). The EPR principle embedded in the PPW Directive led to a complex situation where the industry (private sector) is responsible for an activity that is traditionally carried out by local authorities (public sector). The industry had, therefore, to reimburse waste management operators (local authorities) for the costs of managing packaging waste. The problem is that these costs are hard to determine and sometimes it is difficult to differentiate a "cost" from a "price." Whereas producers should not be responsible for the possible cost-inefficiencies of waste management operators, the spirit of the law is that they should be responsible for the true costs involved in the recovery of their waste. This dimension is mainly addressed in the fourth chapter.

And third, there were environmental impacts arising from the conservation of raw materials and the diversion of waste from landfills. Evidently, it is expected that the recycling of packaging waste will have a favorable balance between positive and negative environmental impacts. Accounting for these impacts is an extremely complex research topic as their magnitude is contingent upon several external factors and assumptions (this is also addressed in the fourth chapter). Having both the financial-economic and environmental costs and benefits balances, it is possible to discuss the degree of success of the EPR and Waste Hierarchy policies for packaging waste management (this is accomplished in the fifth chapter).

The two main authors of this book were actively involved in the EIMPack (Economic Impact of the Packaging and Packaging Waste Directive) Project which lasted for three years and ended in February 2014. Sponsored by the European Investment Bank (EIB) under the EIBURS (EIB University Research Sponsorship) Program, this major R&D Project was the basis of the current book. The nearly two dozen reports produced during the project with the collaboration of various researchers inform several chapters. For this reason, each chapter acknowledges the contributions of the pertinent contributors.

Recycling and Extended Producer Responsibility: The European Experience is useful both to academics and practitioners. Researchers need reliable empirical analyses that provide them with actual unit costs and benefits concerning the preparation for recycling activities. Practitioners and decision-makers from around the globe require *ex post* assessments of recycling policies and programs (to reassess their current strategies or to design their own brand new systems). Indeed, during the last decades, the waste sectors of countries throughout the world have been experiencing significant changes. Among the several international developments, the EU case is particularly interesting given the great efforts that have been undertaken in order to harmonize national legislations and enhance the environmental protection. The assertive, prescriptive, ambitious and wide-ranging EU approach to promote waste recovery (or, more specifically, to divert waste from landfills) finds no parallel elsewhere in the world. Therefore, this book is relevant at the EU level as a test to the recycling policies followed (both at the Community level and in each member state covered in the analysis) and at the international level as a body of knowledge for countries currently considering their options regarding the creation of recycling systems (especially in developing countries where waste management is becoming a serious concern—e.g. the cases of Brazil, India or China).

Acknowledgements

The authors are indebted to the EIMPack research team for their invaluable efforts in gathering all the necessary data and for their successful and professional contribution to the results and analysis reported in this book. Specifically, the work of Marta Cabral, Pedro Simões and Sandra Ferreira must be highlighted. We would also like to particularly acknowledge the contributions of EIMPack's consultants and colleagues from partnering academic institutions, namely: Francis Ongondo and Ian Williams (University of Southampton), Lucia Rigamonti and Mario Grosso (Politecnico di Milano), and Simon De Jaeger (Hubrussel and KULeuven).

The contents of this book were also significantly influenced by the exchanges between all the participants of EIMPack's workshops and conferences held in Lisbon during 2011–2013. We thank them for making this research endeavor so much richer and, ultimately, a vast success. Of particular importance were the participation of Antonio Massarutto, Emma Watkins, Marcos Montenegro, Kátia Campos, Sofia Ahlroth, Thomas Kinnaman and Vanya Veras. Moreover, the cascade of constructive criticism and comments collected at the many international venues where the project findings were showcased was greatly appreciated.

The current research would not have come about without the assistance and cooperation of EIMPack's institutional partners and other allied organizations. Above all, the support of Sociedade Ponto Verde (SPV, the Portuguese Green Dot Agency) in the person of João Letras, Luís Veiga Martins and Manuel Pássaro, the Entidade Reguladora dos Serviços de Águas e Resíduos (ERSAR, the Water and Waste Services Regulatory Authority) in the person of João Rosa, Filomena Lobo and Miguel Nunes, the Agência Portuguesa do Ambiente (APA, the Portuguese Environmental Agency) in the person of Ana Sofia Vaz, Cristina Caldeira and Isabel Andrade. The diligence of AMARSUL, LIPOR, VALORSUL and RECIPAC should also be mentioned.

Finally, this book has been carried out with the financial support of the European Investment Bank University Research Sponsorship (EIBURS) Programme. The guidance provided by Jean Tilly, EIMPack's project manager on behalf of the Bank, was crucial for the fruitful development of the project and, therefore, for the making of this book. The support of Luisa Ferreira and Rosa Mendoza was key to operationalize the project. It should be noted that the views expressed here are those of the authors and do not necessarily reflect the position of the Bank. Furthermore, although we cannot acknowledge enough the various contributions made by all the organizations and individuals mentioned above (and the many others that remain unnamed) any unsubstantiated opinions and/or outstanding errors are the sole responsibility of the authors.

Acronyms

ADEME	Agency for Environment and Energy Management
ANRSC	National Regulatory Authority for Municipal Services
APA	Portuguese Environmental Agency
BATNEC	Best Available Technologies Not Entailing Excessive Costs
BPEO	Best Practicable Environmental Option
CAC	Contributo Ambientale (CONAI Environmental Contribution)
CBA	Cost-benefit analysis
CED	Cumulative energy demand
CH4	Methane
CO2	Carbon dioxide
CONAI	Consorzio Nazionale Imballagi (Italy's National Packaging Consortium)
COPIDEC	Walloon Intermunicipal Companies for Waste Treatment
CTU	Comparative toxic unit
CWR	Controlled Waste Regulations
Defra	Department for Environment, Food and Rural Affairs
DGRNE	Waste Agency of the Walloon Ministry for Natural Resources and Environment
DKR	Deutsche Gesellschaft für Kreislaufwirtschaft und Rohstoffe mbH
DOC	Degradable Organic Carbon
DSD	Duales System Deutschland
EA	Environment Agency
EAP	Environmental Action Programme
EC	European Community
EEC	European Economic Community
EGF	Empresa Geral de Fomento
EIB	European Investment Bank
EIBURS	EIB University Research Sponsorship
EIMPack	Economic Impact of the Packaging and Packaging Waste Directive
EPCI	Intermunicipal Cooperation Agencies
EPA	Environmental Protection Agency
EPR	Extended Producer Responsibility
ERSAR	Water and Waste Services Regulation Authority
EU	European Union

FOD	First Order Decay
FSLA	Financial Support for Local Authorities
FU	Functional Unit
GD	Government Decision
GWP	Global warming potential
IBGE-BIM	Brussels' Institute for Environmental Management
IHK	Chambers of Industry and Commerce
IPC	Interregional Packaging Commission
IPCC	Intergovernmental Panel on Climate Change
IRAR	Regulatory Institute for Water and Waste
LCA	Life Cycle Assessment
LCC	Life Cycle Costing
LCI	Life Cycle Inventory
LCIA	Life Cycle Impact Assessment
LFG	Landfill Gas
LWP	Lightweight packaging
MBT	Mechanical biological treatment
MSW	Municipal Solid Waste
NIEA	Northern Ireland Environment Agency
NMVOC	Non-methane volatile organic compounds
NWRWMG	North West Region Waste Management Group
OVAM	Flemish Public Waste Agency
OECD	Organisation for Economic Co-operation and Development
PAYT	Pay as you throw
PEDMA	Disposal Plans for municipal waste
PERN	Packaging Export Recovery Note
PFI	Private Finance Initiative
PMD	Plastic bottles and flasks, metallic packaging and drinks cartons
PRO Europe	Packaging Recovery Organisation Europe
PPP	Public-Private Partnership
PPW	Packaging and Packaging Waste
PRN	Packaging Recovery Note
QALY	Quality Adjusted Life Year
REOM	Fee for municipal waste disposal
RCRA	Resource Conservation and Recovery Act
SEPA	Scottish Environment Protection Agency
SIRAPA	APA's Integrated System of Records
SIRER	Integrated System of Electronic Record of Waste
SIVU	Single Purpose Intermunicipal Association
SIVOM	Multiple Purpose Intermunicipal Association
SPV	Sociedade Ponto Verde
SWaMP2008	Southern Waste Management Partnership
TEOM	Tax on municipal waste disposal
UDP	Unitary Development Plan

UK	United Kingdom
US	United States
VfM	Value-for-Money
WACC	Weighted Average Cost of Capital
WCA	Waste Collection Authorities
WEEE	Waste Electrical and Electronic Equipment
WDA	Waste Disposal Authorities
WFD	Waste Framework Directive
WTP	Willingness to Pay

Chapter 1

Introduction to Recycling

The Waste Management Problem

According to the Waste Framework Directive (WFD) of the European Parliament and of the Council 2008/98/EC, "waste means any substance or object which the holder discards or intends or is required to discard." It is basically the same definition of the first European WFD from 1975 (75/442/EEC). In turn, municipal waste consists of waste collected by or on behalf of local authorities (and, occasionally, directly by the private sector not on behalf of municipalities). The majority of municipal waste is generated by households, although similar wastes from sources like small commercial businesses, offices, public institutions and municipal services may also be considered as such. The term "Municipal Solid Waste" (MSW) is often used to explicitly exclude wastewater from municipal sewage networks. However, definitions and terminology may well be among the very few things that have not been rapidly changing in the European Union (EU) waste management scene. In fact, the growth in waste generation in Europe posed difficult legal, technical, environmental, financial and social challenges to EU decision-makers.

The collection, treatment and disposal of municipal waste are crucial for the wellbeing of populations. Therefore, the delivery of these services within suitable quality levels is deemed "essential" within the EU. But despite its importance, municipal waste management is fairly complex even when compared to other waste streams, such as the ones arising from the industry flow (Walls, 2006; Lavee, 2007). Indeed, MSW management involves many tasks (different types of collection, transportation, sorting, storing, treatment, recovery and/or final disposal), origins of waste (households, small and medium-sized businesses, municipal facilities, etc.), types of material (food waste, plastic, metal, glass, paper, wood, electrical and electronic waste, etc.) and stakeholders (manufacturers, packers and fillers, retailers, local and national authorities, public and private waste management operators, and citizens/customers).

The other side of the coin of economic development is that it triggers new human consumption patterns that often result in an increase in waste generation. In Europe, this put added pressure on existing landfills and (illegal) open dumps and, in fact, the first main drivers of change in waste management policies and practices were environmental protection and human health issues. But if on the one hand many European countries were facing problems with landfill capacity, on the other hand waste incineration always caused great public contestation due to the inherent air emissions. This led the EU authorities to develop a wide-ranging approach to the problem.

Taking into account the latest years, it is reasonable to say that the EU-27 generates about 250 million tons of municipal waste per year. This corresponds to around 500 kg per capita (it peaked at 523 kg in 2007 and has been decreasing ever since mostly due to the economic crisis, being 492 kg per capita in 2012). Figure 1.1 provides a good illustration of the evolution of municipal waste generation and treatment in Europe. Although loose interpretations should be avoided (because waste generation rates and type of treatment may correlate with many economic and social factors), it seems that the EU policies have been effective in curbing municipal waste generation and diverting waste from landfills and incineration without energy recovery. It also seems that these policies have been somewhat successful in achieving relative decoupling (dissociating waste production from economic growth).

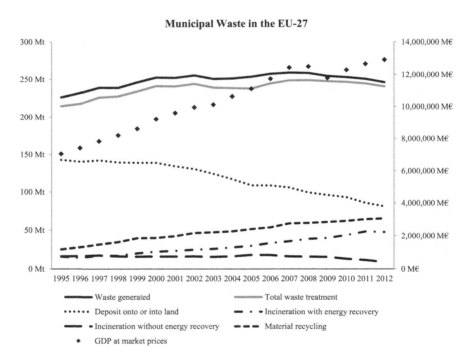

Figure 1.1   Municipal waste generation and treatment in the EU-27

Source: Eurostat

The above-mentioned environmental and human health concerns coupled with the drop in landfill capacity in more urbanized areas led to a new "waste hierarchy" which was introduced by the WFD. This policy sets out waste prevention as the most favorable option followed by reuse, recycling, energy recovery and, finally, disposal. Alongside this, a number of key principles became the basis of EU waste legislation, for instance: precaution, proximity, polluter pays and, quite notably, extended producer responsibility (EPR).

The European Approach to the Problem

The environment has been a matter of great concern in the EU over the last 40 years. One of the first steps of the European environmental policy was taken through the European Commission's Environmental Action Programme (EAP), which was originally introduced in November 1973. The first EAP was an important development, introducing basic principles, such as the polluter pays and the priority of preventing environmental damage at the source.

As argued above, the rise in the rate of waste generation over the last decades had strong implications in the European waste management policy (e.g. see Bailey, 1999). Actually, significant changes in the waste sector have been observed throughout the world. However, the EU case is particularly interesting when compared to other international developments, given the major effort to harmonize national policies and legislations while enhancing environmental protection (da Cruz et al. 2014a). In fact, the "significant changes" in waste management operations in Europe were driven by EU legislation which, in practice, dedicates special attention to diverting waste from landfills.

The harmonization of waste management policies is mainly intended to prevent any internal market distortions or barriers and unbalanced competition amongst the EU member states. Some years after the enactment of the first WFD (from 1975), the Directive on Hazardous Waste (91/689/EEC) established a definition for hazardous waste and its waste management framework. These two Directives and the Regulation on the Supervision and Control of Waste Shipment were the bedrock of the European legislation on waste (Hansen et al., 2002). Many other waste Directives were published after the WFD, setting guidelines and targets for specific waste streams. These included packaging waste, oils, batteries and accumulators, sewage sludge, end-of-life vehicles and electrical and electronic equipment. A set of Directives was also implemented to regulate waste treatment operations, such as landfilling and incineration of municipal and hazardous waste. Table 1.1 briefly reviews some of the main European Directives on waste management.

Indeed, the generalized drop in the availability of compliant landfills (especially in more densely urbanized areas), coupled with the growing volume of municipal waste led to a "revolution" in the EU waste legislation that started in the 1970s (Hansen et al., 2002; da Cruz et al. 2014b). In addition to the rise in landfill area at an accelerated rate, several member states were facing political and social opposition to waste incineration. Regarding municipal waste management, the specific approach to the packaging waste "problem" emerged naturally as the key concern of policy-makers. The share of packaging in municipal waste quantities, the environmental impacts of landfilling this type of material (a significant percentage of packaging waste is not biodegradable), the ever-increasing tipping fees (due to lack of landfill capacity and new environmental taxes), and the opportunity to use this waste as a resource (avoiding the consumption of raw material) made packaging waste management a key focus of European waste policies.

Table 1.1   Examples of EU legislation on waste management and recovery

EU legislation	Scope
WFD 75/442/EEC	Introduces the basic principles on the collection, recycling/processing and disposal of waste.
Directive 91/689/EEC on hazardous waste	Regulates the management of hazardous waste.
Directive 91/157/EEC on batteries and accumulators	Regulates the management of batteries and accumulators waste, imposing collection, recycling and recovery targets.
Council Regulation 259/93/EEC, on the supervision and control of shipments of waste within, into and out of the European Community	Regulates the export of waste out of the EU. The amendment banned hazardous waste destined for final disposal on non-OECD countries, and by January 1998 all exports of hazardous waste destined for recovery on non-OECD countries.
Directive 94/62/EC on packaging and packaging waste	Sets standards for the design of packaging and lays down specific targets for the recycling and recovery of packaging waste.
Directive 99/31/EC on the landfill of waste	Sets standards and limits for the emissions of pollution into the air or into groundwater
Directive 2000/52/EC on end-of-life vehicles	Sets rising re-use, recycling and recovery targets and restricts the use of hazardous substances in both new vehicles and replacement vehicle parts.
Directive 2000/76/EC on the incineration of waste	Sets standards and limits for the emissions of pollution into the air or into groundwater.
Directive 2002/96/EC on waste electrical and electronic	Lays down collection, recycling and recovery targets for electrical and electronic goods.

Forced to find new management strategies for packaging waste, Germany, the Netherlands, Denmark and Belgium were the first countries to define their respective policies and legal frameworks. The German Packaging Ordinance had special importance in this context and it was considered one of the key drivers for the development of the European packaging and packaging waste (PPW) Directive (Eichstadt et al., 2000).

The discussions regarding EU legislation on containers of liquids for human consumption had already commenced in 1975 with the aim of promoting the use of refill packaging. Nevertheless, the first real EU effort to tackle the packaging waste problem corresponds to a Directive on containers of liquids for human consumption, which was only published in 1985 (85/339/EEC). The objective was to encourage the adoption of measures to curb the environmental impacts of packaging waste disposal, and reduce the consumption of energy and raw materials. The member states were supposed to stimulate the reduction of packaging waste generation and the increase of the share of refillable and recyclable packaging in household waste (Eichstadt et al., 2000). However, it was too vague and ineffective in bringing about the harmonization of national policies and, therefore, diverging national legislation appeared in many member states.

As a consequence, only some member states introduced effective legal provisions on packaging waste management with the purpose of reducing its environmental impacts. This originated severe internal market distortions where cheap secondary materials from countries with subsidized recycling schemes appeared on the markets of other member states where no such funding for collection and/or recycling were in place. The economic sustainability of collection and recycling activities was seriously threatened in these countries.

In 1994, the Directive 94/62/EC on PPW was adopted under the article 100A of the Treaty of Rome which means that, in legal terms, it is a "harmonization Directive" and not an "environmental Directive" (Bongaerts and Kemp, 2000). The purpose of this Directive was twofold (da Cruz et al, 2014b): (1) reduce the impact of PPW management on the environment, and (2) harmonize national legislation on PPW to ensure the functioning of the internal market (concerning the free movement of both packaged goods and packaging waste). According to the PPW directive, packaging is defined as all products made of any material, whatever its nature, used to contain, protect, handle, deliver and present goods from the raw materials to the processed goods, from the producer to the final consumer or user. All disposable items used for the same purpose shall also be considered packaging. Furthermore, packaging was categorized as primary (designed to constitute a sales unit in the point of purchase), secondary (designed to group several sales unit) and tertiary (for transport purposes).

The PPW Directive set recycling and recovery targets to be attained by all member states. This piece of legislation corresponded to the main paradigm shift in EU municipal waste management. It was the main driver behind the establishment of the current "recycling systems" present in nearly all EU countries. Although other waste streams, such as batteries and accumulators, waste electrical and electronic equipment (WEEE), end-of-life vehicles were also addressed with a similarly assertive, prescriptive, ambitious and wide-ranging approach that emphasizes recovery, the prominence of packaging waste of day-to-day human activities places the PPW Directive at the core of European recycling efforts. Moreover, the complexity involved in "rescuing" this waste from the municipal circuits required major large-scale investments in new equipment, infrastructure, facilities and specialized personnel throughout Europe.

With the transposition of the PPW Directive to their national legal frameworks, the member states adopted and operationalized the EPR principle, meaning that the necessary provisions to meet the recycling and recovery targets were the responsibility of the industry itself (producers of packaging, packers, fillers, etc.). As stated in the Directive "it is essential that all those involved in the production, use, import and distribution of packaging and packaged products become more aware of the extent to which packaging becomes waste, and that in accordance with the polluter-pays principle they accept responsibility for such waste." To respect the EPR principle, each member state must, therefore, ensure that the industry is not just physically or financially responsible for the waste from the production process and the subsequent use of its products but also for its "end of life" (i.e. a cradle-to-grave or a whole life-cycle approach). The Directive 2004/12/EC amended the first PPW Directive, setting even more ambitious recycling and recovery targets for each packaging material.

Waste Hierarchy

Alongside the EPR principle, the waste hierarchy is also (to a certain extent) embedded in the PPW Directive. As previously mentioned, this concept was introduced by the WFD which became the cornerstone of all the subsequent EU waste legislation. According to it, the member states ought to focus on waste prevention and only then consider reuse, recycling, other types of recovery (mainly energy), per order of preference, where disposal operations, such as landfilling, should be considered as measures of last resort (see Figure 1.2).

Although prevention at the source is the main way to effectively decrease the amount of waste and reduce resource consumption (Jacobsen and Kristoffersen, 2002), with regard to packaging waste this is very difficult to accomplish in practice (because its generation is connected to economic development and consumption patterns, and packaging affects the life-cycle and logistic chain of consumer goods). Measures, such as avoiding or even eliminating certain packaging and/or reducing its weight, have as their main objective helping to produce less packaging waste.

Next, in line in the EU waste hierarchy, is reuse. The applicability of this strategy is higher for the case of transport packaging though it has also been broadly adopted for beverage packaging (Golding, 1999). Along with prevention and reduction, reuse is the only way of managing the end-of-life of packaging without generating waste. Some studies have been carried out trying to discern to

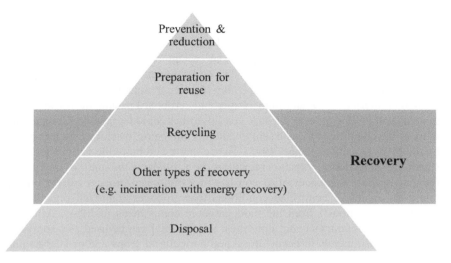

Figure 1.2   Waste hierarchy

Source: adapted from da Cruz and Marques (2014)

what extent reusable containers are preferable to one-way packaging. Although the results are mixed in absolute terms, there are some generally accepted conclusions on the reuse of packaging (COM, 2006). It is not reasonable to claim that reusable packaging is better for the environment than the one-way packaging in all situations. Note that transport distances between filling, consumption, collection and reuse have a great influence in terms of the net environmental impacts (PRO, 2008). In fact, one-way packaging can be better for the environment whenever distances are too long or the rates of return (of used packaging) are low for reusable packaging. Pira and Ecolas (2005) provide a brief description of success stories within the EU (namely, in Germany, Austria, Norway and the UK). However, this report also showed that the market share of non-reusable packaging was growing every year. The fact that the PPW Directive did not establish any targets for reuse rates is noteworthy in this respect.

Recycling in itself does not prevent the generation of packaging waste. Nevertheless, if recycling rates are relatively high, this strategy helps curbing the consumption of raw material. The recycling of trade and industry packaging waste does not present so many challenges (separation at the source is simpler), but the household flow requires the active participation of the populations so that an effective collection and efficient sorting of waste can be achieved. Nevertheless, the optimal recycling (and, therefore, separate collection and sorting) rates, or the ones that minimize the total social costs of packaging waste management (this topic is briefly revisited in Chapter 6), are contingent upon several social, economic, physical and infrastructural factors. This suggests that, from a, purely theoretical, social welfare point of view, each country (or even region) should have its own recycling target. Evidently, this would raise several other pragmatic problems (for example, in the EU, the functioning of the internal market). However, it is undeniable that, besides reducing natural resources consumption (together with other beneficial environmental impacts, see Chapters 4 and 5), higher recycling rates are also associated with lower refuse collection and treatment costs.

The "organic recycling" or composting (aerobic treatment) of municipal waste is another alternative to landfilling. Paper and cardboard packaging waste can be treated through this process because cellulose fiber is biodegradable. Composting reduces the quantities of waste sent to landfills and helps to achieve the targets set by the PPW Directive (Pagga, 1998). Hence, more and more the various member states are considering organic recycling as a fundamental part of integrated municipal waste management. It consists of a biological process carried out by micro-organisms in controlled conditions that produces stabilized organic soil conditioner (compost) from the biodegradable components of MSW. After the removal of contaminants and impurities, this material can be used as a source of nutrients and minerals in horticultural and agricultural crops and/or landscaping activities (Renkow and Rubin, 1998).

In addition to recycling, incineration with energy recovery of packaging waste is also a good alternative to landfilling because it allows using the waste as a resource and seize its energetic value. Some evidence even suggests that this strategy performs better than disposal in landfills, not just concerning opportunity costs but also environmental costs (Mazzanti and Zoboli, 2008). Yet, incineration must be strictly controlled to avoid harmful air emissions. The residues of incineration reduce the original bulk material up to 90 percent in volume and 70 percent by weight. This enables savings in transport costs and landfill requirements. The process also removes organic (biodegradable) waste components which prevents the generation of gas and leachate when the residues are landfilled. Recent studies have been emphasizing that the different waste management strategies should be considered together as integrated solutions and not as mutually exclusive alternatives. Both the incineration of waste (with energy recovery) and the recycling of packaging material are necessary to reduce the amounts sent to landfills and their coexistence makes sense from an economic perspective (Massarutto et al., 2011). In fact, the incineration of waste does not necessarily imply a decrease in recycling rates. Although, in theory, recycling is the most environmentally sound option, it does not allow for the recovery of energy (and it uses energy in the process), which seems to suggest that waste-to-energy should be seen as an important part of waste management strategies.

Whereas it is true that by setting ambitious recycling and recovery targets the PPW Directive aimed at reducing the environmental impacts of packaging waste while avoiding barriers to trade within the EU, the reinforcement of prevention and reuse was somehow limited (because no explicit targets were defined for this, regardless of whether or not this would be feasible). This is why one may state that the waste hierarchy is embedded in the Directive only to a certain extent. Indeed, the PPW Directive did not lead to a reversal of the trend towards one-way packaging and a reduction in packaging volumes, nor did it encourage more "green" packaging materials or promote the design of easier reuse and recycle packaging alternatives (Bongaerts and Kemp, 2000). The priority in most member states was to improve the quality and extent of selective collection since this influences the effectiveness and efficiency of the recycling systems. The prevention and reuse of packaging would require different legal instruments for packaging waste management (ARGUS, 2001). Nevertheless, this piece of legislation has had a major bearing on the EU, both concerning environmental protection (packaging waste recovery and recycling rose abruptly) and macro-economic impacts (e.g. all member states had to undertake high investments in selective collection as well as sorting equipment and infrastructure, which, in turn, gave rise to new recycling markets).

Preliminary Remarks

The municipal "waste management problem" (and packaging waste management in particular) is not exclusive to the EU. The same issues are present in most developed and developing countries from all world regions. However, the prescriptive and ambitious recovery and recycling EU targets common to all member states are unique in the world. For example, in the United States (US) the legal/institutional framework of recycling is handled at a state and local government level. The federal government does not impose targets applicable to all states. The Resource Conservation and Recovery Act (RCRA) was the main US law governing waste disposal (Vogel et al., 2010). Congress approved this law in 1976 to address the increasing problems regarding the growing volume of waste from both municipal and industrial flows.

The RCRA (which amended the Solid Waste Disposal Act from 1965) established national objectives to protect human health and the environment from the potential hazards of waste disposal, conserve energy and natural resources, reduce the amount of waste generated, and ensure that the waste is managed in an environmentally-sound manner (USEPA, 2011). Nonetheless, more prescriptive recycling agendas remain at the discretion of state and local governments because national laws do not allow the US Environmental Protection Agency (EPA) to establish such federal regulations (Vogel et al., 2010). Indeed, to avoid landfilling and incineration, several American states and local governments have developed their own programs, encouraging the recycling of various materials. To accomplish this, a few states banned packaging that is particularly difficult to recycle, such as aseptic drink boxes which are made of paper, foil and plastic layers (the case of Maine). In Connecticut, an analogous process occurred with plastic cans.

A federal executive order was issued in 1991 to increase the level of recycling and procurement of recycled-content products in the US. Afterwards, in 1993, another executive order required federal agencies to purchase paper products with at least 20 percent post-consumer fiber (this increased to 30 percent in 1998) and EPA was requested to create a list of environmentally-sound products. In sum, between 1989 and 2007, all attempts to pass nationwide laws regarding the recycling of beverage packaging were eventually unsuccessful. Nonetheless, the federal government did not prevent any state or local government from pursuing their own recycling strategies. Actually, it is noticeable that the dynamics of the regulation of packaging waste in the US are quite different from the ones in the EU. Whereas the US federal government enjoys far more authority over its states, the European environmental policy is currently more centralized and the EU has *de facto* power to impose recovery and recycling targets to all member states (Vogel et al., 2010).

The European approach, especially with the enactment of the PPW Directive, has had several major impacts. The countries that already had national policies for packaging waste recycling and recovery (e.g. the abovementioned cases of Germany, the Netherlands, Denmark and Belgium) did not experience so many abrupt changes in their waste management legal and institutional settings and the investments outlays required to establish the recycling systems were not so substantial, but these were a minority within the EU 27 (da Cruz et al., 2014b).

In fact, national authorities along with all relevant public and private stakeholders from the various member states had first to design institutional and information management arrangements that allowed them to respect the EPR principle in the pursuit of compliant recycling and recovery rates. Obviously, the market structure of municipal waste management was greatly affected by the PPW Directive, since selective collection and sorting activities had to be carried out to a larger extent. Furthermore, new monitoring mechanisms had to be implemented to control both the quantities of packaging placed onto the market and the quantities of packaging waste effectively recovered (for all the different materials, namely: plastic, paper and cardboard, metal, glass and wood). In the dynamic process of transposing the Directive into national law, some member states seized the opportunity and set more ambitious internal objectives regarding the recycling and recovery of packaging waste (although the PPW Directive sets a maximum for the recycling rates of the EU countries).

Along with the legal and institutional transformations also came major financial impacts. New (or more intensive) selective collection and sorting activities mean new (or higher) costs. In general, these "extra costs" were incurred by local authorities. Even when waste management is carried out by private entities, in Europe (and elsewhere), municipal waste management is usually the responsibility of local authorities. The fact that the extra costs are not directly borne by the industry leads to an immediate problem: the "spirit of the law" (i.e. the EPR principle embedded in the PPW Directive) is not automatically respected. Therefore, some "reimbursement system" must be established between the industry and the waste management operators (local authorities) concerning the costs of managing packaging waste. The difficulty here is that these costs are not evident and it can be difficult to distinguish a "true cost" from a "price" (da Cruz et al., 2012). In other words, being true that the PPW Directive requires the industry to accept responsibility for the recovery of its packaging waste, it is also true that it should not be made responsible for any cost-inefficiencies attributable to waste management operators (Marques et al., 2012).

The recycling and recovery obligations can be fulfilled individually, where each producer develops its own packaging waste management system (this would have to be approved by the respective National Waste Authority), or by delegating the responsibilities to an authorized company (again, licensed by the National Waste Authority). Virtually, all producers of municipal packaging waste in Europe join a "compliance scheme" and transfer their responsibility to another entity (e.g. a Green Dot company). The typical solution was the creation of non-profit Green Dot companies that have the mission of managing the logistic chain of packaging waste (ARGUS, 2001). In general, the scheme works as follows: the producers of packaged goods pay a financial contribution (e.g. contingent on the material, type and quantity of packaging) when placing their products onto the market and, in return, transfer away their responsibility to manage and recover the resulting packaging waste (and, in many cases, earn the right to place a Green Dot symbol on their packaging).

To coordinate these schemes and manage the licensing of the Green Dot trademark, PRO Europe (Packaging Recovery Organisation Europe) was founded in 1995. PRO Europe is the umbrella organization for most European PPW compliance schemes. The presence of the Green Dot symbol on packaging means that a financial contribution (i.e. a Green Dot fee) has been paid to an EPR compliance scheme licensed according to the principles set out in the PPW Directive and respective national laws. However, the absence of this symbol does not necessarily mean that a financial contribution has not been made. In some countries the marking is not mandatory (and it may entail an additional payment to the relevant Green Dot company).

Finally, some major (and positive) environmental impacts were also anticipated with the enactment of the PPW Directive and subsidiary EU waste legislation. With the significant increase in recycling rates (and less than proportional increase in consumption) it was possible to attain enhanced raw materials conservation and greater diversion of waste from landfills. Although "preparation for recycling" activities also entail some negative environmental impacts (e.g. due to the additional transport movements necessary for the selective collection of waste and the subsequent routing to sorting facilities and recycling centers, the energy necessary to process recyclables, etc.), it is expected that the benefits more than compensate for these. Though extremely complex, accounting for the net environmental impacts is a crucial endeavor if one desires to discuss the economic rate of return of the EU approach to recycling. Indeed, knowing the net results of both the environmental and financial-economic balances of the newly-developed recycling systems, it is possible to evaluate the degree of success of the EPR and waste hierarchy policies set out in Europe.

Performing an *ex post* assessment of the above-mentioned impacts within the EU is a topic of great importance for academics and policy-makers.

However, this objective denotes a quite complex research agenda that involves multidisciplinary empirical investigations (e.g. case-studies on the financial and environmental impacts using real data which is difficult to obtain). The financial costs and benefits of collecting, sorting, storing and recycling packaging waste need to be accurately estimated and allocated to the correct stakeholders. After this, for a credible cost-benefit analysis of the enhanced environmental protection achieved with recycling, the environmental externalities need to be factored in. Furthermore, all country case-studies must take into account the specificities and institutional features of the respective countries. The legislation enacted in each member state led to the adoption of different recycling models and strategies that must be considered when accounting for the economic-financial costs and benefits assumed by the local authorities in charge of municipal waste management (collection, treatment and disposal).

For that reason, the current book discusses in detail the recycling systems of seven member states. Among the seven case-studies there are two recycling "champions" (Belgium and Germany), four "compliant" countries (France, Italy, Portugal and the UK) and one "newcomer" (Romania). Two of these countries do not adopt a Green Dot scheme (Italy and the UK) and three have a competitive recycling market (Germany, the UK and Romania). Finally, four of these member states have implemented more ambitious recycling targets than the ones laid down in the PPW Directive (Belgium, France, Germany and the UK). In fact, the set of countries addressed in this book is quite representative of the European recycling scene. Chapter 3 will thoroughly describe the recycling systems of the seven member states. Comparing and contrasting the legal and institutional differences of these countries will provide a great resource for readers both from Europe and elsewhere.

Chapter 2

The European Directive 94/62/EC on Packaging and Packaging Waste

Recovery and Recycling Targets

This chapter will look more closely at the PPW Directive. Undoubtedly, this was the piece of EU legislation with broader impacts on the waste management, packaged goods and recycling markets. As previously mentioned, according to this Directive, packaging is any product used to contain, protect, handle, deliver and present goods (both raw materials and processed goods) from the producer to the user or consumer. It can be made of various materials, such as plastic, paper, cardboard, glass, metal or wood, and classified as follows (Directive 94/62/EC):

a. sales packaging or primary packaging, i.e. packaging conceived so as to constitute a sales unit to the final user or consumer at the point of purchase;
b. grouped packaging or secondary packaging, i.e. packaging conceived so as to constitute at the point of purchase a grouping of a certain number of sales units whether the latter is sold as such to the final user or consumer or whether it serves only as a means to replenish the shelves at the point of sale; it can be removed from the product without affecting its characteristics;
c. transport packaging or tertiary packaging, i.e. packaging conceived so as to facilitate handling and transport of a number of sales units or grouped packagings in order to prevent physical handling and transport damage. Transport packaging does not include road, rail, ship and air containers.

The definition of "packaging waste" is therefore any packaging or packaging material (as described above) covered by the definition of waste in the WFD (excluding production residues). In simple terms, packaging becomes waste when it is perceived by the consumer as valueless and is discarded (Cleary, 2009).

The first version of the PPW Directive (1994) required that, by the end of 2001, all member states should at least have recovered 50 percent and recycled 25 percent of all generated packaging waste (by weight). All countries should recycle no less than 15 percent of each individual packaging material. In 2004, these objectives were updated (through Directive 2004/12/EC) setting new and more ambitious targets for the recovery and recycling of packaging waste. The second version of the Directive set the overall targets of 60 percent for recovery and 55 percent for recycling of packaging waste, all to be achieved by the end of 2008. As shown in Table 2.1, the specific targets for the recycling rates of each packaging waste material were revised as well. The PPW Directive also established ceilings for the recovery and recycling rates of all member states. The maximum rates (65 percent for overall recovery and 45 percent for overall recycling in 2001 and 80 percent for overall recycling in 2008) were set to avoid distortions of the internal market and not hinder compliance by other member states (the ceilings may be exceeded if the proper provision to prevent this are in place, da Cruz et al., 2014b).

Table 2.1   EU recycling and recovery targets by weight of packaging waste

			Recycling targets					
Directive	**Deadline**	**Recovery targets (%)**	**Overall (%)**	**Glass (%)**	**Paper / cardboard (%)**	**Metals (%)**	**Plastic (%)**	**Wood (%)**
94/62/CE	31/12/2001	50 (max. 65)	25 (max. 45)	15	15	15	15	(–)
2004/12/CE	31/12/2008	60	55 (max. 80)	60	60	50	22.5	15

All countries transposed the PPW Directive into their national legislation; however, some countries had already a recycling system at work (e.g. note that the enactment of this Directive was influenced by the German Packaging Waste Ordinance, Eichstadt et al., 2000) while others had to create a new one (e.g. invest in selective collection and sorting equipment and infrastructure). Taking this into account, there were some exceptions to the deadlines that had been set. This was the case of Greece, Ireland and Portugal which, also due to their specific features such as the number of small islands or the widespread presence of rural and mountain areas, were allowed to postpone the 2001 targets to the end of 2005 and the 2008 targets to the end of 2011. Moreover, the new member states were also allowed to postpone the 2008 targets as follows:

- 31 December 2012 for the Czech Republic, Estonia, Cyprus, Lithuania, Hungary, Slovenia and Slovakia;
- 31 December 2013 for Malta and Romania;
- 31 December 2014 for Bulgaria and Poland;
- 31 December 2015 for Latvia.

As discussed earlier, many member states adopted EPR compliance schemes to fulfill the targets of the PPW Directive. In most member states, and regarding the municipal stream, the producers of packaging waste have been indeed transferring their responsibility to licensed entities that take on the responsibility of managing the logistic chain of packaging waste. Nevertheless, there are some noteworthy exceptions, such as the particular case of Denmark (where a deposit system runs for beverage packaging).

Despite the major impacts of the PPW Directive, it should be noted that non-negligible quantities of packaging waste were already being recycled in Europe (COM, 2006) even before this law entered into force. Indeed, recycling has been a commonly used waste management strategy for many decades now (especially for valuable materials, such as metal packaging, and also because, in some circumstances, it can be cheaper than landfilling). For glass packaging, given the specific features of the material (e.g. hygienic, versatile, non-absorbent and inert) the reuse option has also been applied in several jurisdictions and could be superior from an environmental standpoint (followed by recycling when its returnable cycle finishes). Furthermore, although recycling seems to be the preferable treatment option for plastic packaging (also from an environmental perspective), this material has a high calorific value, which increases the attractiveness of incineration with energy recovery.

In general, when reuse is not a feasible option, the recycling of packaging waste seems to be preferable in terms of environmental performance because it enables the production of secondary raw materials as well as the reduction of the consumption of primary raw materials and the amount of waste incinerated and/ or landfilled (with the consequent production of gaseous emissions and leachate). However, from an economic perspective, this treatment option is not necessarily the best in all circumstances. The implications of the ambitious recovery and recycling targets applicable to all member states will be addressed in this chapter.

Extended Producer Responsibility

Generally speaking, the life-cycle of packaging waste can have two types of ending: disposal (i.e. landfilling or incineration without energy recovery) or recovery (i.e. the residual value is recouped as energy—energy recovery—or a useful material—recycling). Figure 2.1 presents a general outline of the possible routes and treatment operations of municipal packaging waste. Not all packaging waste enters the recycling system. In many cases, most of the packaging waste material that enters the undifferentiated (or refuse) collection flow gets landfilled. This packaging waste may still be recovered if it is sent to a waste-to-energy incineration facility (in addition to energy recovery, a significant portion of the bottom ash can also be recycled) or routed to a mechanical biological treatment (MBT) plant (because paper is biodegradable and, in the cases where refuse or mixed waste flows feed the composting or anaerobic digestion facilities, a manual or mechanical sorting process precedes the biological treatment where recyclable materials can be recovered and sent to recycling facilities). Nevertheless, most of the municipal packaging waste sent to recycling comes from the selective collection flow. This selective collection can be accomplished through bring systems (drop-off containers), curbside (door-to-door) and/or drop-off centers and, in most cases, counts on the environmental awareness of citizens/consumers and on their willingness to participate (source separation levels are key for the success of the recycling systems).

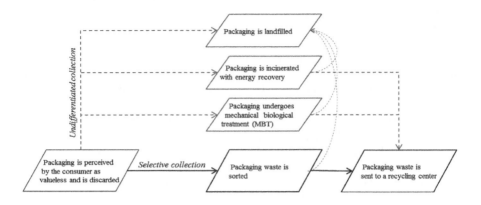

Figure 2.1   Simplified illustration of the life-cycle of packaging waste
Source: adapted from Cabral et al. (2013)

Although the PPW Directive targets are the same for all member states, a few countries established even more ambitious objectives. Moreover, the institutional and regulatory frameworks and, more considerably, the operational strategies developed to achieve those targets may vary substantially from country to country. However, in most countries, the local (or regional) authorities are responsible for municipal waste management. Therefore, being it a public, mixed or private utility delivering the services, the ultimate responsibility for the suitable collection, sorting, treatment and final disposal of municipal waste lies with local authorities (in the cases of mixed capital or private waste management operators, a public-private partnership (PPP) agreement usually has to be established, da Cruz et al., 2013).

To respect the EPR principle inherent to EU legislation, local authorities or waste management operators must receive a financial support from the economic operators placing packaged products onto the market to compensate for the selective collection and sorting activities (among other tasks, such as information management and reporting, packaging waste recovered through MBT or energy recovery operations, awareness raising, etc.). Figure 2.2 provides an example of an EPR scheme applicable to the municipal flow (the packaging waste arising from industrial or large-scale commercial activities—referred to as "trade and industry flow"—does not require such a complex system). As illustrated below, the industry (packers or importers) usually pays a fee based on weight and type of packaging to a licensed entity (e.g. a Green Dot Company) in order to join the compliance scheme. Afterwards, the licensed entity pays the financial support for local authorities (FSLA) again based on the amount (weight) and type (material) of packaging waste collected and/or sorted. In the example given in Figure 2.2, the licensed entity owns the packaging waste after paying the FSLA (which means that the amounts paid include net take-back value of the materials) and so it may sell it to recyclers or guarantors. There are cases, however, where local authorities can decide to whom to sell the recyclables after sorting. All stakeholders must share information with the respective National Waste Authority (frequently the National Environment Agencies), so each member state may account for the attained recovery and recycling rates.

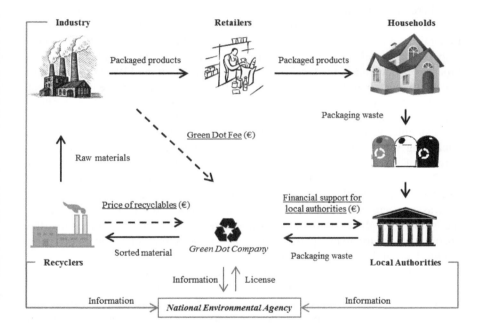

Figure 2.2   Example of an EPR scheme (household flow)
Source: adapted from da Cruz et al. (2012)

Such an EPR scheme can be prone to some criticism both by waste management operators, who often claim that the unit value of the FSLA is not enough to cover all costs, and the industry, which often claims that some waste management operators are inefficient and the producers should not be held responsible for something they cannot control. Another crucial question is whether the industry (i.e. the consumer, through the prices of packaged goods) should just pay for the incremental costs of recycling (i.e. full costs of selective collection and sorting minus the avoided costs with the diversion of waste from the undifferentiated flow) or for the net financial costs of packaging waste management.

Evidently, in the event that the industry pays for less than the incremental costs of recycling, the local authorities (i.e. rate-payers or tax-payers) will have to support the extra costs of recycling. In this regard, it is worth quoting the following statement extracted from the first version of the PPW Directive (1994): "the measures provided for in this Directive should involve and require the close cooperation of all the partners, where appropriate, within a spirit of shared responsibility." The Directive 2004/12/EC amending the original version also states that "[t]he operators in the packaging chain as a whole should shoulder their shared responsibility to ensure that the environmental impact of packaging and packaging waste throughout its life cycle is reduced as far as possible."

Therefore, although the EPR principle is a fundamental aspect of the EU approach to the recycling problem, this reference to "shared responsibility" may raise some doubts. To ascertain whether the EPR principle has been strictly respected in the EU or if the various member states have instead adopted a more broad interpretation of the legal dispositions drawn from the PPW Directive, it is necessary to account for the costs and benefits undertaken by waste management operators concerning the collection and sorting of packaging waste. The literature suggests that the compliance with the EPR principle varies greatly in Europe. For example, whereas in Germany the industry is 100 percent responsible for packaging waste management, in Portugal the industry is financing around 77 percent of the net financial costs of packaging waste management (da Cruz et al., 2012), CONAI (the Italian compliance scheme) finances approximately 20 to 25 percent of total recovery costs with the remaining costs being supported by waste management bills (according to Massarutto, 2010) and in Denmark or the Netherlands the cost of is entirely supported by waste management bills (the encouragement for municipalities to engage in selective collection is given by landfill bans and/or very high landfill taxes, EEA, 2005).

The main theoretical motivation behind the option for an EPR recycling system is that it should encourage innovation within the industry (e.g. less or easier-to-recycle packaging). However, some authors (such as Massarutto, 2014) argue that the price signals from EPR policies have been somewhat weak in encouraging green innovation. To divert waste from landfills (and promote recovery) EPR schemes would not be a requirement and, instead, a waste collection tax incorporating externalities (or a landfill tax, or a tax on raw materials, etc.) could generate similar results without market distortions (Kinnaman, 2009). Yet, the creation of powerful "Producer Responsibility Organizations" (the abovementioned licensed companies responsible for the compliance schemes) was a "side-effect" of the EPR approach that greatly facilitated the development of recycling markets that were unimaginable a few decades ago (Massarutto, 2014).

Finally, it is interesting to note that many local authorities in Europe do not yet reflect the full costs of MSW management on the utility bills. This means that whereas the PPW Directive requires that economic operators accept the (financial) responsibility for their packaging end-of-life, the polluter-pays principle is often not respected when income from local or national taxes is used to subsidize waste management. In other words, although the costs of recycling packaging waste should be included in the retail price of packaged goods (and that moment of taxation can have an impact on consumer behavior), the same kind of awareness is not being imposed in all member states when it comes to pricing mixed waste management (da Cruz et al., 2014b).

Current European Panorama

As depicted in Figure 2.3, the generation of municipal waste per capita across Europe is quite variable, ranging from 279 kg/inh. in Estonia to 694 kg/inh. in Switzerland (in 2012). It is also visible that most countries have succeeded in changing behaviors in order to contain or reduce the rate of municipal waste generation (although there are some exceptions). Considering the seven member states discussed in detail in this book, the variation is low, being Romania the country which generates less waste per capita and Germany the one that generates more.

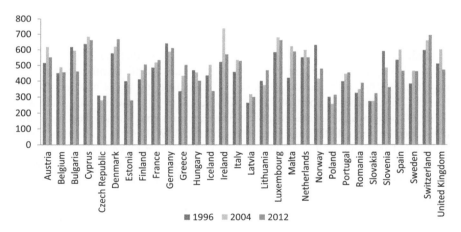

Figure 2.3   Municipal waste generation of European countries in 1996, 2004 and 2012 (kg per capita)

Source: Eurostat

Table 2.2 details the generation and treatment of municipal waste in the year under analysis (2010) for the countries studied in the following chapters. In this year, almost 149 million tons of municipal waste was incinerated or landfilled in the EU-27. In addition, around 97 million tons of municipal waste were composted or sent to a recycling facility, representing 38 percent of the waste generated. Germany achieved the highest recycling rate (63 percent if recycling plus composting materials are considered) and, at the same time, the lowest landfilling rate. Romania had the highest landfilling and the smallest recycling rates.

Table 2.2   Municipal waste generation and treatment in 2010 for the country case-studies (thousands of tons)

	Waste generation	Deposit onto or into land	%	Total incineration	%	Material recycling	%	Composting and digestion	%
EU-27	252,315	92,068	36.5	56,923	22.6	62,695	24.8	34,049	13.5
Belgium	4,973	84	1.7	2,016	40.5	1,807	36.3	1,069	21.5
France	34,535	10,745	31.1	11,730	34.0	6,143	17.8	5,917	17.1
Germany	49,237	206	0.4	18,256	37.1	22,476	45.6	8,298	16.9
Italy	32,479	15,015	46.2	5,387	16.6	6,429	19.8	3,908	12.0
Portugal	5,457	3,381	62.0	1,058	19.4	619	11.3	399	7.3
Romania	6,552	5,003	76.4	0	0.0	107	1.6	1	0.0
UK	31,955	14,686	46.0	4,125	12.9	8,069	25.3	4,786	15.0

Source: Eurostat

Regarding the packaging waste stream, Figure 2.4 shows that the PPW Directive led to an impressive increase of the recycling rates of all member states. For instance, in 1998, only around 30 percent of all packaging waste was recycled in Greece, Italy, Portugal, Spain and the UK, whereas in 2011 the recycling rate was about 60 percent in all these countries. The countries that already had recycling legislation in force before the enactment of the PPW Directive are also easily pinpointed in Figure 2.4 (i.e. the ones with the higher recycling rates). These "recycling champions" had fairly high recycling rates early on (for example, in 1998, Belgium and the Netherlands recycled more than 60 percent of all packaging waste and Germany had a recycling rate of around 80 percent—i.e. higher than nowadays). Currently, most countries comply with the imposed overall recovery and recycling targets. It should be mentioned that the most recent data currently available refers to the year 2011 (each member state must report the quantities to the European Commission within 18 months) and the deadline for some countries is beyond this year.

In 2011 (the last available data), a total of 80 million tons of packaging waste were produced in the EU-27, where only about 62 million tons were recovered and 51 million tons were recycled. Considering the countries studied, in 2010, Germany had the highest packaging waste production followed by France (Table 2.3). Note that these figures include packaging waste from both the municipal and the trade and industry flows.

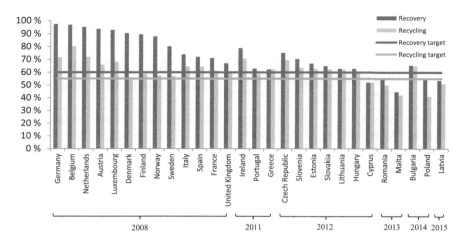

Figure 2.4   Packaging waste recovery and recycling rates in 2011 and PPW Directive targets

Source: Eurostat

Some of the official figures reported for Romania are somewhat surprising. For example, *a priori* there is no reason for the difference observed for the share of packaging waste in the generated MSW. In fact, the percentage of packaging waste in a ton of municipal waste seems to be less than half of the one observed for other countries. One possible explanation might be that the data available for this country are biased due to the presence of "free-riders."

Packers/fillers or other economic operators that do not declare their packaging to avoid paying the license fees to the entities in charge of managing the logistic chain of packaging waste recycling (e.g. a Green Dot company) are commonly referred to as "free-riders." This "free-riding" phenomenon undermines the economic sustainability of the systems, creates market distortions and hinders the calculation of the recovery and recycling rates achieved by the member states (Yau, 2010).

In some cases, the figures relative to the quantities of packaging recovered are higher than the quantities of packaging reported. For instance, Denmark achieved a recovery rate of 108 percent in 2009 and 2010. The import of waste may also influence these figures; furthermore, some non-packaging waste (mainly paper and plastic materials) can be treated as packaging waste since they may be collected in the same containers.

Table 2.3   Packaging waste generation in 2010 for the country case-studies (thousands of tons)

	Packaging waste	Percentage of MSW (%)	Paper / cardboard	Plastic	Wood	Metal	Glass	Other
EU-27	78,672.4	31	31,055	14,847	12,010	4,540	15,980	(-)
Belgium	1,686.0	34	648	316	196	127	386	13
France	12,515.9	36	4,673	2,002	2,413	595	2,829	5
Germany	16,002.6	33	7,196	2,690	2,550	833	2,712	21
Italy	11,411.0	35	4,338	2,071	2,281	568	2,153	0
Portugal	1,664.3	30	704	361	106	95	399	0
Romania	974.9	15	266	281	212	55	160	0
UK	10,824.8	34	3,788	2,479	1,024	800	2,713	22

Source: Eurostat

Concerning the packaging waste generation per capita (Figure 2.5), Germany had the highest value (196 kg/inh.), being closely followed by France (193 kg/inh.). Romania attained the lowest value of 46 kg per inhabitant per year. In addition, Figure 2.5 shows that, in most countries, paper/cardboard is the most used packaging material. However, in Romania the quantity of plastic packaging is higher than the quantity of paper/cardboard packaging.

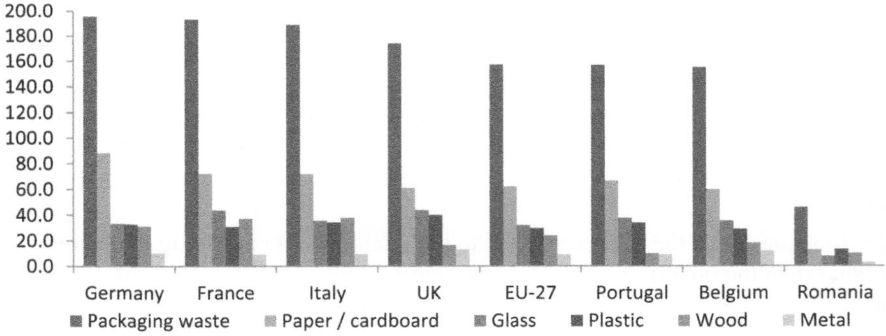

Figure 2.5   Packaging waste generation in 2010 for the country case-studies (kg per capita)

Source: Eurostat

Considering the recycling rates for each packaging waste material, as shown in Table 2.4, all analyzed countries were fulfilling the specific targets in 2010, with the exception of Portugal (for the case of glass) and Romania (for the overall target and also glass packaging waste). In 2011, the recycling rate for glass was 59.7 in Portugal (i.e. just below the target, which should have been met this year). Also in 2011, the recycling of glass packaging waste matched the imposed target of 60 percent in Romania. In a similar fashion, the overall recycling rate in this country raised to 50 percent (note that, according to the PPW Directive, Romania only has to meet all the targets by the end of 2013).

Table 2.4   Packaging waste recycling in 2010 for the country case-studies (thousands of tons)

	Packaging waste	Paper / cardboard	Plastic	Wood	Metal	Glass
EU-27	49,765 (63.3%)	25,920 (83.5%)	11,064 (33.3%)	4,941 (38.1%)	4,575 (71.5%)	3,248 (69.2%)
Belgium	1,345 (79.8%)	582 (89.8%)	386 (41.5%)	131 (63.3%)	124 (94.7%)	121 (100.0%)
France	7,646 (61.1%)	4,293 (91.9%)	1,974 (23.7%)	474 (19.1%)	460 (74.8%)	445 (69.8%)
Germany	11,628 (72.7%)	6,492 (90.2%)	2,336 (49.4%)	1,328 (27.5%)	700 (92.7%)	772 (86.1%)
Italy	7,346 (64.4%)	3,416 (78.7%)	1,471 (34.5%)	715 (58.7%)	1,339 (71.3%)	405 (68.3%)
Portugal	924 (55.5%)	472 (67.0%)	225 (24.5%)	89 (66.0%)	70 (72.0%)	69 (56.6%)*
Romania	423 (43.4%)*	178 (66.8%)	91 (28.2%)	79 (18.1%)	38 (65.7%)	36 (56.8%)*
UK	6,568 (60.7%)	3,103 (81.9%)	1,648 (24.1%)	598 (75.4%)	772 (55.9%)	447 (60.7%)

* below the PPW Directive target

Source: Eurostat

Chapter 3
Packaging Waste Recycling Systems

Belgium[1]

Legal and Institutional Framework

In Belgium, waste policies are the responsibility of the three Belgian regions since 1993 (with the exception of radioactive waste). It was during this year that the country was constituted as a federal state composed of communities (The Flemish, French and German communities) and regions (Flanders, Wallonia and Brussels-Capital). In fact, the national government has limited powers in the field of waste management, mainly related to products standardization and taxing, and to the negotiation and implementation of international commitments (such as the transposition of the European Directives, Criekemans, 2010).

Before the enactment of the PPW Directive, Belgium had already implemented fiscal instruments to encourage green innovation and the ecodesign of products. This Directive was transposed into Belgian legislation through the Interregional Cooperation Agreement established in 1996 among the three regions. The agreement applies to all municipal and industrial packaging waste and has force of law throughout the whole territory, ensuring a harmonized management of packaging waste across the regions (IVCIE, 2012). Afterwards, the Directive 2004/12/EC was transposed to the revised Cooperation Agreement which was published in 2008 and came into force in 2009 (Pinckaers, 2012).

In order to comply with the ambitious recycling and recovery targets, the Interregional Cooperation Agreement imposed "take-back" obligations to all economic operators (such as producers, packers, fillers and importers and industrial consumers) who place packaging and packaged products onto the Belgium market. The economic operators had the possibility to transfer those obligations to a company licensed for managing the household and/or industrial packaging waste (Lavrysen and Misonne, 2004). As a result, the Green Dot company "Fost Plus" was created and granted with a license to manage the household flow (holding 89 percent of the Belgian market share in 2009) while "Val-I-Pac" is the licensed organization to manage the industrial flow (about 84 percent of the market). Only 2 percent of the economic agents with industrial packaging have assumed their own "take-back" obligations through an individual recycling system (Adams, 2011).

---

1 The following scholars contributed with research for this subchapter (in alphabetical order): Marta Cabral, Nuno Ferreira da Cruz, Pedro Simões, Rui Cunha Marques, Sandra Ferreira and Simon De Jaeger.

The economic operators must register and submit data based on the quantities of packaging or packaged products handled to one of the three regional authorities (the Brussels' Institute for Environmental Management—IBGE/BIM; the Flemish Public Waste Agency—OVAM; or the Waste Agency of the Walloon Ministry for Natural Resources and Environment—DGRNE). These authorities ensure the participation of the respective region in the Interregional Packaging Commission (IPC). The IPC was created to ensure a uniform management of packaging waste between the three Belgian regions and the fulfillment of the Cooperation Agreements, playing a regulatory role. The main responsibilities of the IPC are (Adams, 2011):

- Certifying the competent entities for managing the packaging waste stream (Fost Plus and Val-I-Pac) and auditing their activities to suspend or renew their licenses;
- Controlling all procedures including their efficiency, checking the declaration forms of compliance (delivered by the members of the Fost Plus and Val-I-Pac systems) and performing *in-situ* audits;
- Approving the prevention plans submitted every three years by all economic operators that handle at least 300 tons of packaging and all producers or packers that handle at least 100 tons of packaging or packaged products (IBGE/BIM, 2011);
- Ensuring that the financial transfers arising from the packaging recycling systems are carried out correctly and fairly.

The national agreement from 1996 had already imposed more ambitious recycling and recovery targets than the EU Directive. The minimum recycling rate should increase from 35 percent in 1996 to 50 percent in 1999. In the same period, the recovery target raised from 50 percent to 80 percent. These targets were once again raised by the national legislation currently in force (Cooperation Agreement from 2008). The recycling and recovery targets of municipal packaging waste for 2009 were 80 percent and 90 percent, respectively. The recycling and recovery targets of the industrial flow in 2010 were 80 percent and 85 percent, correspondingly (Adams, 2011).

Waste Management Operators

The local governments are responsible for the collection and treatment of municipal waste. There are 589 municipalities in Belgium. The Brussels region has 19 municipalities, whereas the Flemish and Walloon regions encompass 308 and 262 municipalities, respectively (Wayenberg and De Rynck, 2012). According to the Belgian Constitution, the municipalities can cooperate for all issues of local interest, including municipal waste management. Indeed, nearly all Belgian municipalities share their waste management responsibilities through inter-municipal associations. By joining together, the municipalities form inter-municipal authorities (the *intercommunales*) and share or transfer all their competencies regarding urban waste services to these associations. The industrial waste collection and treatment is the responsibility of the private sector (CSD, 2009).

Since 1993 several municipal waste services have been provided by *intercommunales* (through in-house delivery, outsourcing to private companies or other governance arrangements) in Flanders and Wallonia. Currently, there are 26 *intercommunales* in Flanders and eight in Wallonia. In the Flemish region, about 555 kg per capita of household waste has been generated every year (CSD, 2009). The collection is carried out by curbside collection and drop-off containers. Regarding waste treatment in this region, around 72 percent of household waste selectively collected has been reused or recycled, including composting (CSD, 2009). Respecting the Flanders waste principles, only a small fraction of household waste has been landfilled (1.2 percent, OVAM, 2009). In 2012, Flanders had 340 container parks, 27 paper and cardboard sorting and/or processing facilities, 97 sorting and processing facilities of non-hazardous waste, 149 composting plants, 10 incineration plants, 15 glass processing plants and four landfills (OVAM, 2012).

In Wallonia, around 538 kg per capita of household waste has been generated every year (CSD, 2009). According to the Walloon Intermunicipal Companies for Waste Treatment (COPIDEC), the *intercommunales* in this region provide curbside refuse and selective collection services as well as bring systems. Moreover, they manage several sorting and treatment infrastructures. Currently, about 64 percent of waste collected is recycled, 22 percent is incinerated and 14 percent is landfilled in Wallonia. In 2012, there were 202 container parks, 341 drop-off containers for three packaging waste fractions, 7489 drop-off containers for waste glass, three sorting stations for packaging waste, nine composting centers, four energy recovery plants and eight landfills in this region (COPIDEC, 2012).

In the Brussels region, about 475 kg per inhabitant of household waste has been produced every year (CDS, 2009). Around 25 percent of this waste has been reused or recycled (including composting) and 75 percent has been incinerated. In Brussels, household waste is not landfilled. The municipalities have delegated MSW services to a single public company (the ABP) since 1990. In 2012 this company managed two drop-off centers, one sorting station, one composting center and one incineration plant with energy recovery (IBGE, 2012).

Compliance Scheme

As mentioned above, there are two licensed packaging waste entities in Belgium: Fost Plus and Val-I-Pac. These entities should ensure the collection of packaging waste and its adequate final disposal in order to comply with the national and EU recycling and recovery targets. Fost Plus is a non-profit organization that promotes, coordinates and finances the selective collection, sorting and recycling of municipal packaging waste. It was created in 1994 as a private sector initiative (mostly, producers and importers of packaging, packaging materials, and packaged products, retailers, and trade federations). In 1997, Fost Plus officially became the Green Dot company, assuming the economic operators' obligations regarding municipal packaging waste.

All economic operators can join the Fost Plus system through a membership contract and by accepting to submit an annual declaration of reusable and non-reusable packaging placed onto the Belgian market. In order to meet its obligations, Fost Plus establishes contracts (eight year terms) with all inter-municipal authorities for the collection and/or sorting of the municipal packaging waste flow. The last version of the Interregional Cooperation Agreement introduced a new threshold of 300 kg of packaging per year placed in the Belgian market. Below this threshold the companies are exempted from the legal obligations of recycling and recovery.

The members of the Fost Plus scheme have to pay an annual contribution based on the types and quantities of packaging put onto the market. The minimum yearly contribution was fixed in €30 for the case of companies which handle less than 300 kg/year of packaging or only handle reusable packaging and want to use the Green Dot trademark (PRO Europe, 2010). The contributions of the economic operators and the revenue arising from the sale of sorted packaging waste materials must cover the costs of the selective collection and sorting services provided by the *intercommunales* (Fost Plus pays a FSLA per flow of packaging material).

Fost Plus has two declaration schemes: the "detailed" declaration and the "fixed-price" declaration. The first scheme is applicable to all operators whereas the second one is only applicable to companies with a turnover of a maximum of €12.5 million. According to the standard scheme (detailed declaration), the operators have to declare the number of consumer units (the smallest unit that can be sold to the consumer) per packaging placed on the market and the financial contribution (i.e. the Green Dot fee) is calculated according to the materials and weights of the packaging (see Table 3.1, Fost Plus, 2012a).

Table 3.1   Green Dot fees for 2010 in Belgium

Packaging material	Green Dot fees (€/ton)
Glass	18.40
Paper/cardboard	17.60
Steel	37.60
Aluminum	137.90
PET	199.40
HDPE	199.40
Beverage cartons	272.80
Others (recoverable)	313.50
Others (non-recoverable)	441.70

In the fixed-price declaration scheme, the operators have to declare the number of consumer units per product family (also called product group or product line) placed onto the market (excluding the producers/importers of empty "service packaging"). These operators pay a fixed-price per unit declared, depending on the product family (Fost Plus, 2012b). Table 3.2 shows the fixed contributions in 2010.

Table 3.2   Fixed contributions from 2010 in Belgium

Packaging material	Fixed contribution (€/unit)
Food	0.0031
Drinks 1: Sodas, lemonades, fruit juices and vegetables, syrups, milk, water, beer	0.0056
Drinks 2: Wine, champagne, spirits, aperitifs	0.0100
Drinks in reusable packaging	0.0000
Cleaning and maintenance (including accessories)	0.0127
Body care (hair care, teeth, samples and accessories included)	0.0047
Pharmaceuticals	0.0038
Garden items (products and garden tools)	0.0073
Adhesives, paints, varnishes and related products	0.0144
Miscellaneous (equipment included)	0.0049
Clothing, footwear, textiles and accessories	0.0026
Electro 1: Major appliances (TV, HiFi included)	0.1736
Electro 2: Small appliances (radio, telephone included)	0.0085
Electro 3: Accessories for appliances (lamps, batteries)	0.0015
Kitchenware	0.0027
Indoor and outdoor furniture	0.0333
Lighting	0.0054
Animals	0.0023
Tobacco	0.0006
Others	0.0022

In addition to the financial contributions from the industry, Fost Plus establishes contracts with the recyclers who pay for the packaging waste materials collected and sorted according to the respective materials price index. In agreement with the Belgian system, these two sources of revenue must cover the full costs of packaging waste collection and sorting undertaken by the *intercommunales*.

Furthermore, Fost Plus has costs concerning coordination, quality management, public communication and awareness.

The *intercommunales* receive a financial contribution (the FSLA) by Fost Plus to support the municipal packaging waste services. In principle, Fost Plus reimburses the exact full costs involved in the selective collection and sorting of packaging waste for a standard level of service. The reimbursements are carried out according to one of the four following schemes (IVCIE, 2008):

1. "Real and complete cost": when the utilities outsource their services to a third party, Fost Plus reimburses them according to the costs per material as set in the outsourcing contract.
2. "Mutual agreement": Fost Plus and the utility negotiate a mutual agreement on the costs to be reimbursed by Fost Plus.
3. "Standard cost": the various utilities may differ on the level of service provided in their jurisdiction (e.g. the number of collection rounds or the number of pick-up points). Fost Plus only reimburses the costs of a "standard" level of service. This reference cost is paid for each type of packaging material and calculated per ton (40 percent of the value—the variable part of the standard cost) and per inhabitant (60 percent of the value—the fixed part of standard cost). This value corresponds to the average cost of the collection scenarios reimbursed to the "real and complete cost." If the utility can provide evidence for an atypical cost structure, Fost Plus may use an alternative proportion of the fixed and variable components.
4. "Special fixed reimbursement": a utility can receive two types of special contributions. (1) If a utility decides to complement the standard level of service with additional collection rounds, Fost Plus reimburses the "real and complete cost" for the standard level of service per flow of packaging waste and the additional quantities are reimbursed with a special contribution. For plastic and metal, the contribution corresponds to (at least) 50 percent of the standard cost per ton. For the other type of materials, the cost per ton is fixed at 160€. (2) The costs arising from household cardboard collected separately via container parks (i.e. via a bring system and not via the standard door-to-door collection) are reimbursed according to the "standard cost."

The average FSLA per ton of packaging waste material and per activity are summarized in Table 3.3. Note that the exact value is different for each *intercommunal* since this depends on the scheme adopted (although, in general, it should cover the full costs of selective collection and sorting). For the case of paper/cardboard selectively collected, Fost Plus only reimburses 30 percent of the costs because not all paper waste is from packaging. Since the Green Dot company owns the waste and deals directly with recyclers, the revenue from the sale of packaging materials is included in the financial contributions paid to *intercommunales*.

Table 3.3   FSLA in 2010 in Belgium

Packaging material	Average FSLA (€/ton)
Glass collection	49.33
Paper/Cardboard collection	52.95
PMD* collection	199.79
PMD* sorting	168.71

* plastic bottles and flasks, metallic packaging and drinks cartons

Source: IVCIE (2011)

In addition to the main financial supports described above, Fost Plus pays some complementary fees to *intercommunales* as follows (IVCIE, 2008):

- An additional fee of 0.1€ per inhabitant each year, which can be used for increasing the level of service for glass collection (e.g. curbside collection, additional cleaning and/or acquisition of containers, etc.);
- Compensation for the costs of monitoring the outsourcing contracts;
- 0.25€ per inhabitant each year for communication and information campaigns;
- A bonus if the PMD (plastic bottles and flasks, metallic packaging and drinks cartons) residue after sorting is below certain thresholds;
- Reimbursement of the collection and transportation costs for metal packaging materials collected at incineration (or other waste treatment) facilities;
- Partially reimbursement of additional packaging waste collection rounds (which are not included in the standard level of service).

Current Situation

Belgium is one of the most effective recyclers of municipal waste in the EU. Furthermore, it has shown a municipal waste generation per capita below the European average (as well as the quantity of landfilled waste). As shown in Figure 3.1, during 18 years, the generation of municipal waste reached the highest value in 2007 (494 kg/inh.). However, Belgium per capita rates were always below the EU-27 average.

Belgium has been at the forefront regarding the management of municipal waste. Recycling has steadily increased over time while landfilling has decreased significantly. As described in the previous chapter, in 2010, 36.5 percent of municipal waste generated in Europe was landfilled, whereas in Belgium this rate was only 1.7 percent. Nowadays, this percentage is even lower (approximately 1.2 percent). The percentage of waste incinerated has remained approximately constant over the years.

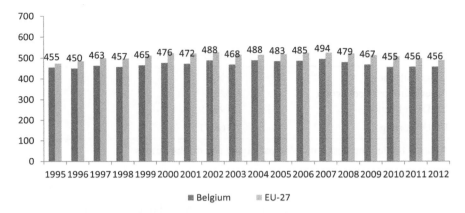

Figure 3.1   Generation of municipal waste in Belgium (kg per capita)
Source: Eurostat

For the particular case of packaging waste, Belgium had already overcome the targets of the PPW Directive in 1999. Currently, it is the country with the highest packaging waste recycling rate in the EU. As shown in Table 3.4, paper and cardboard packaging are the most commonly used in this country. Belgium has achieved very high recycling and recovery targets. Glass (100 percent since 2005) and metal (more than 90 percent since 2006) packaging are the materials with the highest recycling rate (see Figure 3.2).

Table 3.4   Generation of packaging waste by material in Belgium (thousands of tons)

Year	Packaging waste	Paper / cardboard	Plastic	Wood	Metal	Glass
2002	1,490	569	258	166	138	323
2003	1,624	593	278	176	141	419
2004	1,632	614	281	187	137	396
2005	1,659	637	290	192	136	388
2006	1,666	635	302	191	136	385
2007	1,669	640	309	201	136	367
2008	1,690	643	302	197	132	400
2009	1,642	628	304	180	121	396
2010	1,686	648	316	196	127	386
2011	1,703	656	316	202	128	388

Source: Eurostat

Despite the fact that plastic is a problematic material due to its chemical composition (which hinders recycling) Belgium far exceeded the Directive's specific objective for 2008. These results demonstrate the success of the political efforts towards recycling (at least in terms of effectiveness) and the public awareness towards environmental issues in Belgium.

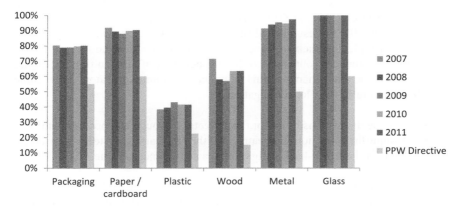

Figure 3.2   Recycling rate of packaging waste by material in Belgium
Source: Eurostat

France[2]

Legal and Institutional Framework

Before the PPW Directive was published, France had already adopted recycling-related legislation. In 1975, the Law No. 75-633 on the elimination of waste and material recovery included some dispositions with relevance for packaging waste management (Nikolaides and Associates, 2010). Later on, the Law No. 92-646 amended the law from 1975 and introduced the EPR concept into the national legislation. Its main goals were the following:

- To predict or reduce the production and toxicity of waste, by acting on the manufacture and distribution of products;
- To organize the transport of waste and limiting distance and volume;
- To recover the waste by reuse, recycling, or other action for waste from reusable materials or energy;

---

2   The following scholars contributed with research for this subchapter (in alphabetical order): Marta Cabral, Nuno Ferreira da Cruz, Pedro Simões, Rui Cunha Marques and Sandra Ferreira.

- To provide public information on the effects on the environment and public health operations of production and waste disposal, subject to the rules of confidentiality provided by law, as well as measures to prevent or to offset the adverse effects.

There are two crucial decrees in the history of French legislation regarding packaging waste management: Decree No. 92-377, which regulated the municipal flow, and the Decree No. 94-609, which dealt with the trade and industry flow. The Decree No. 92-377 established the obligation of each producer or importer responsible for placing packaged goods (for households) onto the French market to assume or somehow contribute to the management of all resulting packaging waste. Since the enactment of this law, the economic operators have three possibilities to fulfil their legal obligations:

- Assume the responsibility for the collection through a deposit system;
- Assume the collection and treatment of their packaging waste by themselves;
- Transfer their take-back obligation to a compliance scheme.

Economic operators responsible for packaging and packaged goods have to communicate to the Agency for Environment and Energy Management (ADEME) the quantity of packaging (and subsequent packaging waste) placed onto the market and the quantity of packaging waste collected and recovered. In France, there are three licensed organisms for the management of the collection and recovery of municipal packaging waste: Eco-Emballages, Adelphe and Cyclamed. However, Adelphe joined Eco-Emballages Group in 2005 and Cyclamed handles expired medicines and their packaging waste. When selecting the compliance scheme, the economic operator has to specify the type of packaging and the estimated volume of waste produced annually.

The Decree No. 94-609 establishes the obligation that each end-user of non-household packaging waste (i.e. from the trade and industry flow) has to sort its packaging waste separately from other types of waste and to ensure its recovery. In the event that the non-household end-user generates less than 1,100 liters of unsorted waste per week the packaging waste can enter the municipal flow. In the other cases, the end-users have three possibilities to fulfil their legal obligations:

- Recover their packaging waste on their own licensed treatment facility;
- Sign a contract with an officially licensed treatment facility;
- Sign a contract with an intermediary that is responsible for the transport and trade of the packaging waste.

In 2007 the French government facilitated a democratic debate on environmental issues known as *le Grenelle Environnement* (Grenelle Environment Round Table). The Grenelle Environment was firstly operationalized through the "Grenelle 1" Act (planning law No. 2009-967). The major concerns of the "Grenelle 1"

Act were (MEEDDM, 2009): climate change, biodiversity, ecosystems and natural environments, environmental and health risks, and policy for reducing waste, developing an ecologically-responsible democracy with new governance approaches and better public information. Furthermore, the "Grenelle 1" established a consistent and clear set of measures:

- Reduce the waste production of households (and similar waste sources) by 7 percent per capita during the next five years;
- Increase organic and material recycling to 75 percent for municipal packaging waste until 2012;
- Reduce the amount of waste incinerated or landfilled by 15 percent until 2012;
- Extend the financing needs by the contributors to household packaging waste from non-household production;
- Cover the costs of collection, sorting and treatment by 80 percent of the net benchmark costs for an optimized collection and recycling service until 2012.

The 2009–2012 Waste Action Plan was the result of the effort made by working groups formed by the State and all relevant stakeholders. It specified actions to be taken in the corresponding period in order to achieve the objectives set by the "Grenelle 1" Act. The National Waste Council is responsible for supervising the implementation of this type of plans. The 2009–2012 plan had the following general objectives:

- Reduce waste production;
- Increase and facilitate recycling;
- Improve organic waste recovery;
- Reform the planning and effectively treat residual waste;
- Improve the management of waste from construction.

The ensuing Law No. 2010-788, known as the "Grenelle 2" Act, also defined some measures related to waste management:

- Wastes landfilled and incinerated are limited to 60 percent;
- Local authorities are authorized, for three years, to implement a tariff system based on weight and/or volume of municipal waste (commonly known as a Pay as You Through system—PAYT);
- Retail stores covering a surface area greater than 2,500 m^2 have to install a voluntary collection point for packaging waste (from products purchased in the establishment);
- Endeavor to model the contributions from the package producers based on the product design and its impact on the environment by the end of life, including the material recovery.

The Decree No. 2011-828 transposed to the national legislation the WFD from 2008. This law introduced regulatory measures promoting the traceability of waste and the transparency of the different actors involved in the waste management chain. Finally, the Environment Code sets the "waste management policy priorities and provides for the establishment of departmental and regional waste disposal plans. It clarifies the nomenclature of the various classes of facilities for environmental protection and sets the procedures for issuing permits prior to operating waste treatment and storage facilities" (Djemaci, 2009: 7).

In France, local administration has a three-layer structure. The country is divided in regions which are then split into departments where the municipalities are the lowest tier. The General Councils (The Regional Council in the Region of Paris) are responsible for preparing the Disposal Plans for municipal waste (PEDMA). The PEDMAs are designed to coordinate and schedule the treatment of municipal waste from five to 10 years. They set targets for prevention, recycling and recovery of waste and guidelines for the equipment required for this purpose.

Waste Management Operators

The French municipalities transferred the waste management-related activities to intermunicipal cooperation agencies (EPCI). There are two main categories of EPCIs:

- Associations of municipalities: Single Purpose Intermunicipal Association (SIVU) and Multiple Purpose Intermunicipal Association (SIVOM);
- EPCIs with their own tax scheme: communities of municipalities, metropolitan communities, agglomeration communities, new agglomeration associations and urban communities.

Mixed associations are intermunicipal cooperation structures that are composed of municipalities and EPCIs (closed regime) or include the participation of the private sector (open regime). A local (or regional) authority responsible for the collection and treatment of municipal waste has three ways of financing the waste services (Le Bozec, 2008): (1) the general budget; (2) a tax on municipal waste disposal (TEOM); and/or (3) a fee for municipal waste disposal (REOM).

The general budget income comes from taxes collected by municipalities (such as the housing tax, trade tax, real estate tax on built-up property, and real estate tax on land that has not been built upon), from the revenues of waste recovery and from the financial support of eco-organizations (Eco-Emballages/Adelphe). The TEOM is a flat-tax that is added to the land tax on built properties, therefore it is collected with the real estate tax. If the TEOM does not cover the cost of managing the household waste, the authority may have to resort to the general budget. The REOM is a fee due to the services provided. The producer of waste pays a fee for the actual use of the service "which is usually calculated according to the number of people living in the household, in the case of household waste, and according to the size of the bin in the case of public establishments and businesses" (Djemaci, 2009: 18).

By the end of 2009, more than 99 percent of the French population was already covered by a selective waste collection service via curbside collection or bring system. In the same year 36,269 municipalities had a multimaterial contract with Eco-Emballages or Adelphe (ADEME, 2010). The private sector in the waste sector in France has been very active. Several operators develop outsourcing contracts with private companies. Besides, some of these companies are very significant international players in the waste sector.

Municipal waste is usually collected through curbside and/or bring systems. The drop-off centers contribute with a small percentage of packaging waste (mainly cardboard) for recycling. In brief, packaging waste can be collected through the following methods:

- Bi flow (two flows): the glass flow is collected separately from the multimaterial flow which includes all types of packaging as well as newspapers and magazines;
- Tri flow (three flows): a glass flow, a multimaterial flow, and a newspapers and magazines flow;
- *Corps creux/corps plats*—also a tri flow where the glass is collected separately, the cardboard is collected together with newspapers and magazines, and the third flow is composed of metal and plastic packaging.

Compliance Scheme

In 1992, several economic operators (packers, importers, etc.) created an organization in order to fulfil their environmental responsibilities, the non-profit organization named Eco-Emballages (the French Green Dot company). Adelphe was founded in 1993 by the wines and spirits manufacturers in order to meet their legal obligations concerning packaging waste generated by their products. In 2005, Adelphe joined the Eco-Emballages Group that now holds 84.,5 percent of Adelphe's capital, being the remaining shares divided between the wines and spirits network and the company's directors. In 2010, the license of Adelphe and Eco-Emballages was renewed for six years (from January 1, 2011 to December 31, 2016). Both companies have to report annually the results attained for packaging waste collection and recovery to the Minister of the Economy, Finances and Industry, to the Ministry of Ecology, Sustainable Development and Energy and to ADEME.

The goal of Eco-Emballages is to meet the recycling targets and to carry out campaigns to increase public awareness about environmental issues. It supports the entire packaging waste logistics chain in France. This chain involves the industry, local authorities and citizen/consumers. To operationalize the recycling system Eco-Emballages establishes various contracts (Eco-Emballages, 2010a):

- Economic operators (the producers responsible for the packaging) who contribute financially with the green dot value;
- Local authorities (individual municipalities or associations) who are responsible for the collection and treatment of municipal waste. By signing a contract with Eco-Emballages they get financial support (the FSLA) to collect and sort the packaging waste;
- Industrial firms that collect the sorted packaging waste for recovery (Eco-Emballages receives information about the process).

In 2010, the industry (encompassing 49,200 economic operators—covered by 22,771 contracts—that are members of the compliance scheme) transferred a total of 518 million Euros in contributions to Eco-Emballages (Eco-Emballages, 2011). Local authorities have to set up selective collection systems for the materials defined in the contracts (paper and cardboard, glass, plastic and metals).

In simple terms, the management of municipal packaging waste is financed through the Green Dot fee (from the industry), the sale of sorted materials and local taxes on refuse collection (Eco-Emballages, 2010a). Economic operators calculate their contribution based on a variable component (weight fee) and a fixed component (unit fee). The weight fee is determined by multiplying the total weight of each packaging placed onto the market by the respective fee that varies with the type of material, as shown in Table 3.5 (values for 2010). Concerning the unit fee, it is contingent upon the value achieved for the weight fee. If the weight fee is greater than or equal to 0.0014€, then the unit fee is a flat rate of 0.0014€. When the contribution on weight is less than 0.0014€, the unit fee is equal to the weight contribution and the total fee is twice the weight fee. If packages weigh more than 1kg their contribution to the weight fee is limited to 1kg.

Table 3.5   Green Dot fees for 2010 in France

Packaging material	Green Dot fees (€/ton)
Glass	4.5
Paper/cardboard	152.6
Steel	28.2
Aluminum	56.6
Plastics	222.2
Others	152.6

Eco-Emballages must use these financial resources to cover its operating expenses and fund the selective collection and sorting activities carried out by local authorities. The year 2010 was a transitional one where Eco-Emballages was still adapting to the requirements of the Grenelle Act. During this year the Green Dot company only had to cover 60 percent of the efficient benchmark costs due to selective collection and sorting (this value should raise to 80 percent by the end of 2012). In addition to this significant source of revenue, local authorities also rely on the sale of sorted materials (and on the tax-payers and/or rate-payers contributions). So, in 2010, the FSLA was calculated based on the per capita performance (of selective collection) and the take-back quantities for different packaging materials. The model for the calculation of the FSLA is presented in Table 3.6.

Table 3.6   FSLA in 2010 in France

Level	Performance (P) in kg/inh./year	Financial support (S) in €/ton
1	$P \leq Nb$	$S = Sb$
2	$Nb < P \leq Nh$	$S = \dfrac{(Nb \times Sb) + (P - Nb) \times Si}{P}$
3	$Nh < P \leq Np$	$S = \dfrac{(Nb \times Sb) + (Nh - Nb) \times Si + (P - Nh) \times Sp}{P}$
4	$P > Np$	$S = \dfrac{(P - Np + Nb) + (Nh - Nb) \times Si + (Np - Nh) \times Sp}{P}$

Where: Sp is the plafond support; Si is the intermediary support; Sb is the bottom support; Nb is the lower level; Nh is the higher level; and Np is the plafond level.

Source: Eco-Emballages (2010b)

The quality of materials taken back should be in accordance with material standards (see Eco-Emballages and Adelphe, 2011) documented and reported by local authorities and guarantors. The values indicated in Table 3.7 are the unit support for each material (Sb, Si and Sp) and the different thresholds designed to encourage higher performances (Nb, Nh and Np). For local authorities with different selective collection systems for colored and colorless glass, the financial support was 7 €/ton for the colorless flow. The financial support for the colored glass flow was calculated according to the model shown in Table 3.6.

In addition to the recycling of packaging waste, Eco-Emballages funds the activities involved in the incineration of packaging waste with energy production (for electricity, heat or both through cogeneration) and the recovery of packaging waste through MBT processes (see Table 3.8). These financial supports are calculated based on the amount of packaging waste treated (in tons) and a unit support fee (in €/ton). It should also be noted that other (less relevant) supports were also conveyed by Eco-Emballages during 2010. Indeed, local authorities may have their funding increased depending on their global performance rate or if they serve a restricted group of population (buildings and/or dispersed rural housing).

Table 3.7   Values of the variables to calculate the 2010 FSLA per material in France

Material	Nb	Nh	Np	Sb	Si	Sp
Steel	1	2	7	45	62.5	80
Aluminum	0.1	0.2	1	230	280	330
Paper / cardboard	4	8	18	120	200	280
Plastic	1.6	3.2	8	310	575	840
Glass	15	30	45	3	5	7
EMR*	4	8	18	60	100	140

*Mixed recovered paper and board (unsorted paper and board, separated at source).

Source: Eco-Emballages (2010b)

Table 3.8   Additional support to French local authorities in 2010 (metals from incineration and composting)

Packaging material	Additional support (€/ton)
Steel (from incineration)	12
Aluminum (from incineration)	75
Steel (from MBT)	45
Aluminum (from MBT)	230

Other transfers are carried out by the Green Dot company in 2010 concerning optimization and communication. Supports for optimization are given to local authorities that serve more than 10,000 inhabitants and accept, by a contract with Eco-Emballages and ADEME, to report all detailed costs of their waste management systems (including selective collection and sorting of household waste) and to identify the main factors that enable a technical, economic and social improvement of their systems. The support provided for communication compels the local authorities to develop annual communication plans specifying all measures, tools and resources required to raise awareness concerning the selective collection of household packaging waste. To make local authorities eligible to receive support for capacity building, they were required to develop an annual report, including all the communication activities developed by the "sorting ambassadors."

In 2010, the direct funding paid to local authorities amounted to 416 million Euros (Eco- Emballages, 2011). The new system developed by Eco-Emballages to comply with the "Grenelle 1" agenda aims to encourage a higher performance of the local authorities (along with the increase of the FSLA) and to strengthen preventive measures that promote the eco-design (increasing the green dot fees of certain packaging types).

The sale of sorted packaging waste to guarantors/recyclers corresponds to another financing source for local authorities beyond FSLA from the Eco-Emballages. The take-back prices of materials depend on the specific take-back scheme adopted by local authorities. They have three options to sell recyclables: Option *Filières*, Option Federations and Option Individual. However, the same local authority can select different options for different materials. Table 3.9 shows the 2010 take-back prices of several packaging materials for each take-back option. In some cases, the actual take-back values vary significantly since the negotiation of the price of the materials is made directly with the recycling industry in the last two options (either through the national federations—*Fédération Nationale des Activités de la Dépollution et de l'Environnement* and *Fédération de la Récupération, du Recyclage et de la Valorisation*—or individually). Nevertheless, the quality of the sorted materials should not differ in the three options because, in general, the recycling operators are the same. The values presented in Table 3.9 were the highest after 18 months of economic crisis, leading to a strong increase in the revenue generated by local authorities which was around 158 million Euros in 2010 (Adelphe, 2010).

Table 3.9   Take-back prices in France according to the take-back scheme option and material (€/ton)

Packaging material	Option *Filières*	Option Federations		Option individual	
		Average price	Price range	Average price	Price range
Steel (selective collection)	111,6	126,4	79–174	159,3	124–195
Steel (bottom ashes)	41,5	49,3	6–93	69,1	47–92
Aluminum (selective collection)	451	499,3	348–651	337,9	205–471
Aluminum (bottom ashes)	552	635,8	573–698	(-)	(-)
Plastics	196,3	189,6	151–229	(-)	(-)
Paper/cardboard	72,3	75,6	55–96	51.4	35–68
Glass	22,42	(-)	(-)	(-)	(-)

Source: Adelphe and Eco-Emballage (2011)

Current Situation

Municipal waste generation has increased over time in France, although the rate somehow stabilized since 2007 (which can be related to the economic crisis). Despite that, as illustrated in Figure 3.3, the municipal waste generation per capita has remained above the European average since 2004. The percentage of material recycled has also increased over time in this country.

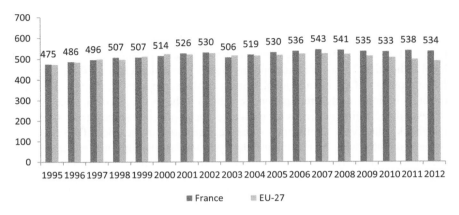

Figure 3.3   Generation of municipal waste in France (kg per capita)

Source: Eurostat

For the particular case of packaging waste, France met the targets of the PPW Directive in 2007. Since then the overall recycling rate has been somewhat constant and is currently (2011) about 60 percent. Among the various packaging materials, the paper/cardboard is the most used material, as shown in Table 3.10. Paper/cardboard packaging is the material with the highest recycling rate, reaching 88 percent in 2011 (see Figure 3.4).

All specific targets have been met by France in recent years with the exception of wood packaging in 2009. According to the latest available data, plastic is the material with the smallest slack between the minimum recycling target and actually achieved rate.

Table 3.10   Generation of packaging waste by material in France (thousands of tons)

Year	Packaging waste	Paper / cardboard	Plastic	Wood	Metal	Glass
2002	12,275	4,234	1,867	2,068	734	3,372
2003	12,334	4,210	1,951	2,240	688	3,240
2004	12,383	4,257	1,980	2,295	711	3,135
2005	12,361	4,295	2,007	2,218	685	3,151
2006	12,668	4,419	2,064	2,306	669	3,205
2007	12,797	4,472	2,114	2,388	673	3,145
2008	12,828	4,284	2,047	2,642	718	3,133
2009	12,278	4,379	1,877	2,474	670	2,873
2010	12,516	4,673	2,002	2,413	595	2,829
2011	12,811	4,882	2,032	2,418	593	2,881

Source: Eurostat

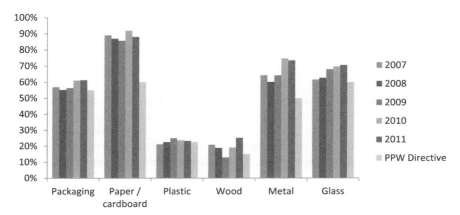

Figure 3.4   Recycling rate of packaging waste by material in France
Source: Eurostat

Germany[3]

Legal and Institutional Framework

The EU "waste hierarchy" (which has prevention, reuse, recycling, recovery and disposal as last resort) is also the basic foundation of waste management policies in Germany. In fact, Germany aims to achieve full waste recovery in 2020 (at least for municipal waste), avoiding disposal in landfills. The ban on the landfilling of untreated waste approved in 2005 is in line with this strategy.

The aim to ban uncontrolled waste dumps dates back to 1972, when the first independent Waste Disposal Act was enacted, imposing the tight supervision and control of landfills for waste treatment (Schnurer, 2002). A few years later (1986), the Waste Avoidance and Management Act set out the legal framework for waste treatment. The waste hierarchy was established by putting waste prevention before waste recovery and waste disposal. All "recoverable" waste must follow this sequence. This Act also introduced take-back obligations and the EPR in the national legislation (Hempen, 2005).

During these legislative changes incineration became the main solution for municipal waste treatment. Therefore, in order to regulate waste incinerators, the Seventeenth Federal Emission Control Ordinance, came into force in 1990, introducing the world's most demanding emission limits (for dioxins, furans and heavy metals). The incinerators had to be upgraded in line with the new specifications or to be closed in a six-year transitional period.

---

3   The following scholars contributed with research for this subchapter (in alphabetical order): Marta Cabral, Nuno Ferreira da Cruz, Pedro Simões, Rui Cunha Marques and Sandra Ferreira.

The Technical Instructions on Waste from Human Settlements were enacted in 1993 with the objective of assuring that the landfills in Germany were established according to several requirements in terms of location, design and composition and characteristics of the waste accepted. It also imposed the pre-treatment of waste prior to landfilling.

The Closed Substance Cycle and Waste Management Act, which came into force in 1996, integrated the accountability of waste producers before the economy, forcing them to pay for the waste placed into the market. This Act stated that waste producers/owners were responsible for the prevention, recycling, reuse and disposal of waste produced. It was the basis for a series of ensuing ordinances and voluntary agreements. Furthermore, several specific regulations were developed for different sectors, namely: packaging, end-of-life vehicles, batteries, electrical and electronic equipment, waste oil, wood waste, commercial waste, biodegradable waste, sewage sludge, hazardous waste and waste from construction and demolition.

The PPW Directive was introduced into German legislation through the so-called Packaging Ordinance in 1998. However, Germany had already packaging legislation in force before the enactment of this EU Directive (the Ordinance on the Avoidance of Packaging Waste of 1991). The Packaging Ordinance was amended five times (in 2000, 2002, two times in 2005 and in 2009) and the fourth revision transposed the Directive 2004/12/CE (updating the targets for packaging waste recycling).

The German Packaging Ordinance requires that manufacturers and distributors provide a collection and disposal system, managing all the one-way packaging that is placed onto the market for consumers. "Sales packaging" is defined in the Packaging Ordinance as "the packaging that is made available as a sales unit and arises at the final consumer (...) shall also include such packaging provided by retailers, restaurants and other service providers as facilitates or supports the transfer of goods to the final consumer." Secondary packaging is defined as "Packaging that is used as packaging additional to sales packaging and is not necessary for transfer to the final consumer for reasons of hygiene, durability or the protection of goods from damage or contamination." Distributors are also required to take-back the secondary packaging (free of charge) at the point of sale or nearby. Furthermore, the Packaging Ordinance defines and distinguishes the terms "final consumer" and "private final consumer." Whereas, in general, the final consumer is any person (or entity) who is the last user of the packaging (i.e. the packaging is not sold to anyone else), the private final consumer are specifically households (or equivalent waste producers).

Concerning the selective collection of sales packaging, the Packaging Ordinance allows manufacturers or distributors to participate in a "sector-specific collection" scheme for sales packaging waste arising at household-equivalent places (e.g. restaurants, hotels, canteens and others). However, these economic operators must obtain a certificate issued by an independent expert confirming that there is a collection system (free of charge) and that sales packaging recovery is assured.

All entities responsible for placing sales packaging onto the market have to submit a Declaration of Compliance to the Chambers of Industry and Commerce (IHK in the German acronym). If the amount of sales packaging is below the threshold quantities, the Declaration of Compliance must be submitted only if the authorities responsible for monitoring waste management request it. The economic operators with values above the threshold have to declare their compliance and register in the IHK's internet platform. The thresholds regarding the various materials are as follows:

- Glass—80 tons/year;
- Paper/cardboard—50 tons/year;
- Aluminum, plastics, steel and composites—30 tons/year.

The submission of the Declaration of Compliance requires an audited activities report of the companies. There are about 4,500 German companies in this situation. Even though they only represent 5 percent of the total number of economic operators, they are responsible for 97 percent of the sales packaging tonnage (MS2 and Perchards, 2009). The Declaration of Compliance must include information about the material type and weights of packaging placed onto the market and clarify the following aspects:

- Participation in a compliance scheme for household sales packaging (dual system);
- Participation in sector-specific collection system;
- Participation in a compliance scheme for non-household sales packaging.

The minimum national recycling targets for each material of household sales packaging waste (as established in the Packaging Ordinance) are the following:

- Glass—75 percent;
- Tinplate—70 percent;
- Aluminum—60 percent;
- Paper/cardboard—70 percent;
- Composites—60 percent;
- Plastics—60 percent recovery and 36 percent recycling.

In 1991 the Ordinance on the Avoidance of Packaging Waste stated that a mandatory deposit would be in force if the recycling targets set to the Duales System Deutschland GmbH (DSD—see the following subchapters) were not met and if the market share of refillables remained under the 72 percent level. In 1997, these goals were not met, thus a mandatory deposit system was firstly introduced in 2003. Currently, a deposit of 0.25€ on non-reusable drinks packaging is in force. This deposit is applied to all non-ecologically favorable packaging containing mineral water, beer, soft drinks and alcoholic mixed drinks for sizes between

0.1 and 3.0 liters. The Packaging Ordinance defines "ecologically advantageous one-way drinks packaging" as "drinks carton packaging (brick packs, gable-top cartons and cylindrical packaging), drinks packaging in the form of polyethylene bags and stand-up bags." In 2010, the target for the market share of refillables and environmentally favorable non-refillables was 80 percent.

The Ordinance on Environmentally Compatible Storage of Waste from Human Settlements came into force in 2001, introducing some modifications to the Technical Instructions on Waste and transposing the EU Landfill Directive into national law. In addition to the ban on the landfilling of untreated waste going to (not authorized after 1 June 2005), the Ordinance contained additional criteria for the classification of landfills and disposal rules which encouraged the MBT of waste. The law requires that the organic portion has to be biodegraded, demanding a separation of the higher calorific value materials (plastics, wood and paper) that represents a share of 40–50 percent (BMU, 2006). These materials should be used in co-incineration and incineration facilities. By the end of 2009, the landfills that did not meet the criteria were closed.

The 2008 WFD requires that reuse and/or recycling of waste materials (paper, metal, plastic and glass from households and similar) shall be increased to a minimum of 50 percent by weight until 2020. This Directive is being transposed to German legislation through the Act for Promoting Closed Substance Cycle Waste Management (the draft was published in 2010). This Act introduces even more ambitious recycling and recovery targets (more demanding that the requirements of the WFD), particularly: 65 percent of all municipal waste and 70 percent of all building and demolition waste has to be recycled (preparation for reuse is included) or recovered by 2020.

Waste Management Operators

Germany is a Republic with 16 federal states, each with its own legal framework, governments and parliaments. The administrative and political structure of each state is different. There are three levels of government, the Federal, the states and the local governments. Concerning waste management, Federal and State Governments are responsible for the legal framework at their respective levels (prevailing the national law in case of missing points).

The local authorities are responsible for waste management and have autonomy to issue local regulations to complement state legislation. These regulations may define the collection frequency, collection points and the fees applied to businesses and households for the waste management services.

Despite the growth observed after the landfill ban of 2005, Germany faces a problem related to the balance between the capacity of the incineration facilities and the growth of recycling which has been deviating the waste (in particular, packaging waste). Currently the waste incineration capacity is about 18.8 million tons and the MBT capacity is around 6 million tons per year (UBA, 2012).

Until 2015 an increase of approximately 6 percent in the incineration treatment capacity is expected to take place, corresponding to 19.6 tons/year (Prognos AG, 2008). It is also estimated that, by this year, around 31 percent of the incineration capacity (of a total of 69 facilities) will be managed directly by municipalities or public companies, 38 percent delivered through public-private arrangements and the remainder 31 percent by privately owned plants. The market structure of MBT is projected to be around 44 percent (of a total of 60 MBT facilities) of direct public management, 35 percent through PPP arrangements and 21 percent of private investors.

According to the Packaging Ordinance, packaging manufacturers and distributors are solely responsible for their waste and have to comply with a system that ensures its recycling and recovery. Indeed, in Germany, the recycling system (including the selective collection and sorting of waste) is 100 percent financed by the industry, which also has the responsibility to operationalize it. To accomplish this, a dual (separate) system for the collection of packaging waste was established throughout the country. Local authorities are only responsible for the refuse (mixed waste) flow.

Compliance Scheme

To cope with the obligation of collecting and recovering their sales packaging waste, the German economic operators created the first ever Green Dot company in 1990: the DSD. Initially this Green Dot company was a non-profit organization responsible for the entire compliance dual system in Germany. The Deutsche Gesellschaft für Kreislaufwirtschaft und Rohstoffe mbH (DKR), a DSD's subsidiary, is responsible for the recovering of the materials. DKR started with the plastic packaging recycling process and has now extended its scope to other packaging materials, such as tinplate, glass, paper and lightweight packaging (LWP) sorting refuse.

Participation in a dual system is open to all manufacturers and distributors responsible for placing household sales packaging onto the market. Regarding imported sales packaging the participation in a dual system is the responsibility of the importer. The compliance scheme company coordinates with the local authorities across the country and is responsible for the collection, sorting and recovery of the sales packaging of their clients. The dual system is financed by the participation fees paid by the manufacturers. The fees are set according to the material and weight of the sales packaging introduced in the market.

DSD used to be the only company coordinating the packaging waste collection with all the local authorities across the country and to be responsible for the sorting and recovery of all sales packaging on behalf of the industry (and it still carries out this activity by contracting private and MSW management companies). However, in 2004 the market was liberalized and DSD was "privatized" (i.e. producers are no longer the sole owners of the EPR companies, as in most Green Dot schemes).

The objective was to introduce competition in the market. Presently (2014), there are nine (for-profit) dual system companies licensed to manage packaging waste:

- DSD;
- Landbell AG für Rückhol-Systeme;
- Redual GmbH;
- BellandVision GmbH;
- Vfw GmbH;
- Eko-Punkt GmbH;
- Interseroh Dienstleistungs GmbH;
- Veolia Umweltservice Dual GmbH;
- Zentek GmbH & Co. KG.

Nevertheless, detaining the highest market share for all the waste stream materials, DSD continues to be the major player having more than 18,000 members (see Table 3.11). Companies participating in the dual systems report the quantities of each packaging material they want to place onto the market to the respective managing organization so that these entities can calculate the applicable fees. The companies involved in the recycling process report the amount of packaging waste delivered for recycling and the recycling rates are calculated with this information.

Table 3.11   Operators of dual systems and market shares in the last quarter of 2010 (%)

Dual system	LWP	Glass packaging	Paper/Cardboard
DSD	56.04	54.69	43.13
Landbell	4.98	5.13	6.92
Interseroh	7.13	10.60	6.56
Eko-Punkt	1.13	16.37	5.53
Redual	10.80	5.21	4.17
Vfw	7.35	1.85	11.19
BellandVision	6.54	2.75	7.16
Zentek	5.30	3.40	8.17
Veolia	0.73	0.00	2.17

Source: BVSE (2011)

In order to keep their licenses the EPR companies have to provide the mass flow verification to the state governments that have the responsibility to monitor the recycling system. Dual systems are only responsible for sales packaging. Industry and transport packaging are collected and recycled separately (transport packaging is defined in the Packaging Ordinance as "packaging that facilitates the transport of goods, protects the goods from damage during transport or is used in the interest of transport safety and arises at the distributor"). The non-negative market value of most packaging materials contributes to the high recycling rates achieved in Germany (R3 and CM, 2009).

The dual systems provide various options for the collection of sales packaging. For instance, the LWP, comprising plastics, aluminum, tinplate and composite materials, are mainly collected via curbside or bring system. The household sales packaging collection system was built up in Germany by DSD. Today, the other dual systems also use this collection infrastructure. The collection system depends on the agreements firmed with the municipalities as well as on the existent infrastructure. Each compliance scheme needs to have the permission of the local authority to organize the collection of the household packaging waste. Currently, there are around 450 local authorities with a particular waste collection system (PRO Europe, 2010). Nevertheless, the most common system is as follows:

- Glass is collected in dedicated containers (bring system);
- Paper/cardboard packaging waste is collected in a "blue bin" along with non-packaging waste paper;
- LWP is collected in a "yellow bin" or "yellow bags" (curbside collection).

Whereas glass and paper are rather "easy" to recycle, the recovery process for LWP is the most complex. LWP is first sorted in sorting facilities according to the material used for packaging: different types of plastic, metals (aluminum and tin plate), beverage liquid containers, paper/cardboard packaging and other residues. The sorted materials are then recovered by waste operators contracted by the compliance schemes. Five of the nine dual systems are owned by waste management companies (that sometimes carry out the sorting and recovery services "in-house").

The paper/cardboard packaging waste is collected with the other (non-packaging) waste whose responsibility for collection lies with the municipalities. In this case, the dual systems have to pay for the collection based on the share of the packaging waste collected. Since 2004, DSD has tendered collection services and organized the collection infrastructure in three-year contracts which have been shared by the remaining compliance schemes. The sharing of the collection infrastructure is done on a market share basis. From then on, the costs (or prices) of collection have been reduced by 30 percent compared with the years before competition was introduced in the market (Bundeskartellamt, 2011).

After collection, the packaging waste is sent to each compliance scheme (being processed in a transfer station) according to the Dual System market share. The costs with containers and with communication are supported by the EPR companies (also based on the market share). Each compliance scheme has organized the sorting and recycling of its share of waste.

With the last amendment to the Packaging Ordinance, DSD no longer detains the exclusive competence for tendering the collection services. In the new system each compliance scheme organizes tenders in a number of districts. Since this alteration, there were several tendering agreements submitted by the compliance schemes with the aim of organizing the new system, but only in 2011 did eight of the EPR companies (representing 99 percent of the packaging quantities) sign the "Tendering Agreement" that met the key requirements of the national competition law. Each compliance scheme is responsible for the tender process in its lot and has to design the collection system in coordination with the local authorities, draft the tender documents, award the contract and monitor its implementation during the three-year period. A joint tender platform supports the tendering process which is operated by an outside service provider and monitored by an independent third party. The bids are submitted under this platform and the organizer of the tender will only have access to the information about the name of the best bidder and not the price (Bundeskartellamt, 2011).

The number of districts for which a compliance scheme is responsible for organizing the tenders is determined according to the market share. As the market shares depend on the packaging waste material, separate procedures are carried out. The collection districts allocated by lot are determined in a draw, conducted by a third party. The prices of collection from different tender organizers are not disclosed. The third party organizing the draw has access to the prices but have to sign a confidentiality clause. The first draw took place on 30 November 2010 and only involved three compliance schemes (which had signed the Tendering Agreement by that date); the tender procedures started to be organized by the end of April 2011 (Bundeskartellamt, 2011). The tender organizer bears 50 percent of the collection costs, whereas the other 50 percent will be charged to all the compliance schemes based on the market share structure. The calculation of the quantity of the waste collected and handed over to the respective compliance schemes remains the same.

The municipalities are responsible for the household (mixed) waste management and the services provided are funded by local taxes or fees. The tariff systems may vary based on the number of household members, the land size and/or the quantity or volume of waste generated. In some municipalities the households have the option to choose their bin size and the waste collection frequency (CCC, 2009). Indeed, there are two models in use for the calculation of the household waste disposal charges (Eunomia, 2009): (1) flat rate charging or (2) charging based on the quantity of waste disposal. In the flat charging model the households are charged depending on the number of people per household. According to Eunomia (2009) this model is applied to the majority of the municipalities in Germany. In this model the waste fees are composed of an annual fee per household and a fee for the waste container (that can be of different volumes). The PAYT fee depends on the volume of waste disposed.

The selective collection flow, however, is totally financed by the industry (i.e. the compliance schemes). The packaging waste management operations are financed by the license fees paid by the dual systems' clients. Since the liberalization of the market DSD (as the other EPR companies) ceased to be a non-profit company which had some implications regarding the transparency and communication of market information. The dual systems currently do not publish the license fees, being these negotiable between the producer and the EPR company (MS2 and Perchards, 2009). Therefore, due to the competitive nature of the market, the EPR companies only issue price information to actual customers. The last publicly available list of the Green Dot fees (DSD's fees from 2007) is shown in Table 3.12.

In Germany, the use of the Green Dot symbol is not mandatory (since DSD is the Green Dot company and there are eight more compliance schemes). Any economic operator who wishes to use it has to pay a trademark fee (see Table 3.13), in addition to the license fee based on the weight and the type of packaging material.

Table 3.12   Green Dot fees for 2007 in Germany

Packaging material	Green Dot fees (€/ton)
Glass	74
Paper / cardboard	175
Tinplate	272
Aluminum, other metals	733
Plastic	1,296
Composites cartons with special acceptance and recycling guarantee	752
Other composites	1,014
Natural materials	102

Source: PRO Europe (2010)

The fees for the trademark usage (paid to DSD) are not enough to fulfil the requirements of the Packaging Ordinance. These fees only represent the "economic value" of using the Green Dot symbol on the packaging of the goods. The manufacturers and distributors have also to pay a fee for the participation in a dual system (the economic operators can choose among the previously listed companies).

Table 3.13   Trademark fees *Der Grune Punkt* by material

Packaging material	Green Dot fees (€/ton)
Glass	1
Paper / cardboard	3
Tinplate	5
Aluminum	13
Plastic	17
Composites	13

Source: PRO-Europe (2011)

Despite the unavoidable issues (e.g. related to free-riders, lack of transparency, etc.), it seems that competition brought relevant cost savings and technology innovation to the selective collection and sorting of packaging waste (BMU, 2011a). During the DSD's monopoly, the total fees paid in Germany were about 2 billion Euros per year. With the competition between the nine Dual Systems, the fees represent now about half that amount (Bundeskartellamt, 2011).

The sorting of approximately 2.25 million tons of LWP collected is done in the almost 100 nationwide sorting facilities. In 2009, almost 90 percent of the amount collected was sorted in 50 facilities. The sorting is done with the aim of producing marketable material fractions which have a positive value, except for portions of mixed plastics with a negative value of 50€/ton and beverage composites that have approximately "zero" value (BMU, 2011b).

The (household) dual systems companies also have solutions for manufacturers and distributors supplying commercial end-users comparable to households (the so-called "branch solution"). In these cases, the EPR companies organize the separate waste collection at the supplied places. The fee of this waste management service is considerably lower than waste collection from the households (MS2 and Perchards, 2009) because the source separation is better and the level of contamination of packaging waste is lower. The number of compliance schemes in the branch solution (encompassing to large users, such as hospitals) is higher than the operators of the dual system, corresponding to about 120 EPR companies. When the dual systems perform both services, it can become difficult to distinguish household packaging from non-household packaging.

Current Situation

Taking into account the most recent years, approximately 600 kg of municipal waste are generated per capita in Germany. With a rate of 46 percent, the material recycling of municipal waste in Germany is the highest in the EU. The share of incineration is about 37 percent (there were 69 incineration plants in Germany in 2010; UBA, 2012). Landfilling has decreased since 2005, being in 2010 only 0.4 percent of the total municipal waste generated. The number of landfills has also reduced significantly (e.g. from 297 in 2004 to 160 in 2007). Despite this, the municipal waste generation per capita is considerably above the European average (see Figure 3.5). Nevertheless, the higher per capita values from 1996 to 2002 have been avoided in the ensuing 10 years.

Among the various packaging materials, the paper/cardboard is the most widely used, whereas the metal is the material with the lowest share. Table 3.14 shows the quantities of packaging waste produced between 2002 and 2011 for each material.

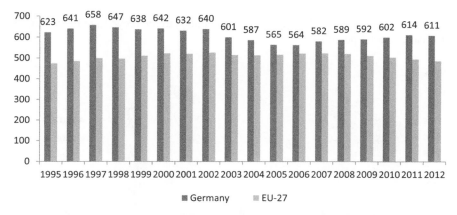

Figure 3.5   Generation of municipal waste in Germany (kg per capita)
Source: Eurostat

Table 3.14   Generation of packaging waste by material in Germany
(thousands of tons)

Year	Packaging waste	Paper / cardboard	Plastic	Wood	Metal	Glass
2002	15,435	6,607	2,073	2,382	1,091	3,266
2003	15,466	6,789	2,071	2,508	950	3,130
2004	15,517	6,947	2,255	2,319	904	3,073
2005	15,471	6,896	2,368	2,408	898	2,879
2006	16,133	7,104	2,591	2,633	887	2,895
2007	16,113	7,148	2,644	2,620	853	2,825
2008	16,045	6,940	2,732	2,571	912	2,869
2009	15,052	6,634	2,621	2,110	810	2,857
2010	16,003	7,196	2,690	2,550	833	2,712
2011	16,486	7,347	2,776	2,791	881	2,670

Source: Eurostat

Complying with the overall recycling targets of the PPW Directive was never really a challenge for Germany that in 1997 already presented a recycling rate of 80.6 percent (i.e. even higher than the one depicted nowadays, around 70 percent). As shown in Figure 3.6, currently, Germany maintains comfortable slacks between the achieved recycling rates and the minimum requirements for all packaging waste materials. Glass, metal and paper and cardboard all achieved a recycling rate of nearly 90 percent. In terms of recovery, only glass is below 90 percent (the recovery rate of glass packaging waste corresponds to the recycling rate which, in this case, is 88.4 percent).

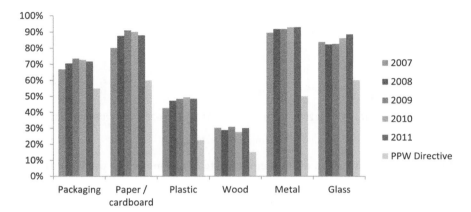

Figure 3.6   Recycling rate of packaging waste by material in Germany
Source: Eurostat

Italy[4]

Legal and Institutional Framework

The PPW Directive was first introduced in the Italian legislation by the *Ronchi* Decree (legislative Decree 22/97) which was amended in 2006 by the legislative Decree "Environment Regulations" (legislative Decree 152/06). The Italian Government has set more stringent targets for the recycling of plastics (26 percent) and wood (35 percent). As in most EU countries, the responsibility for packaging waste management in Italy is transferred by the industry to an entity duly licensed for this activity. However, this is one of the very few countries where there is no official Green Dot company. Indeed, despite being based on the principles of the PPW Directive, the National Packaging Consortium (CONAI in the Italian acronym) does not formally participate in the Green Dot scheme (Comieco, 2011).

This is due to a number of reasons and political decisions, namely the fact that (arguably) the full embracement of the Green Dot scheme would have resulted in higher fees for the economic operators (for example, leading to possible free-riding). Therefore, when CONAI was established back in 1997, the industry decided to opt for a different (supposedly lower) calculation of license fees.

---

4   The following scholars contributed with research for this subchapter (in alphabetical order): Lucia Rigamonti, Mario Grosso, Marta Cabral, Nuno Ferreira da Cruz, Pedro Simões, Rui Cunha Marques and Sandra Ferreira.

According to the Italian legislation, municipal waste management services and the awareness campaigns (e.g. in terms of source separation practices) are the exclusive responsibility of local authorities. However, the CONAI system must contribute financially to the expenses related to a proper (i.e. efficient and economic) packaging waste collection and management. The industry is not required to pay excess costs due to poor quality collection, inefficient sorting, over-costly transport, etc. The "collection fee," which is paid by CONAI to the municipalities, is based on the quality of collected materials. The lower the quality is, the lower the FSLA will also be.

Waste Management Operators

In 2010, 32 percent of the residual waste (refuse or undifferentiated collection flow) was treated in MBT facilities, 10 percent was incinerated and 58 percent was landfilled. Indeed, landfilling still plays a major role for the disposal of residual (mixed) waste in Italy. The residual waste sent to MBT facilities may still be sorted for further material recovery. Thus, the packaging waste included in this flow can be sent back to the recycling system. Regarding the incineration process, the combustible packaging materials in waste (such as plastic) will contribute to energy production due to their high calorific value, while metallic packaging recovered from bottom ash can also be sent to the recycling system.

Municipal waste collection in Italy is carried out through curbside and/or bring systems managed by local authorities. The drop-off centers contribute with a small percentage of packaging waste for recovery. Furthermore, packaging waste can be collected either as a mono-material flow or as a multimaterial flow (the latter meaning that two or more material fractions are co-mingled in a single bin). A number of different multimaterial schemes exist in Italy, for instance:

- Paper and plastic;
- Paper, plastic, aluminum, steel;
- Plastic, aluminum, steel;
- Glass, paper, aluminum, steel;
- Glass, aluminum, steel;
- Paper, glass, plastic, aluminum.

When a multimaterial collection scheme is employed, the packaging waste flow requires a preliminary step of separation between the different materials. In general, this separation step is something different from what one usually refers to as sorting operations. However, in some cases, the sorting of single material and multimaterial flows take place in the same facilities. In Italy, the CONAI system manages the collection, sorting and recovery of packaging waste in two different ways (according to the origin of the packaging):

- The selective collection of primary packaging from municipal waste is managed on the basis of the ANCI-CONAI agreement. That is, the local authorities that wish to join the CONAI system must sign a convention with the respective Material Consortium. This allows the municipalities to receive a "collection fee" (paid by the industry) for each ton of material collected and delivered to the relevant consortium.
- The secondary and tertiary packaging arising from private premises (industrial facilities, shopping malls, etc.) is managed optionally through a platform system.

CONAI is a private non-profit organization established in 1997 with the aim of promoting the selective collection, sorting, recovery and recycling of packaging waste in Italy (encompassing packaging of both fast moving consumer goods and industrial products). For the recovery operations of individual materials, CONAI co-ordinates the activities of the six Material Consortia:

- RICREA for steel;
- CiAL for aluminum;
- Comieco for paper;
- Rilegno for wood;
- COREPLA for plastic;
- COREVE for glass.

Table 3.15 shows the current coverage of CONAI and of the Material Consortia.

Table 3.15   Direct management by CONAI

Consortium)	Share of inhabitants	Share of municipalities
Steel (Ricrea)	73%	61%
Glass (Coreve)	82%	73%
Aluminum (Cial)	73%	60%
Plastics (Corepla)	96%	90%
Paper (Comieco)	89%	80%
Wood (Rilegno)	71%	59%

Source: EIMPack (2013a)

Compliance Scheme

CONAI operates under the "polluter pays" and the "shared responsibility" general principles. According to the first principle, any person/entity responsible for environmental pollution must also bear the costs of "decontamination." In the case of packaging waste, this corresponds to the cost of collection and recovery or landfilling. Economic operators that produce goods have the greatest responsibility for pollution, and thus they should bear the greater part of the cost of packaging waste management. But other players in the system hold part of the responsibility as well, and they should share the costs proportionally.

This means that, in Italy, economic operators cannot be fully and unconditionally charged with packaging waste management costs. Indeed, the local authorities are required to organize the selective collection systems "efficiently and economically," and private citizens should follow the instructions of local authorities regarding the proper way of sorting the materials prior to collection.

CONAI is funded through the "CONAI Environmental Contribution" (CAC in the Italian acronym) applied to the packaging sold by the "last producer" (manufacturers and importers of raw materials for packaging, manufacturers and importers of half-processed products for packaging, the producers of empty packaging, importers, and retailers of empty packaging) to the "first user" (dealers, distributors, fillers, users of packaging and importers of filled packaging). CONAI will then transfer the respective amounts to the competent Material Consortium, after deducting a certain percentage for its own administration. The value of the contribution for each material is defined every year by the CONAI Board of Directors. Table 3.16 presents the values in effect in 2010. The procedure is implemented as follows:

1. When issuing an invoice, the economic operator adds an amount (in Euros) equal to the weight (in kilograms) of the packaging sold, multiplied by the value (in Euro/kg) set for that particular material;
2. The economic operator pays the resulting amount to CONAI, which will then transfer it to the competent Material Consortium after deducting a percentage for its own administration;
3. The Material Consortia use these funds to pay the "collection fee" to the local authorities as defined by the ANCI-CONAI agreement for selective collection.

Table 3.16   License fees for 2010 in Italy

Packaging material	Environmental contribution (€/ton)
Steel	31.00
Aluminum	52.00
Paper	22.00
Wood	8.00
Plastic	160.00
Glass	15.82

Source: EIMPack (2013a)

As mentioned above, regarding the management of primary packaging resulting from the municipal waste stream, the local authorities that wish to join the CONAI system must sign a convention with the corresponding Material Consortium/a. This will allow them to receive a "collection fee," paid by the Consortia, for each ton of material collected and delivered to the appropriate Consortium. The various fees, quality standards, methods and procedures are stipulated in the ANCI-CONAI agreement (signed every five years). Indeed, among other technical aspects, the agreement defines the following:

- The "collection fees," in €/ton, for the quantities of packaging waste of a particular material collected and taken back by the relevant Consortium. The fees are also based on the quality of the collected material (i.e. to the impurities it contains). Quality is checked through analyses carried out periodically. No "collection fee" is payable if the percentage of impurities exceeds the maximum threshold and the Consortium may choose not to take back the material;
- Any other charges payable to municipalities depending on distance and transport costs, or other additional costs (e.g. due to waste compressing, sorting/cleaning, etc.).

Actually, the "collection fee," paid by CONAI to the municipalities for the selective collection of packaging waste that they carry out, corresponds to the FSLA (already mentioned for other member states). When paying the FSLA the industry ensures that the collected packaging waste will be, in fact, recovered through material recycling or energy recovery, in order to fulfil the legal requirements of the PPW Directive. As previously explained, packaging waste can be collected both as mono-material flow and as a multimaterial flow. When multimaterial collection is employed, the packaging waste must undergo a preliminary step of separation between the different materials. The FSLA is paid in both cases, but when multimaterial collection is in place the unit fees are based on the quality of the materials after the multimaterial separation.

The quality levels attained for each material, which affects the amount of the FSLA, as shown in Tables 3.17 to 3.21, might also affect the financial responsibility for the disposal of the sorting residues. However, this is not applicable to all six materials (only to steel, paper and plastic). In general, when a good quality of collection is achieved, the disposal of residues will be paid by the Consortium; whereas for poor quality levels, the disposal is under the responsibility of the local authority. This gives a double penalization to the local authorities, thus encouraging all efforts to attain a very high quality of the collected materials. Tables 3.17 to 3.21 show the FSLA (or, as referred to in Italy, the "collection fee") for each material based on the amount of impurities (other materials) present in the packaging waste collected.

Table 3.17   FSLA for steel in 2010 in Italy

Category	% of other fractions	FSLA (€/ton)	Responsibility for the disposal of sorting residues
1	≤ 5	82.68	Consortium (Ricrea)
2	>5–10	70.04	Local authority
3	>10–15	57.41	Local authority
4	>15–20	37.89	Local authority

Source: EIMPack (2013a)

For aluminum packaging waste (Table 3.18), other services may be paid by the consortium (CiAl) to the local authorities in charge of the collection, for example due to:

• Reduction of volume;
• Transport from small islands;
• Reward if the material falls in categories A or B and a total yield higher than 250 g per inhabitant and per year is achieved.

Table 3.18   FSLA for aluminum in 2010 in Italy

Category	% of other fractions	FSLA (€/ton)
1	≤ 4	422.56
2	>4–10	281.31
3	>10–15	172.24

Source: EIMPack (2013a)

Table 3.19   FSLA for glass in 2010 in Italy

Category	% of the fine fractions	% of other fractions	FSLA (€/ton)
Excellence	< 15 mm max 5%	max 1%	37.20
1	< 10 mm max 5%	max 1.5%	34.18
2	< 10 mm max 7%	max 2.5%	17.84
3	< 10 mm max 8%	max 5%	0.5

Source: EIMPack (2013a)

Also for plastic packaging waste (Table 3.20), other services may be paid by the consortium (Corepla) to the local authorities in charge of the collection, namely due to:

- Reduction of volume;
- Transport;
- Other logistic activities.

Table 3.20   FSLA for plastics in 2010 in Italy

Category	% of other fractions	FSLA (€/ton)	Responsibility for the disposal of sorting residues
Mono-material	≤ 5	277.87	Consortium (Corepla)
	>5–16	195.77	Consortium (Corepla)
	>16	0.00	Local authority
Multimaterial* (already in place)	≤ 10	277.87	Consortium (Corepla)
	>10–20	195.77	Consortium (Corepla)
	>20	0.00	Local authority
Multimaterial* (new implementation)	≤ 10	277.87	Consortium (Corepla)
	>10–16	195.77	Consortium (Corepla)
	>16	0.00	Local authority

* Depending on whether it was already in place at the date of signing of the Technical Annex plastic packaging (ANCI-CONAI Agreement) or if it was launched at a later stage.

Source: EIMPack (2013a)

The paper recyclers or guarantors pay 19 €/ton to the local authorities for non-packaging paper (average value in 2010). For wood, a specific agreement exists for packaging and non-packaging waste; both are paid by the Consortium (Rilegno) at 3.33 €/ton. Furthermore, there is no sorting for this material and all the collected wood is directly sent to recycling/recovery.

Other packaging and non-packaging waste that is recovered via the undifferentiated or refuse collection flow (e.g. through MBT or incineration) is also included in the ANCI-CONAI agreement. This is the case of packaging and non-packaging steel and aluminum recovered in MBT plants or from bottom ash of combustion plants (see Table 3.22). These materials may be sent to the respective consortium which will pay a fee to the operator depending on the quality of the material. Concerning steel, the value of the fee is defined by specific agreements, whereas the value of aluminum is defined within the ANCI-CONAI agreement.

Table 3.21   FSLA for paper in 2010 in Italy

Material	Category	% of other fractions	% of FSLA*	Responsibility for the disposal of sorting residues
Only packaging (after sorting of non-packaging)	1	≤ 1.5	100	(-)
	2	>1.5–4	75	Local authority (the fraction > 1.5%)
	3	>4–10	50	Local authority (the fraction > 1.5%)
Packaging and non-packaging (packaging are assumed equal to 25%)	1	≤ 3	100	(-)
	2	>3–6	75	Local authority (the fraction > 3%)
	3	>6–10	50	Local authority (the fraction > 3%)
	4	> 10	0	The sorting plant can reject the load. If it accepts it, the local authority pays for the fraction > 3%

* Financial support in 2010: 90.48 €/ton
Source: EIMPack (2013a)

Table 3.22   FSLA for aluminum recovered in MBT plants or from bottom ash of combustion plants in 2010 in Italy

Category	% of other fractions	FSLA (€/ton)	
		From MBT plants	From bottom ash*
A	≤ 15	154.26	154.26
B	>15–30	128.56	143.97

* Moisture of the material shall be ≤ 15%; if it is included between 15% and 25%, only the 60% of the financial support will be given
Source: EIMPack (2013a)

Current Situation

In 15 years the recycling rate of packaging waste in Italy has increased immensely (from practically no recycling in 1997 to 64.5 percent in 2011). Recovery also increased significantly in the same period (from 31.8 percent to 74.0 percent). Indeed, the global targets of the PPW Directive were somewhat easy to achieve in this country (also taking into account that specific national targets for plastic and wood are more ambitious than those set by the EU Directive). The effects of the EU policies in terms of avoiding municipal waste generation were not so successful. In fact, as shown in Figure 3.7, Italy has been depicting higher per capita rates in recent years.

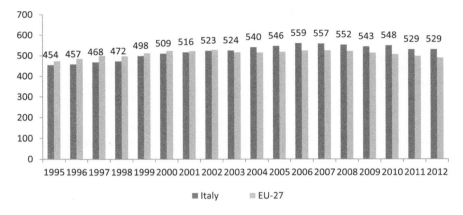

Figure 3.7   Generation of municipal waste in Italy (kg per capita)
Source: Eurostat

As shown in Table 3.23, paper and cardboard are also the most commonly used packaging materials in this country. These were also the materials with the highest recycling rates, followed by metal packaging waste (see Figure 3.8).

Table 3.23   Generation of packaging waste by material in Italy (thousands of tons)

Year	Packaging waste	Paper / cardboard	Plastic	Wood	Metal	Glass
2002	11,367	4,218	1,951	2,603	625	1,970
2003	11,537	4,208	2,000	2,570	640	2,107
2004	11,989	4,333	2,054	2,787	674	2,141
2005	11,953	4,315	2,099	2,788	634	2,117
2006	12,220	4,400	2,202	2,852	633	2,133
2007	12,541	4,619	2,270	2,860	635	2,157
2008	12,169	4,501	2,205	2,720	604	2,139
2009	10,862	4,092	2,092	2,094	519	2,065
2010	11,411	4,338	2,071	2,281	568	2,153
2011	11,638	4,436	2,075	2,306	555	2,266

Source: Eurostat

The recycling rates of all materials are comfortably above the minimum EU targets. The effects of the higher national targets for plastic and wood packaging waste are mainly observed in the case of the latter.

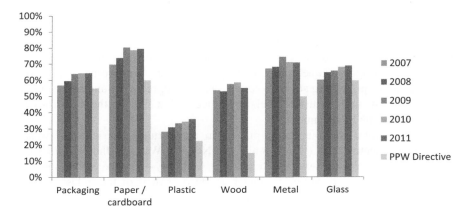

Figure 3.8   Recycling rate of packaging waste by material in Italy
Source: Eurostat

Portugal[5]

Legal and Institutional Framework

The legal framework for waste management was first approved in Portugal in 1985 through the Decree-Law No. 488/85. After the accession to the EU, in 1986, the national legislation on waste had to be substantially upgraded. For example, and more recently, the EU Directive No. 2006/12/EC on waste was transposed by the Decree-Law No. 178/2006 which set the national Waste Framework Law. This framework stipulated the creation of the National Waste Authority (currently within the scope of the Portuguese Environmental Agency—APA) and regulated the "waste market" envisaging the preservation of natural resources. This law led to the creation of SIRER (Integrated System of Electronic Record of Waste) which gathers information on the waste generated and imported and on the entities operating in the waste sector. Later on, this system evolved to SIRAPA (APA's Integrated System of Records), a single portal reserved to organizations and establishments with legal obligations relating to the environment (including the users of the old SIRER). Producers of municipal waste employing more than

---

5   The following scholars contributed with research for this subchapter (in alphabetical order): Marta Cabral, Nuno Ferreira da Cruz, Pedro Simões, Rui Cunha Marques and Sandra Ferreira.

10 workers, businesses whose waste production exceeds 1,100 liters per day and producers of hazardous waste from agriculture and other origins are required to have a register in SIRAPA.

The PPW Directive was transposed into national law by the Decree-Law No. 366-A/97 (initial EU targets) and the Decree-Law No. 92/2006 (new EU targets). According to the national legal framework, economic operators have to accept responsibility for the management of their packaging waste which can be transferred to an entity duly licensed for this activity. The Sociedade Ponto Verde (SPV), the Portuguese Green Dot company, is a private, non-profit organization with the aim of promoting separate collection, sorting, recovery and recycling of packaging waste at the national level. It was licensed in 1997 by the Ministries of Economy and the Environment.

In brief, there are four major players in the Portuguese packaging waste management sector: APA (which is also the National Waste Authority), ERSAR (the Water and Waste Services Regulation Authority—i.e. the sector-specific regulator), SPV (the recycling promoter acting on behalf of the industry) and, ultimately, the local authorities (i.e. the municipalities).

In the context of waste management, APA's competences are to develop and monitor the implementation of the national waste management strategies (although it also has other responsibilities regarding environmental protection). Its responsibilities include the licensing of waste management operations and the operators of specific waste flows, as well as the operational and administrative control of waste transfers. According to the Ordinance No. 29-B/98, packers and/ or those responsible for placing packaged products onto the domestic market shall report annually to APA the statistics on the quantities of reusable and non-reusable packaging, the quantities of packaging effectively used that were reused and recovered and also the quantities delivered to entities responsible for recovery or disposal. Those responsible for placing packaging in the market can transfer their liability to a licensed entity or adopt their own recovery system (which has to be approved by APA; currently, all packers/importers choose to join the SPV system). The responsibility of the licensed entity regarding the collection and recovery of household packaging waste is materialized through contracts with municipalities or with multimunicipal or intermunicipal systems (see below) that have been awarded the concession for the selective collection and sorting of municipal waste and with recyclers or guarantors to ensure the recovery of reclaimed materials. SPV, who is currently solely in charge of managing this logistic chain, is required to deliver an annual activities report to the licensing authorities.

The Decree-Law No. 362/98 approved the statute of IRAR (Regulatory Institute for Water and Waste), which was created as a public institute with administrative and financial autonomy but subject to the supervision of the Minister for Environment, Planning and Regional Development. IRAR had competence for "issuing binding instructions to correct the irregularities found in the design, implementation, management and operation of multimunicipal and municipal systems under concession arrangements." Among other amendments, the Decree-Law No. 207/2006 renamed the sector-specific regulator to ERSAR. In addition to the functions of economic and quality of service regulation for the water and waste sectors, this legislation also assigns ERSAR as the competent authority to supervise the quality of drinking water, ensure the structural regulation of the water and waste sectors and promote the comparison and public disclosure of the operators' performance through periodic reports (sunshine regulation via yardstick competition, see Marques and Simões, 2008). ERSAR has the main mission of protecting the users' interests, fostering the quality of service while guaranteeing the economic sustainability of the companies. The Decree-Law No. 277/2009 extended the scope of intervention of ERSAR to all managing bodies of these services regardless of the management model, and provided the regulator with greater regulatory power. ERSAR is an unusual regulator if one considers the usual lack of regulators for the waste sector throughout the world (Simões and Marques, 2012).

SPV is the main actor involved in the recycling of packaging waste (encompassing packaging of both fast moving consumer goods and industrial products). There are, however, two other entities responsible for specific packaging waste streams: Valorfito (agricultural packaging) and Valormed (pharmaceutical packaging) but these types of packaging waste do not enter the municipal flow. In addition, there are other entities licensed for the management of other specific waste streams, for example: Amb3E and ERP (electrical and electronic equipment), Ecopilhas and Valorcar (batteries and accumulators), Valorcar (vehicles), Sogilub (mineral oils) and Valorpneu (tires).

The current institutional framework of waste management includes municipal and intermunicipal systems (controlled by local governments), and multimunicipal systems (controlled by the central state). Taking into account the legal responsibilities and competences of local authorities in Portugal, the municipalities are required to ensure the proper management of urban waste. Nevertheless, many municipalities rely on multimunicipal systems (where the central state is the majority shareholder) for waste treatment and disposal and, very often, for selective collection. In terms of management models, the array of options is wide, especially for municipal (or intermunicipal systems): in addition to the direct management of the services through municipal services (with or without financial autonomy), there is also the possibility of corporatizing the municipal systems that provide these services (i.e. delivery by municipal and intermunicipal companies owned by the local governments), resorting to user groups (e.g. cooperatives) and contracting out to the private sector through concession agreements.

Waste services can be categorized into "wholesale" and "retail" services, depending on the activities carried out by the operators (da Cruz et al. 2012). In Portugal, the waste sector is clearly divided in these two segments. The retail services cover the activities of collection and transportation of household (or similar) waste and are performed primarily by municipal systems. The wholesale segment (managed by intermunicipal or multimunicipal entities) encompasses the storing, transportation, sorting, recovery, treatment and disposal of household waste, as well as other waste similar in its nature and composition to that from households whose daily production does not exceed 1,100 liters per producer.

Waste Management Operators

Since the PPW Directive has been published, large investments have taken place in the waste management sector in Portugal in this scope. After the elimination of the waste dumps at the end of the 1990s, several multimunicipal and intermunicipal systems have been established for municipal waste management, along with new compliant landfills, selective collection routes and equipment and sorting facilities.

The wholesale segment of urban waste management is dominated by multimunicipal companies. The entities consist of partnerships between a public company owned by the central state (Empresa Geral do Fomento—EGF) and the municipalities covered by the respective waste system. EGF owns 51 percent of the shares in these companies and, therefore, the municipalities have a minority participation (da Cruz et al., 2013). In 2014, there were 12 multimunicipal concessionaires, eight intermunicipal companies (indirect public management), four associations of municipalities (direct public management) and one private concessionaire in this segment. In addition to the typical wholesale services many of these entities are also in charge of selective collection.

Most operators providing waste retail services (mainly refuse collection) are municipal services (i.e. specialized departments of local governments), covering 230 municipalities (there are 278 municipalities in mainland Portugal and 308 in total). Municipal and intermunicipal companies are also frequent providers of these services, encompassing 31 municipalities in 2010. Although wholesale companies are usually responsible for selective collection in Portugal, in some cases municipalities also assume this particular service (either directly or through delegation to another public or private company).

Regarding the infrastructure and equipment employed in municipal waste management, in 2010, there were 40,278 drop-off containers, 204 drop-off centers, 33 sorting stations, 91 transfer stations, 14 MBT facilities, three incineration units with energy recovery and 41 landfills in Portugal (ERSAR, 2011). With the application of PERSU II (the national Strategic Plan for Urban Solid Waste currently in force) it is expected an increase in the number organic recovery units.

Compliance Scheme

SPV was created to take on the responsibility for managing packaging waste and ensure its proper destination, contributing to the achievement of recovery and recycling targets. The scope of the initial license granted to SPV (in 1997) only concerned the municipal flow. However, SPV was later licensed to extend its scope of operation to trade and industry packaging waste. The Green Dot company currently manages all types of material of non-reusable packaging placed onto the market. Thus, those placing packaging in the market shift the responsibility for waste management to SPV under the Green Dot scheme. At the end of 2010 there were 10,008 contracts signed with packers/fillers.

The Green Dot fees vary for each type of packaging material, namely: glass, plastic, paper and cardboard, composite packaging, steel, aluminum, wood and other materials. The unit fees also differ for some materials depending on whether the package is for fast moving consumer goods or for industrial products. In the case of packaging for fast moving consumer goods, the value is also different for primary, secondary or tertiary packaging. SPV provides three different membership arrangements:

1. Detailed statement: the packer/importer reports the weight of all packaging placed onto the national market in a given year, classifying it as fast moving consumer goods and/or industrial products packaging, and as primary, secondary and tertiary and detailing the type of material (or materials);
2. Simplified declaration: if the packer/importer places onto the domestic market up to 20,000 kg of packaging a year, it can choose to join the simplified system. In this case, in the first year the packer/importer just has to report the total weight of packaging put in the market and its materials (without detailing the type or category of packaging). In subsequent years, the value of the statement is automatically calculated by SPV based on estimates of growth of the sector where the company operates. Every year the producer will just have to approve SPV's estimate, indicate and state officially that it did not place onto the national market more than 20,000 kg of packaging;
3. Minimum Contribution: if the producer's sales volume is less than or equal to 100,000 €/year, it can opt for the minimum contribution scheme. In this case, it is not necessary to calculate weights of packaging or deliver any statement. The single annual payment will correspond to the minimum fee defined for that year.

SPV is also responsible for VERDORECA, a Green Dot subsystem, known as HORECA channel, with the aim of promoting the sorting of packaging waste discarded in hotels, restaurants, and similar businesses and forwarding it for recycling. This integrated system covers non-reusable packaging for all packaged or imported products for immediate consumption in those locations.

Adherence to VERDORECA does not imply any financial contribution to the Green Dot Company by those who want to join it. The members just have to ensure the separation of the packaging waste they produce, by type of material, and put them in appropriate containers at times determined by the entity responsible for collection in the area where they are located. The goal is to recycle all packaging waste after consumption. Thus, all establishments that use non-reusable packaging must be part of the VERDORECA system.

In short, the economic operators that make up the recycling system supported by SPV are the following:

a. Packers and/or other entities responsible for placing packaged products onto the Portuguese market;
b. Manufacturers of packaging and of raw materials used for the manufacture of packaging;
c. Packaging waste management operators;
d. Local authorities and/or management companies of multimunicipal or intermunicipal systems;
e. Hotels, restaurants and similar facilities (HORECA establishments).

The recycling system managed by SPV is mainly based on the following financial flows: (1) the Green Dot Fee (paid by the industry); (2) the Net take-back value (paid by recyclers/guarantors—when sorted material have a positive market value); (3) the FSLA (municipal flow), (4) the Information and Motivation fee (trade and industry flow); and (5) the Complementary fee (for the information about the amount and type of materials sent for recovery but not coming from selective collection).

The Green Dot Fee corresponds to the amount of financial compensation paid by packers or importers of packaged products to the SPV. The Green Dot Fees were established in the license granted in 2004 for the following materials: glass, paper and cardboard, steel, aluminum, plastic, wood and others. During the last years, the lessons learned and increased know-how gathered by all stakeholders led to more complex Green Dot Fees. The unit values set for the current Green Dot fees can be found in Table 3.24. Packers and importers calculate their annual contribution by multiplying the total weight of each type of packaging material placed onto the market by the respective fee. The objective is that the financial transfers made by the industry to SPV match the costs of the waste management operators (household flow, and trade and industry flow) and any investment made by SPV (including costs with marketing and R&D).

In the case of the municipal packaging waste, SPV establishes partnerships with local authorities (intermunicipal and multimunicipal systems and/or their concessionaire companies) that carry out the selective collection and sorting of packaging waste separated by the population within its area of intervention. Municipal packaging waste sent for recycling can have three different sources: selective collection, pretreatment of MBT and incineration. Packaging waste from selective collection comes from drop-off containers, curbside collection (there were some pilot experiences throughout the country) and drop-off centers. The waste coming from the selective collection flow is supported financially by SPV based on a model that relies on the efficiency of collection and sorting systems and on their potential generation per capita (as well as on the type of packaging waste material).

The FSLA is calculated using the values that correspond to a certain per capita generation of packaging waste. Evidently, the financial support also depends on each type of material, as shown in Table 3.25 (values set in 2009). In brief, the model is based on the efficiency of the waste management systems and their per

Table 3.24   Green Dot fees for 2010 in Portugal

Packaging material	Primary (€/ton)	Secondary (€/ton)	Tertiary (€/ton)
Packaging of fast moving consumer goods			
Glass	18.3	(-)	(-)
Paper/Cardboard	86.3	35.2	7
Plastic	228.2	92.3	23.8
Composite Food Packaging	129.4	(-)	(-)
Steel	96	41.7	24.4
Aluminum	164.4	(-)	(-)
Wood	15.4	14.2	9.1
Others	260	260	260
Packaging of industrial products and raw materials			
Glass	13.5	(-)	(-)
Paper/Cardboard	7.0	7.0	7.0
Plastic	23.8	23.8	23.8
Steel	24.4	24.4	24.4
Aluminum	49.4	(-)	(-)
Wood	9.1	9.1	9.1
Others	55	55	55
Packaging of industrial products; hazardous raw materials			
Glass	13.5	(-)	(-)
Paper/Cardboard	7.0	7.0	7.0
Plastic	23.8	23.8	23.8
Steel	24.4	24.4	24.4
Aluminum	49.4	(-)	(-)
Wood	9.1	(-)	(-)
Bags			
Plastic	228.2	228.2	228.2
Paper/Cardboard	86.3	86.3	86.3

capita potential (SPV, 2010). In Table 3.25, the "X" columns represent the take back per capita of each material and the "P" columns represent the corresponding financial compensation. The "X1" threshold provides the national average of waste sorted and sent to recycling by the local authorities (before 2009); "X2" corresponds to the take-back per capita required to comply with the targets of the PPW Directive; "X3" is the potential market for packaging (total packaging generated in Portugal divided by the population). Arguably, this "stairway payment" scheme promotes efficiency and it also allows for different levels of incentives regarding each type of packaging waste material. Note that SPV also defines a "P4" (assuming the same value of "P1") for the levels of performance that exceed "X3." This procedure has as main goal to reduce the incentives to the creation of a parallel market of packaging waste.

Table 3.25   FSLA in 2010 in Portugal

Packaging material	Kg/inhabit/year			€/ton		
	X1	X2	X3	P1	P2	P3
Glass	14.3	24.5	40.8	35.00	48.00	60.00
Paper/Cardboard	8.0	10.0	15.0	122.00	136.00	149.00
Plastic	2.1	3.6	15.3	732.00	782.00	832.00
Steel	0.4	0.7	4.1	540.00	580.00	619.00
Aluminum	0.02	0.04	0.86	689.00	914.00	1155.00
Composite Food Packaging	0.3	1.8	3.0	693.00	741.00	788.00

Considering SPV's recovery and recycling objectives, undifferentiated waste collection is a complementary flow to selective collection. For instance, the mechanical and manual sorting carried out in MBT facilities recovers packaging waste that is sent for recycling; furthermore, steel and aluminum can be recovered after incineration. The local authorities receive a complementary report fee per ton of packaging waste sent to recovery. In these cases, SPV does not get involved in the process of sending this waste to the duly licensed recovery entities (with the exception of metal slag requested for take back). The financial support is mainly due to the sharing of information. Indeed, the packaging waste that is recovered or recycled through the "traditional" refuse collection chain also needs to be considered (to compute the final rates achieved by the country). Hence, the Green Dot company pays a Complementary Report fee to the entities in charge of the waste management systems (see Table 3.26).

In the case of trade and industry packaging waste, contracts are set up with waste management operators that carry out the selective collection at the producers facilities. These waste management operators receive an Information and Motivation Fee per ton and type of packaging waste material and can only receive trade and industry waste for which their premises are licensed to. Similarly to what happens with packaging waste not coming from selective collection circuits, SPV does not have a direct intervention regarding non-municipal packaging waste. However, it collects information from the waste management systems on the trade and industrial packaging waste sent for recycling (SPV, 2010). The waste management operators (65 had an agreement with SPV in 2009) report the amounts of all trade and industry materials collected and sent for recycling or

Table 3.26   Complementary Report fee for 2010 in Portugal

Packaging material	Support (€/ton)
Incineration slag (requested take-back)	
Steel	85.0
Aluminum	575.0
Incineration slag (direct transaction by collection operator)	
Steel	15.0
Aluminum	35.0
Composting (direct transaction by collection operator)	
Glass	5.0
Cardboard	5.0
Film	275.0
HDPE	275.0
PET	180.0
Steel	15.0
Aluminum	35.0

Table 3.27   Information and motivation fee for 2010 in Portugal

Packaging material	Support (€/ton)
Glass	5.0
Paper/cardboard	5.0
Plastic	15.0
Steel	15.0
Aluminum	35.0
Wood	5.0

valorization and receive an information and motivation fee for this reporting (see Table 3.27).

Current Situation

In recent years there has been an increase in the generation of municipal waste and in 2009 the per capita production reached 520 kg/inhabitant in Portugal. However, probably as an effect of the stringent economic crisis that hit the country, these per capita values have been decreasing ever since. In the last 18 years, only in 2009 and 2010 the per capita generation of municipal waste in Portugal was higher than the EU-27 average (and only very slightly).

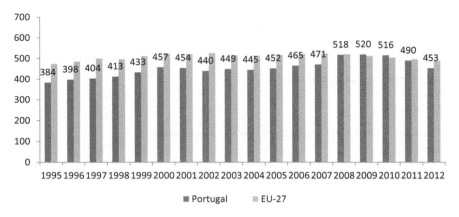

Figure 3.9   Generation of municipal waste in Portugal (kg per capita)
Source: Eurostat

Paper and cardboard packaging waste represented about 44 percent of all packaging waste generated in Portugal in 2011 (this share is similar to previous years). Despite the oscillations in the recycling rates of practically all materials, glass packaging waste has clearly been the main challenge for Portugal. However, it seems that the minimum admissible recycling rate for this material was precisely matched in 2011 (the deadline for Portugal).

Table 3.28   Generation of packaging waste by material in Portugal (thousands of tons)

Year	Packaging waste	Paper / cardboard	Plastic	Wood	Metal	Glass
2002	1,298	507	325	(-)	103	363
2003	1,406	515	330	83	105	372
2004	1,430	520	345	91	106	367
2005	1,498	525	356	125	106	384
2006	1,733	762	377	87	110	394
2007	1,713	697	378	117	113	405
2008	1,785	718	388	138	110	431
2009	1,719	711	378	110	100	420
2010	1,664	704	361	106	95	399
2011	1,566	687	357	55	93	374

Source: Eurostat

With the exception of wood and metal, all the achieved recycling rates are somewhat close to the PPW targets. Therefore, it is clear that Portugal will have to continue its efforts and improve the whole recycling system in order to comply with the EU legislation in the following years.

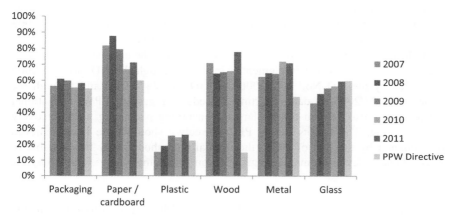

Figure 3.10   Recycling rate of packaging waste by material in Portugal
Source: Eurostat

Romania[6]

Legal and Institutional Framework

Romania signed the Accession Treaty in 2005 and entered effectively into the EU on 1 January 2007. In addition to the Treaty, other protocols were signed setting commitments to implement the *Acquis Communautaire*. Consequently, the EU legislation on waste management has also been transposed into the national law. Among other commitments, the closures of 150 non-compliant landfills and of 1,500 illegal dumpsites were some of the accession requirements concerning waste management. Some transitional periods were set to achieve full compliance, namely, 2009 for the closure of illegal dumpsites and 2017 for the closure of all non-compliant municipal landfills (TWB, 2011).

The WFD was transposed into Romanian legislation through the Law No. 426/2001 which approved the Emergency Ordinance No. 78/2000 and through the Government Decision (GD) No. 123/2003 which approved the National Waste Management Plan. The Directive 1999/31/EC on waste landfilling (transposed

---

6   The following scholars contributed with research for this subchapter (in alphabetical order): Marta Cabral, Nuno Ferreira da Cruz, Pedro Simões, Rui Cunha Marques and Sandra Ferreira.

into national law through GD No. 349/2005, modified and completed by GD No. 210/2007), requires a reduction of the quantities of landfilled biodegradable waste, imposing targets to be achieved in 2010 and 2013. Indeed, since 2010 over 0.8 million tons of biodegradable waste have been diverted from landfills and from 2013 onwards over 2 million tons of biodegradable waste should be recovered annually (REPAB, 2010). The Directive No. 2000/76/EC on waste incineration was transposed by the GD No. 128/2002 and by the Ordinance No. 1215/2003 which approved the technical norms of waste incineration.

Following the requirements of the PPW Directive, the national legislation on packaging waste was first implemented in 2005 through the GD No. 621/2005 (amended by the GD No. 1872/2006 and GD No. 247/2011) and through the Order No. 927/2005 on data reporting procedures regarding PPW. Transitional periods were also defined for the targets concerning packaging waste recovery and recycling. The targets of the PPW Directive should have been achieved by Romania by the end of 2013 (the official data should only be available in 2016). Other relevant Romanian legislation on packaging waste is framed by the following regulations:

- The Ordinance No. 1032/2011 from the Ministry of Environment and Forests defines the methodology for determining the Environmental Fund contribution (2 RON/kg) in case of non-fulfilment of the recycling/recovery objectives by the required companies. This law amends the Ordinance No. 578/2006 and approves the computational model of the corresponding contributions and taxes;
- The Government Emergency Ordinance No. 196/2005, with later modifications and an addendum, introduces new yearly recycling and recovery objectives for the "required companies" (which are higher than the national objectives);
- The Ordinance No. 2742/2011 from the Ministry of Environment and Forests concerns the approval of Licensing Procedures for Recovery Organizations (acting as intermediaries in the fulfilment of the producers' and packers' obligations in order to attain the recycling and recovery targets).

The required companies minimum recycling and recovery objectives for packaging waste (overall and per material) are given in Table 3.29.

The national minimum recycling and recovery objectives for packaging waste (overall and per material) are provided in Table 3.30. In order to achieve the targets, several instruments were developed, particularly, the National Waste Management Plan and the National Waste Management Strategy. Afterwards, to implement the National Waste Management Plan, eight Regional Waste Management Plans were created, including targets to comply with the national and the EU objectives.

Table 3.29 Recycling/recovery objectives of packaging waste for required companies in Romania

Year	Paper (%)	Plastic		Metal		Glass (%)	Wood (%)	Overall recycling (%)	Overall recovery (%)
		Total (%)	Share of PET (%)	Total (%)	Share of aluminum (%)				
2010	60	14	(-)	50	(-)	44	12	42	48
2011	60	22.5	42	50	17	54	15	50	57
2012	60	22.5	55	50	21	60	15	55	60
2013	60	22.5	55	50	21	60	15	55	60

Table 3.30 National recycling/recovery objectives of packaging waste in Romania

Year	Paper (%)	Plastic (%)	Metal (%)	Glass (%)	Wood (%)	Overall recycling (%)	Overall recovery (%)
2005	15	(-)	(-)	(-)	(-)	18	22
2006	15	(-)	15	15	(-)	26	32
2007	60	10	22	15	5	26	34
2008	60	11	32	50	7	33	40
2009	60	12	38	50	9	38	45
2010	60	14	50	44	12	42	48
2011	60	16	50	48	15	46	53
2012	60	18	50	54	15	50	57
2013	60	22.5	50	60	15	55	60

According to the GD No. 621/2005 "economic agents that place commercial packaging on the market are responsible for these packaging." The recycling and recovery objectives can be achieved by the economic agents individually, through the collection of the packaging waste generated or, alternatively, by delegating their responsibilities to an agent licensed by the Ministry of Environment and Forests (responsible for environmental policy and waste legislation). These agents are then required to provide annual information on PPW management. Eco-Rom Ambalaje is the entity which manages the Green Dot Scheme in Romania. However, in 2012 there was a total of seven companies duly licensed for packaging waste management, acting as intermediaries in the fulfilment of the producers' and packers' legal obligations in order to attain the targets set out for packaging waste recovery and recycling.

The GD No. 247/2011 requires the economic operators with sales areas over 1,000 m², as well as the purchasers of packaged products to direct importers or local manufacturers, to ensure that these suppliers are registered in the Fund for Environment Administration. This list has a record of the companies that must fulfil the recycling and recovery targets set by law (Eco-Rom, 2011a).

Economic operators (who meet their responsibilities individually or through a third party duly licensed), local authorities and other entities managing packaging waste are required to provide information annually to the Ministry of Environment and Forests. The procedure for reporting the data is determined by the Ministry and the information is stored in a database managed by the National Environmental Protection Agency.

The Law No. 132/2010 on selective collection of waste states that local authorities are required to set a selective collection system for the following types of municipal waste: paper, cardboard, plastic, metal and glass. The selective collection system can be performed directly by the local services or by delegating the responsibility to authorized companies.

Waste Management Operators

Romania is organized in eight regions, 41 counties and 314 municipalities and cities. The 41 counties are grouped in seven regions plus Bucharest and the county of Ilfov (representing the eighth region). According to the Law No. 101/2006, local authorities have the exclusive competence for managing and setting up municipal waste services. These services include the following operations:

- Municipal waste collection and transport;
- Municipal waste sorting and storage;
- Waste treatment and transactions of the products from sorting and energy recovery.

The Law No. 101/2006 on local waste services determines that local councils have the power to design and approve local strategies regarding the development of waste management services in the medium and long terms. The regional associations (composed of municipalities) and the county councils manage the disposal facilities and the transfer stations (TWB, 2011). According to the National Waste Management Strategy, the (financial) responsibility for waste management activities shall be assigned to waste producers adopting the polluter pays and the EPR principles.

The Ordinance No. 87/2001 (replaced by Law No. 101/2006 currently in force) established the principle that local authorities can delegate the management of municipal waste services to licensed operators (the National Regulatory Authority for Municipal Services—ANRSC—issues these licenses) through public tenders based on management or concession contracts of waste services. The duration of the delegation contract should not be higher than 49 years (the period necessary to depreciate the investments). Among the 400 licensed operators of waste services, the 10 top companies represent more than 80 percent of the waste management market (collection, transport and disposal). Regarding packaging waste collection, more than 1,000 companies are licensed and, for the case of paper and metal, collection and recycling activities have been assured by a large network of companies (Agentschap, 2011).

Irrespective of the management model adopted (direct management or delegation to public or private entities), the waste service activities are organized and performed in accordance with regulations and technical specifications, approved by local councils in compliance with the regulatory framework. The operators of the waste services have to prove their technical and organizational skills, that their staff is qualified and that they have the appropriate technical equipment in order to provide the services, meeting the qualitative and quantitative standards stipulated in the waste service regulation (REPAB, 2010).

In 2009, the amount of municipal waste collected by municipalities or through contracted waste services was 6.93 million tons. Around 63 percent of the national population was served by waste services during this year, where the share is 84 percent for the urban areas and only 38 percent for the rural areas (ANPM, 2012a). During the period 2004–2006 the selective collection of municipal waste for packaging waste recovery from households (paper, cardboard, glass, metals and plastics) was performed through pilot projects initiated by Eco-Rom Ambalaje in cooperation with waste companies and municipalities. Since 2007, selective collection began to expand and in 2007 selective collection was implemented in 183 villages. In 2010, it was already carried out in 698 villages. During this year several containers for selective waste collection were placed nationwide in 698 localities (including the six areas of Bucharest). There are also on-going pilot projects in 27 municipalities (ANPM, 2012a). Eco-Rom (2011b) estimates that four million inhabitants (approx. 20 percent of the total population) have access to the selective collection system. Household selective waste collection is proving to be particularly challenging, mainly due to the underdevelopment of the collection system, the relatively poor road infrastructure (especially in rural areas) and the lack of education/awareness.

In densely populated areas the waste collection service is generally provided through bring-systems, in collection points with several drop-off containers (for selective packaging waste collection—batteries of containers igloo and/or 1,100 liter containers: blue for paper and cardboard, yellow for metal and plastic and green for glass). For the single-family houses located in the suburbs and rural areas, the waste collection is provided through curbside collection systems. For bring-systems, the collection frequency has to be done on a daily basis. For curbside collection systems, the vehicles carry out two collections per week. In rural areas, the figures on waste collection service diverge widely; for instance, the collection frequency can differ from once every two weeks or twice a week. Moreover, household waste collection in rural areas is generally performed by horse cart (REPAB, 2010).

Concerning biodegradable waste, in early 2011 there were a total of 60 composting facilities (authorized or pending authorization) with a capacity of 166,000 tons per year (ANPM, 2012a). During 2010 there were 106 non-compliant municipal landfills in operation, 26 of which have stopped operating on July 2010. Sanitary landfills are mostly owned by local authorities, being operated by private companies (Agentschap, 2011). According to ANPM (2012b), there are 30 compliant landfills (from which five are under an authorization process and two have exceeded the waste disposal capacity). The current dumping fee is around 10 €/ton (Agentschap, 2011), which is not profitable for the companies that manage these facilities. With the implementation of the new landfill tax it is expected that more foreign companies decide to operate in the market for other waste treatment solutions and that the recycling of waste becomes more appealing.

Compliance Scheme

As previously mentioned, in Romania, there are seven licensed companies with the responsibility of managing the packaging waste generated by the industry. Among them, the most important are EcoRom Ambalaje and Ecologic 3R (Agentschap, 2011). The full list of companies is given below:

- Eco-Rom Ambalaje;
- Ecologic 3R;
- Intersemat;
- Sota Group;
- Eco X;
- Eco Pack Management;
- Respo Waste.

Eco-Rom Ambalaje (Eco-Rom) is an organization founded by a group of companies (Argus S.A., Ball Packaging Europe, Chipita Romania S.R.L., Coca-Cola HBC S.R.L., Heineken S.A., Mars Romania S.R.L., Munplast S.A., Quadrant Amroq Beverages S.A., Romaqua Group S.A., Tetra Pack Romania S.R.L. and Titan S.A., Unilever South Central Europe S.R.L.) with the objective of taking on the responsibility of the industry for packaging waste resulting from the respective products placed onto the market. To fulfil the national recovery and recycling objectives, Eco-Rom introduced the Green Dot System in the country in 2004. In 2010 Eco-Rom had 1,809 members and established contracts with 190 waste management operators (the Green Dot company holds about 65 percent of the market share). The Eco-Rom members were responsible for 617,103 tons of packaging during this year, where 331,781 tons were recycled through the Eco-Rom system (only 22,000 ton came from the household selective collection flow, Eco-Rom, 2011b).

Eco-Rom's members (or clients) are the economic operators that are required by law to recover and recycle the packaging waste arising from their products. The clients have to pay a fee based on the weight and the material of the packaging placed onto the market. To achieve the national recycling and recovery targets for the packaging waste under the responsibility of Eco-Rom, they have contracts with waste management companies. Eco-Rom Ambalaje partially supports the costs of selective collection, performed by the local authorities, signing a contract with waste operators. The support includes some equipment (containers, bags and communication forms), a fee paid per ton sorted, as well as consultancy and technical services. Eco-Rom also organizes and finances awareness campaigns among the population (PRO-Europe, 2010).

Regarding the national (legal) recycling and recovery targets, Eco-Rom has exceeded them for all type of materials. In 2010 there were 93 selective collection systems (8,111 containers) in 72 towns and 78 municipalities in Romania supported by Eco-Rom (Eco-Rom, 2011b). In that year, Eco-Rom had 1,809 clients and had signed contracts with 190 waste management operators in the packaging waste management system.

The Romanian Green Dot company takes over the economic operators' responsibility regarding packaging waste recovery and recycling obligations through the "Responsibility Takeover Contract." The economic operators have to provide to Eco-Rom documents that support the traceability of packaging waste. If they fail to fulfil this requirement, economic operators will have to pay a contribution of 0.48 €/kg to the "Environment Fund Administration." Eco-Rom's clients have the right to use the Green Dot symbol in their packaging (which explicitly informs the consumer that the price of the products includes a financial contribution to support the recovery of the respective packaging waste). The green dot fees for 2010 are indicated in Table 3.31. The economic operators pay for the quantity and type of packaging (material) introduced onto the national market every year. In 2010, the industry paid a total of 8.3 million euros in contributions to Eco-Rom (Eco-Rom, 2011b).

Table 3.31   Green Dot fees for 2010 in Romania

Packaging material	Green Dot fees (€/ton)
Glass	16.29
PET	21.47
Plastics	11.68
Cardboard paper	13.27
Steel	10.27
Aluminum	10.27
Wood	10.53

The companies authorized to carry out waste management operations (collection, sorting, recovery and recycling) from the municipal or industrial flows can be part of Eco-Rom's waste management system and consequently receive financial support. These companies can benefit from a long-term agreement, which offers some predictability and stability to the operators (compensating the instability of the secondary raw materials market), in exchange for reliable information and documentation that certifies the quantities of waste managed and recycled/recovered.

According to the model adopted by Eco-Rom, the authorized companies are entitled to receive a "bonus payment" for the packaging waste management services. This financial support is contractually agreed between the parties based on operational costs and on the market share of each packaging material. The payment is based on the quantity and type of material sent to recycling/recovery. Table 3.32 presents the financial support per ton of each packaging waste material in 2010. During this year Eco-Rom paid to the waste management operators around 4.4 million euros (Eco-Rom, 2011b).

Table 3.32   SLA in 2010 in Romania

Packaging material	"Bonus payment" (€/ton)
Glass	23.89
PET	32.40
Plastics	15.39
Cardboard paper	13.67
Steel	13.88
Aluminum	13.89
Wood	10.60

Source: WMC (2012)

In addition to the "bonus payment" (arising from the green dot fees paid by the industry), the costs of selective collection and treatment (including sorting and baling operations) undertaken by the waste management operators are supported by the sales of sorted packaging waste material. The waste management operators deal directly with recyclers or guarantors. The average price of each packaging material in 2010 is shown in Table 3.33.

Table 3.33   Average take-back prices in Romania in 2010

Packaging material	Take-back price (€/ton)
Glass	6.9
PET	333.5
Plastics	253.0
Paper and cardboard	126.5
Steel	218.5
Aluminum	977.5
Wood	29.9

Source: WMC (2012)

Current Situation

In Romania, not all municipal waste generated is actually collected. A relevant share of the population is not served by waste services. In 2009, the waste generated and not collected was 0.9 kg/person/day in urban areas and 0.4 kg/person/day in rural areas; the estimated total quantity of municipal waste generated and not collected was approximately 1.5 million tons (ANPM, 2012a). Furthermore, the large majority of the waste collected is landfilled (more than 76 percent in 2010). Nevertheless, as shown in Figure 3.11, the per capita rates of generation of municipal waste are significantly below the EU-27 average (and the difference seems to have been accentuated in recent years).

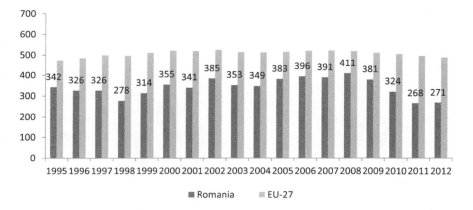

Figure 3.11   Generation of municipal waste in Romania (kg per capita)
Source: Eurostat

Table 3.34   Generation of packaging waste by material in Romania (thousands of tons)

Year	Packaging waste	Paper / cardboard	Plastic	Wood	Metal	Glass
2005	1,141	270	332	137	103	249
2006	1,309	412	355	181	73	285
2007	1,287	387	375	213	76	233
2008	1,171	352	333	216	76	193
2009	999	272	294	188	63	180
2010	975	266	281	212	55	160
2011	993	293	279	226	55	140

Source: Eurostat

Concerning the packaging waste stream, in 2008–2009, the waste generation rate decreased considerably compared to the previous years. In Romania, packaging waste is composed mainly of paper/cardboard and plastic (the share of wood packaging for transport is also substantial). The material with the lowest percentage is metal (see Table 3.34).

In 2011, Romania had not yet reached the 55 percent overall recycling target (note that the EU legislation only imposes that this rate is attained in 2013 for this country). However, all the specific objectives for each packaging material had already been achieved in this year (where the 60 percent target for glass was attained for the first time). Moreover, the annual (and progressive) national targets have always been respected. Because the selective collection of household waste is still incipient in Romania, most targets have been reached mainly due to the performance of the trade and industry flow.

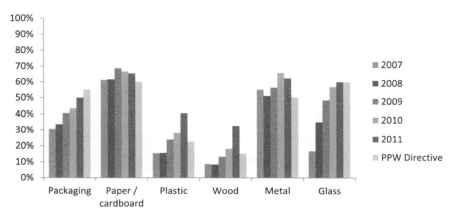

Figure 3.12   Recycling rate of packaging waste by material in Romania
Source: Eurostat

United Kingdom[7]

Legal and Institutional Framework

The main legislation concerning waste management in the UK was introduced by the Environmental Protection Act of 1990. Among other measures, this law demanded the preparation of a national waste strategy by the Secretary of State for England and Wales (Reading, 2001). Following this Act, the Controlled

---

7   The following scholars contributed with research for this subchapter (in alphabetical order): Francis Ongondo, Ian Williams, Marta Cabral, Nuno Ferreira da Cruz, Pedro Simões, Rui Cunha Marques and Sandra Ferreira.

Waste Regulations (CWR) of 1992 provided a list of types of household waste that local authorities can collect (and charge a fee) but not to dispose of. In these regulations, "household waste" includes the waste flow from households and the non-household waste flow from specific sources, such as schools, hospitals and prisons (Defra, 2010). Recently, the new CWR for England and Wales (came into force in April 2012) gave local authorities the power of charging for the collection as well as for the disposal of waste from the non-household flow.

The Waste Management Licensing Regulations of 1994 required all waste management facilities (e.g. landfills, transfer stations, recycling and recovery plants) to be licensed to operate. The regulations also established the procedure to obtain this license, identifying the activities exempt from licensing. Historically, the predominant method of waste disposal in the UK had been landfilling. In the 1990s, more than 80 percent of municipal waste was landfilled. To change this tendency, focusing on the reduction of waste production, the waste hierarchy was introduced for the first time in 1992, through a Governmental White Paper "The Common Inheritance."

The WFD was transposed into British legislation through the Environment Act 1995 which defined the objectives of the national waste strategy. It intended to establish more comprehensive regulations in terms of waste minimization and recycling rates, involving the various stakeholders, namely: the local authorities, the industry (businesses) and the households (Smallbone, 2005). In order to divert waste from landfills towards more sustainable disposal options (encouraging waste minimization, recycling and recovery), the UK government published the "Making waste work: A strategy for sustainable waste management in England and Wales" (Read, 1999). The main objectives defined in this strategy were to stabilize household waste production at 1995 levels, reduce the proportion of controlled waste going to landfill to 69 percent by the year 2005, recover 40 percent of municipal waste by the year 2005, provide close-to-home recycling facilities for 80 percent of the households by the year 2000, and achieve 40 percent of domestic properties with a garden to carry out composting by the year 2000.

The national strategy also developed the first ideas presented in the "Sustainable Development: the UK Strategy" of 1994, setting indicative targets for waste management (Morris et al., 1998). However, those targets proved to be unrealistic and were reduced. Later, in 1996, the British government introduced the Landfill Tax, through the Finance Act 1996 and the Landfill Tax Regulations 1996 (Morris and Read, 2001). However, landfilling continued to be the most common final destination of municipal waste (Defra, 2012). In order to decrease the amount of biodegradable municipal waste sent to landfills, complying with the Landfill Directive targets, the Waste and Emissions Trading Act 2003 was implemented (Bulkeley and Gregson, 2009). This Act established a system of tradable permits, the Landfill Allowance Trading Scheme. The British government assigns to each local authority an allowance in tons of biodegradable waste which can be sent to landfill. The local authorities can trade their allowances with each other if they have more or less capacity than they need. However, they can also save (banking) their unused allowances for future years or even bring forward (borrowing) up to five percent of their future allocations (FOE, 2007).

The Special Waste Regulations of 1996 established the requirements on hazardous waste management, transposing the EU Directive 91/689/EEC, since this type of waste requires special procedures regarding management operations (storage, treatment and disposal; ODPM, 2004). Those regulations were subsequently amended by the Special Waste Regulations of 1997 and 2001. In 2005, the regulations of 1996 were replaced by the Hazardous Waste (England) Regulations, due to the revision of the EU Hazardous Waste List and the waste control system (Defra, 2005a). These regulations were again amended by the Hazardous Waste (England and Wales) Regulations of 2009.

Regarding packaging waste, the targets and requirements of the PPW Directive were transposed into the UK legislation through the Producer Responsibility Obligations (Packaging Waste) Regulations of 1997 (Wilson et al., 2011). These regulations introduced the concept of shared responsibility for all producers involved in the life cycle of packaging (importers of packaging, manufacturers of packaging and packaging materials, packers or fillers and retailers). It also imposed packaging waste recycling and recovery targets in order to comply with the EU objectives. Therefore, all English, Welsh and Scottish producers had to: (1) register in a relevant environment agency (e.g. Environment Agency—EA—or Scottish Environment Protection Agency—SEPA); and (2) declare annually the quantities of packaging waste recycled and recovered with a certificate of compliance (Defra, 2003). The regulations also stated that producers could transfer their responsibility to a licensed company (i.e. join a compliance scheme). The equivalent legislation for Northern Ireland was introduced in 1999.

The new recycling and recovery targets of the Directive 2004/12/CE were transposed by the Producer Responsibility Obligations (Packaging Waste) Regulations of 2005. These regulations were replaced by the Producer Responsibility Obligations (Packaging Waste) Regulations of 2007 (Wilson et al., 2011), which were later amended in 2008 and 2010. Table 3.35 presents the recovery and recycling targets as defined in the various versions of the packaging waste regulations.

The Household Waste Recycling Act of 2003, amending the Environmental Protection Act of 1990, required that the waste collection authorities ensure the selective collection of at least two types of recyclable materials until 31 December 2010 (Warwickshire Waste Partnership, 2006). The main objective was to increase the level of recycling of household waste, helping local authorities to achieve the recycling targets anticipated by the Waste Strategy 2000 (Defra, 2005b).

The Waste Management (England and Wales) Regulations of 2006, also known as "Agricultural Waste Regulations 2006", were implemented to regulate the management of the industrial, commercial and agricultural waste. These regulations were introduced mainly to fulfill the requirements of the WFD and the Landfill Directive. The new Waste (England and Wales/Scotland/Northern Ireland) Regulations of 2011, transposing the latest version of the WFD, defined

Table 3.35 **Packaging recovery/recycling targets according to the Producer Responsibility Obligations Regulations**

	Targets (%)		
	1997	**2010**	**2011**
Paper	15	69.5	69.5
Glass	15	81	81
Plastic	15	29	32
Aluminum	15	40	40
Steel	15	69	71
Wood	15	22	22
Minimum recycling	25	29	29
Total recovery	50–65	74	74

Source: Secretary of State (2010)

the new waste hierarchy: prevention, preparing for reuse (checking, cleaning or repairing operations, by which products or components of products that have become waste are prepared so that they can be re-used without any other pre-processing), recycling, other recovery (e.g. energy recovery) and disposal. These regulations require that companies declare that the waste management operations have followed the new waste hierarchy through a waste transfer note or a hazardous waste consignment note.

The UK has adopted a decentralized form of government, transferring some competences and responsibilities of the central government to each country (Nothern Ireland, Scotland and Wales). Therefore, each country has developed its own waste management strategies based on the same fundamental principles: the Best Practicable Environmental Option (BPEO), the waste hierarchy and the Proximity principle. The BPEO is a procedure to help identify the best waste management option that confers more benefits or less damage to the environment at a reasonable cost (Phillips et al., 2001). The best option varies with the type of waste and location. The waste hierarchy seeks to achieve a sustainable and environmentally friendly waste management, reducing the waste produced and increasing the amount of waste reused, recycled and recovered. The Proximity principle requires that the waste is managed (or disposed) as close as possible to the location where it is produced due to the significant environmental impact caused by the transportation (ERM, 2005). It is related to the principle of self-sufficiency, which requires that regions have the competence to manage the waste produced (ODPM, 2002).

These principles should be followed to achieve a sustainable waste service. The main objectives imposed by the UK waste policies were to inform consumers, retailers and producers about how to reduce, reuse and recycle waste, to set up voluntary agreements with producers and retailers, to use government procurement to accelerate the development of products which use less natural resources, to invest in local government waste collection and disposal, to provide incentives to producers, consumers, and disposers to reduce, reuse, and recycle waste and divert from landfill through tax or trading, and, if incentives are insufficient, to regulate both upstream (materials) and downstream (landfill) flows (Defra, 2007).

The Waste Strategy 2000 was published by the British Government and sets out its vision on the best waste management strategy for England and Wales (ODPM, 2004). This strategy defined ambitious objectives, emphasizing the local authorities' role in waste recycling (Perrin and Barton, 2001). It also intended to reduce the quantities of waste sent to landfill, encouraging recycling, composting and energy recovery from waste (ODPM, 2002). In 2001, those objectives were translated into the performance standards for compliance by local authorities, according to the Best Value Framework (Bulkeley and Gregson, 2009). The waste management targets for recycling and composting of household waste were at least 25 percent by 2005, 30 percent by 2010 and 33 percent by 2015. The Waste Strategy 2000 also established that the volume of biodegradable municipal waste sent to landfill should be reduced to 75 percent by 2010, 50 percent by 2013 and 35 percent by 2020.

The Waste Strategy 2007 for England continued to stress the importance of the waste hierarchy, and the importance of reducing the consumption of natural resources and waste production (Bulkeley and Gregson, 2009). Furthermore, this strategy intended to stimulate the investment in collection, recycling and recovery equipment and infrastructure. In addition, it envisaged to clarify the institutional framework and the responsibilities of national, regional and local governments in order to improve the coordination between them (Defra, 2009). Nevertheless, in 2010, the government (through the Department for Environment, Food and Rural Affairs—Defra) launched a profound Waste Policy Review in England. Therefore, the Waste Strategy 2007 was replaced by the Government Review of England Waste Policy in 2011. This revision highlighted a series of actions to move towards a "zero waste" economy, according to the principles mentioned above. Wales, Scotland and Northern Ireland have adopted similar waste management strategies.

The competences regarding the definition of waste sector policies are distributed by several entities in the UK. According to the Environment Act of 1995, the EA and SEPA were assigned as the waste regulation authorities of Great Britain (Adams et al., 2000). Indeed, since 1996, the EA and SEPA took over the attributions of the National Rivers Authority, the Waste Regulatory Authorities and Her Majesty's Inspectorate of Pollution (ENSR, 1997). The main objectives of their action plans are to protect and improve the environment in Great Britain, contributing to the sustainability of natural resources (Ofgem and EA, 2001). SEPA also took the responsibility for air pollution control in Scotland. In England and Wales that responsibility is a competence of local authorities (ENSR, 1997). Simultaneously, the Environment and Heritage Service (EHS) was established, an agency within the Department of the Environment in Northern Ireland, with similar responsibilities to the Great Britain agencies. On July 1, 2008, this agency was reformed in accordance with a Ministerial decision and renamed to the Northern Ireland Environment Agency (NIEA).

Among other responsibilities, the environment agencies are responsible for licensing all activities related to waste treatment and disposal pursuant to the Waste Management Licensing Regulations of 1994. Moreover, these agencies have the legal duty to ensure the compliance with all EU waste legislation. According to the Producer Responsibility Obligations (Packaging Waste) Regulations of 1997 (1999 for Northern Ireland), the producers involved in the life-cycle of packaging are required to register individually or through a compliance scheme approved by the respective UK environment agency (Anderson et al., 1999). Therefore, an electronic National Packaging Waste Database was created, where the operators must demonstrate the compliance with their packaging waste recycling/recovery obligations and submit the required operational plans. Their environmental agencies also manage the Waste Data Flow database which contains information on MSW submitted by the local authorities.

Waste Management Operators

The Environmental Protection Act of 1990 established that local authorities are responsible for the collection and transport of MSW and the development of waste plans for final disposal. These plans should encourage recycling and the minimization of waste production (Adams et al., 2000). In the UK, there are waste collection authorities (WCA) and waste disposal authorities (WDA). The WCA are responsible for collecting the household waste and some commercial waste, delivering them to the WDA. The latter have the responsibility of planning and performing waste treatment and disposal. In some cases, the WDA are the same as the WCA (the so-called called unitary authorities). These entities are represented by the Local Government Association.

Each British country (England, Wales, Northern Ireland and Scotland) has its own organization regarding local government. Currently, there are 232 local authorities in the UK, of which 152 (WCA and WDA) are located in England. In Wales, there are 22 unitary authorities represented by the Welsh Local Government Association. The 26 councils (unitary authorities) in Northern Ireland, which are grouped into three sub-regional groups, are represented by the Northern Ireland Local Government Association. And finally, in Scotland, there are 32 unitary authorities (councils) represented by the Convention of Scottish Local Authorities. Waste services can be delivered by these authorities or through contracts with external companies (Smallbone, 2005) selected "under the compulsory competitive tendering regime" (Adams et al., 2000, p.221).

In 1992, the British government launched the first PPP projects through the Private Finance Initiative (PFI). The PFI was announced in the Autumn Statement and emerged as a form of private financing of public infrastructure (including waste services), arguably contributing to a greater private sector involvement in the provision of public services. Furthermore, the main objective of this initiative was to reduce the costs of the public sector, maintaining the investment level and avoiding the financing constrains (Bing et al., 2005). The public and private partners enter a long-term agreement (usually 25–30 years), where the private partner is responsible for the construction (when necessary), operation, maintenance and financing of the assets. Generally, it receives a regular financial contribution from the public sector in return. These partnerships should be structured to ensure a high quality of provided service for the contract period. At the end of this period, the ownership of the assets reverts to the public sector (Harris, 2004).

In England, local authorities have gathered through a Waste Partnership in order to improve the quality of service, promote sustainable development, instigate waste reduction, reuse and recycling and ensure the reporting of all information on waste and environmental services. All Waste Partnership members work together in order to set the "best" waste management strategy for their territory, to promote a higher efficiency of the service, reduce the service costs and meet the landfill diversion targets.

The 22 local authorities in Wales are grouped into three regional waste planning areas: the North Region, the South East Region and the South West Region, composed of seven, 10 and six councils, respectively. The Powys County Council is divided into two areas; North Powys is integrated in the North Region and South Powys belongs to the South East Region. The three Regional Waste Groups were formed through the Technical Advice Note 21 on Waste. They are also responsible for the preparation and publication of the Regional Waste Plans. These plans are developed to meet the British and the EU targets. Moreover, they contribute to a sustainable land use and to an efficient and effective waste management, providing the basis for the Unitary Development Plan (UDP). The UDP is a development plan which contains the strategic planning policies. Despite a new system of development where local plans are already in effect, the UDP remains into force in many areas due to the transitional provisions of the Planning and Compulsory Purchase Act of 2004.

In Northern Ireland, the 26 councils are grouped into three sub-regional waste management groups: Arc21, North West Region Waste Management Group (NWRWMG) and Southern Waste Management Partnership (SWaMP2008). The arc21, originally called the Eastern Region Waste Management Group is composed of 11 councils, the NWRWMG is a voluntary coalition of seven councils and the SWaMP2008 (formerly called Swamp) represents eight councils. These sub-regional groups are responsible for developing the waste management system, meeting the needs of the region and contributing to the economic and social development.

Finally, in Scotland there are 32 councils organized into 11 Waste Strategic Areas: Orkney and Shetland, Western Isles, Highland, North East, Tayside, Forth Valley, Fife, Lothian and Borders, Ayrshire, Dumfries and Galloway, Glasgow and Clyde Valley, Argyll and Bute. Each one developed a Local Waste Plan, defining the waste management system in force. These plans seek to contribute to a more sustainable development of the region, improving the efficiency of the waste management models and stimulating the reduction of service costs.

Packaging waste collection in the UK is mainly done via curbside systems (Defra, 2009) offered either by the local authorities or their contracted private companies. However, some packaging waste is also collected via bring bank systems. In 2009, in Scotland, waste collection in nearly all local authorities was delivered in-house, compared to almost 50 percent in England with the remaining proportion contracted out to waste management companies (Defra, 2009). Non-household packaging waste is collected and disposed on a commercial charge basis mostly by the private sector and to a small extent by some local authorities contracted to do so.

There are various types of curbside collection of packaging waste. However, some packaging waste still ends up in the residual waste stream either by being disposed in the general waste bins/bags or by being rejected at material recycling facilities where contaminated packaging waste is considered to be inappropriate for recycling. Contamination occurs when packaging waste is mixed with other waste such as food or contamination of paper by shards of glass, etc.

Around 90 percent of the UK homes are covered by packaging waste curbside collection schemes (WRAP, 2012). These collection schemes can be classified according to two main types of collection: co-mingled (mixed materials) and curbside sort collections. The debate over which system is better (financially, environmentally, operationally, etc.) and the frequency at which packaging waste is collected (weekly versus every two weeks) has been going on in the UK for several years (WYG Environment, 2010; letsrecycle.com, 2009).

In 2008 the co-mingled system was used by around 46 percent of local authorities (35 percent single stream comingled and 11 percent two-stream partially comingled). In co-mingled systems, packaging waste is collected mixed together, then sent to a material recycling facility for sorting and subsequent recycling. Some co-mingled systems include glass collection whereas others do not (WRAP, 2008a).

Also in 2008, around 44 percent of councils operated a curbside sort collection system where packaging waste is separated into different material streams. These are then loaded onto special recycling vehicles with compartments for each type of recycling (WRAP, 2008a). Curbside sort systems utilized in the UK can typically be classified according to the following three streams (Campaign For Real Recycling, n.d.; WRAP, 2008a):

1. Curbside source separated: Multiple-stream for various packaging wastes;
2. Twin-stream system:
   a. paper, light card, pamphlets;
   b. cans, tins, plastic bottles, drink cartons, glass bottles and jars.
3. Triple-stream system:
   a. paper, light card, pamphlets;
   b. cans, tins, plastic bottles, drink cartons;
   c. glass bottles and jars.

Compliance Scheme

According to the Packaging Waste Regulations, producers are responsible for the environmental impact of their waste and are required to register directly with the relevant agency (the EA in England and Wales, the SEPA in Scotland and the NIEA in Northern Ireland), or through an approved compliance scheme. The compliance schemes are managed by companies licensed to take on all legal obligations of packaging operators (i.e. raw material manufacturers, convertors, packers, fillers, sellers and importers) who join the scheme. When producers opt to register directly, they have to comply with their legal packaging obligations by implementing an individual management system. All producers (with direct registration or under a compliance scheme) must prove the fulfilment of their recovery and recycling obligations (in tons), submitting certificates or statements of compliance and operational plans through the electronic database (the National Packaging Waste Database) by January 31st of each year.

The Producer Responsibility Obligations (Packaging Waste) Regulations of 2007 posit that operational plans must provide an estimate of the recovery/recycling obligations of the producers and information concerning the financial resources and technical expertise available to enable the prosecution of those obligations. It must also describe the solutions for the recovery and recycling of each packaging material. This plan must be submitted by all producers with recovery and recycling obligations greater than 50 tons of packaging waste in the preceding year.

The certificates/statements of compliance are obtained through the Packaging Recovery Note (PRN) or Packaging Export Recovery Note (PERN) systems. Only reprocessors and exporters of packaging material accredited by the environment agencies can issue the PRNs and PERNs, respectively (NIEA, 2010). Valpak was the first producer compliance scheme for packaging waste obtaining its license in late August 1997. Currently there are more than 20 licensed schemes (e.g., in addition to Valpak: Betapack, Biffpack, Budget Pack, Compliance Link, Comply Direct, Complypak, Kite Environmental Solutions, Paper Collect, Paperpak, Pennine-Pack, Recycle 1st, Recycle-Pak, Recycle Wales, SWS Compak, Synergy Compliance, TaG Pack, Toddpak, Valuepack, Veolia Environmental Services, Wastepack and Wespack). However, Valpak has a market share of approximately 50 percent (PRO-EUROPE, 2010) and is responsible for the licensing of the Green Dot trademark in the UK. Note that the UK does not operate a "traditional" Green Dot recovery system, such as other EU member states. The use of the Green Dot symbol is not mandatory and it does not necessarily imply compliance with the UK packaging regulations.

As mentioned above, the Valpak's mission (as any other licensed scheme) is to take on the responsibility for the compliance with packaging regulations, acting as an intermediary between the producers and the governmental agencies. This responsibility involves:

- Registering the business in the relevant environment agency;
- Acquiring PRNs and/or PERNs on behalf of the operator;
- Submitting the data in the electronic database;
- Providing technical expertise;
- Providing certificates of compliance;
- Representing the operators' interests at the government level.

In order to achieve its objectives, the Valpak works with several stakeholders involved in the packaging supply chain. It has established partnerships with local authorities, offering its technical expertise to assess the local needs and to suggest the cost-efficient solutions for their obligations. It also contracts directly with the reprocessors and exporters, purchasing the PRNs and PERNs on behalf of the businesses that joined the scheme of Valpak.

PPW is managed in the UK based on a unique and complex system of shared producer responsibility. Operators which have a turnover of less than £2 million a year and handle less than 50 tons of packaging and/or packaging materials in the previous calendar year are not required to register (WMP1, 2010). Operators which have a turnover between £2 million and £5 million a year can choose to register as a small producer and must calculate their obligations using the allocation method (WMP1, 2010). The remaining operators, with a turnover above £5 million must calculate their obligations according to the calculation method described below.

Recovery and recycling obligations (in tons) are calculated based on the recovery/recycling target multiplied by the percentage corresponding to one of the activities listed in Table 3.36 (2011 values). Therefore, these obligations can be subject to changes every year. The UK recovery/recycling rates imposed by the packaging regulations currently in force are shown in Table 3.35. For small producers, the obligations are calculated by the allocation method based on their turnover. The current recycling allocation is 29. Thus, the obligation is calculated by the following formula:

$$\text{Operator obligation (in tons)} = \frac{\text{Economic operator turnover}}{1,000} \times 29$$

Table 3.36   Recycling obligations of the economic operators in 2011

Packaging material	Obligation (ton)
Raw material manufacturing[1]	Amount handled x 6% x UK target
Packaging conversion[2]	Amount handled x 9% x UK target
Packaging/filling[3]	Amount handled x 37% x UK target
Selling[4]	Amount handled x 48% x UK target
Importing[5]	Amount handled x % (the exact percentage is contingent upon the material's "rolled up" obligation, i.e. all activities carried out on the material prior to its import) x the UK target
Service provider[6]	Amount handled x 85% x the UK target

[1] Produce raw materials;
[2] Convert raw materials into packaging;
[3] Place goods in packaging;
[4] Sale of packaging to the end user;
[5] Import packaged goods or packaging materials;
[6] A business that supplies packaging by hiring or loan.
Source: WMP1, 2010;

All producers with direct registration and under the compliance schemes have to pay a registration fee each year to the relevant environment agency. The registration fees are presented in Table 3.37.

In contrast, producers who decide to join a compliance scheme (e.g. Valpak) have to pay a membership fee (instead of the registration fee in the relevant environment agency) based on their obligation level which is invoiced quarterly across the year. Valpak's membership fees are shown in Table 3.38.

Table 3.37   Annual registration fees in 2011

Packaging material	EA and SEPA (€)	NIEA (€)
Individual registration		
For each economic operator	882.69	1,080.62
For each small operator who uses the allocation method	641.55	641.55
For each operator registering as a group of companies	882.69	1,080.62
For each of the first four subsidiaries	204.75	204.75
For each of the fifth of the 20th subsidiaries	102.37	102.37
For each of the 21st and subsequent subsidiaries	51.19	51.19
Resubmission	250.25	250.25
Changes to membership made after 7 April	125.12	125.12

Scheme registration

For each scheme member	641.55	882.69
For each small scheme member who uses the allocation method	392.44	641.55
For each scheme member registering as a group of companies	641.55	882.69
For each small scheme member who uses the allocation method	392.44	641.55
For each of the first four subsidiaries	204.75	204.75
For each of the fifth to the 20th subsidiaries	102.37	102.37
For each of the 21st and subsequent subsidiaries	51.19	51.19
Resubmission*	250.25	250.25
Changes to membership made after 7 April		125.12 (until April 15)

Application for accreditation

Issue of PRN or PERN for 400 tons or less in the year for which accreditation is granted	574.43	
Obligation to recover up to 24,999 tons in the year for which conditional approval is granted		1,751.74
In other cases (i.e. issue of PRN or PERN for more than 400 tons)	2,975.68	
Obligation to recover between 25,000 and 249,999 tons in the year for which conditional approval is granted		2,627.61
Where an initial application to issue up to 400 tons or PRN/PERN has been made, and the applicant subsequently issues more than 400 tons, a top up fee.	2,975.68	
Obligation to recover over 250,000 tons in the year for which conditional approval is granted		3,503.48

*When the previous submission failed to meet the requirements of regulation.
Conversion rates (£1 = €1,14)

Source: WMP1 (2010) and NIEA (2011

Table 3.38   Annual membership fee bandings

Membership fee	Bandings
€455.00	Small and medium enterprises (SME)*
€568.75	0—400 tons
€853.12	401—1,000 tons
€1,137.49	1,001—2,000 tons
€1,706.24	2,001—4,000 tons
€2,843.73	>4,000 tons

* Any operator who has a gross annual turnover of less than £5 million (€5.69 million) and handles under 50 tons of packaging; conversion rates (£1 = €1,14)

Source: Valpak (2011)

Compliance costs in the UK are based on the purchase and sale of PRNs and PERNs. Valpak manages these transactions on behalf of its clients. In the beginning of each year, the demand for PRNs is established and supply depends on the amount of packaging materials to recycle. When the recycling capacity reaches its maximum, the PRN price tends to increase and demand exceeds supply. This dynamic process encourages more suppliers to enter the market, thus increasing supply. With the increase in capacity, the collection and recycling rates also increase, reducing the PRN prices again. Average PRN prices, by type of material (as predicted by Valpak in 2010) are presented in Table 3.39. These prices, however, are subject to fluctuations.

Table 3.39   Average PRN prices predicted for 2011

Material	Average PRN price (€/ton)
Paper	3.80
Plastic	5.00
Glass	23.29
Steel	21.82
Aluminum	16.10
Wood	1.20

Source: PRO-Europe (2010)

As mentioned above, the use of the Green Dot symbol is not mandatory in the UK. Nevertheless, producers can place the Green Dot trademark in their products for free if they are members of the Valpak system. Conversely, an operator who is not a Valpak member can pay an annual license fee of £225 to use the trademark.

Current Situation

According to the latest available data (displayed in Figure 3.13), the UK has managed to reduce the gap to the EU average in terms of municipal waste generation per capita. In fact, 2011 and 2012 the UK per capita values were below the EU average, which suggests that somehow the waste management policies have been successful in meeting the first objective of the waste hierarchy: prevention (although one should stress the fact that waste generation may be contingent upon many other factors, both observed and unobserved). The fact is that waste generation per capita has been persistently decreasing since 2004.

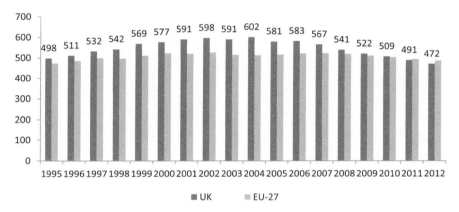

■ UK   ■ EU-27

Figure 3.13   Generation of municipal waste in the UK (kg per capita)
Source: Eurostat

Regarding the packaging waste stream, as shown in Table 3.40, paper/cardboard is the most used material although plastic and glass packaging also depict high absolute values in this country. With the exception of wood packaging waste, for which the UK presents a much higher recycling rate than the one imposed by the PPW Directive, for all the other materials the targets have been consistently met throughout the years with a comfortable though not so expressive slack (see Figure 3.14).

Table 3.40   Generation of packaging waste by material in the UK (thousands of tons)

Year	Packaging waste	Paper / cardboard	Plastic	Wood	Metal	Glass
2002	9,897	3,726	1,740	1,398	818	2,191
2003	10,059	3,726	1,792	1,404	813	2,300
2004	10,230	3,726	1,846	1,404	833	2,400
2005	10,280	3,726	1,901	1,404	828	2,400
2006	10,471	3,763	2,080	1,180	825	2,600
2007	10,610	3,801	2,121	1,192	823	2,650
2008	10,724	3,839	2,185	1,227	821	2,630
2009	10,787	3,758	2,442	1,056	824	2,686
2010	10,825	3,788	2,479	1,024	800	2,713
2011	10,930	3,818	2,516	1,024	810	2,740

Source: Eurostat

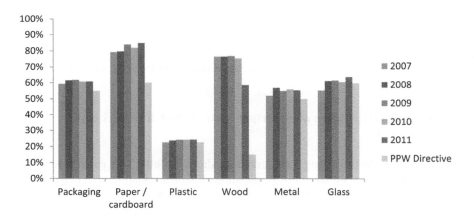

Figure 3.14   Recycling rate of packaging waste by material in the UK
Source: Eurostat

Chapter 4
The Costs and Benefits of Recycling

Financial Flows[1]

System Boundaries

In the current book, the costs and benefits of recycling are compared for Belgium, France, Italy, Portugal, Romania and the UK using the same methodological approach. Notice that these costs and benefits are considered from the perspective of local public authorities. It is necessary to adopt this perspective for the analysis because a major aim of this document is to take note of who is paying for the "incremental cost" of recycling (total cost of preparation for recycling minus savings due to diverting waste from other treatment options). Is it the market (i.e. costs are recovered via the sale of sorted packaging waste materials)? Is it the consumer (i.e. the industry reflects the costs on the price of the products)? Is it the citizens in general (i.e. through higher waste management fees or through taxes)? Perhaps a combination of these? Another interesting query, with potential policy implications, is to ascertain whether the industry is paying for the "net financial cost" of packaging waste management (cost of selective collection and sorting minus benefits attained with the sale of sorted material). The answers to these questions will shed light on the issues of compliance with the provisions of the PPW Directive and the interpretation of the EPR principle in Europe.

To accomplish these objectives, the same system boundary was used for both the economic-financial and the environmental analyses. Figure 4.1 illustrates the system boundary adopted in the forthcoming analyses. It comprises only the activities carried out by the waste management operators (local authorities or other entities on behalf of local authorities) in charge of collecting and sorting the municipal packaging waste. However, as discussed in the following chapters, the environmental impacts linked to the recycling of the sorted materials were also considered in the investigation. This operation was not taken into account in the economic analysis because it is not under the responsibility of the local authorities. Nevertheless, one should bear in mind that the benefits for the environment achieved with recycling are the main goal of all the packaging waste recycling systems. Furthermore, it is reasonable to assume that recycling activities are balanced from

---

1 The following scholars contributed with research for this subchapter (in alphabetical order): Marta Cabral, Nuno Ferreira da Cruz, Pedro Simões, Rui Cunha Marques and Sandra Ferreira.

the financial point of view, otherwise private recyclers or reprocessors would go bankrupt (da Cruz et al., 2012).

In line with what is stated above and considering the availability of information, the packaging materials production, the packaging waste transportation from the production point (households) to the respective containers, the manufacturing and maintenance of drop-off containers and the composting process were excluded from the analysis. The transport of waste to recyclers and the recycling process itself were excluded from the system boundary of the economic-financial analysis but, as just mentioned, these processes were assessed in the environmental perspective. The assessment excluded the long term emissions (over 100 years) because the study intends to quantify the actual environmental impacts for a particular year (2010).

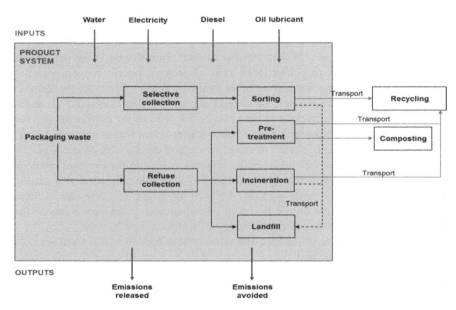

Figure 4.1   System boundary defined for economic-financial and environmental analyses
Source: adapted from EIMPack (2014a)

The methodology applied to the six countries analyzed in this book is based on a model which establishes a balance between the costs and benefits arising from the activities of selective collection and sorting. Only the household packaging waste flow was considered, with exception of Romania where the industry flow was also included. As stated in Chapter 3, the vast majority of packaging waste managed by the Romanian Green Dot company (Eco-Rom Ambalaje) is still originated by industrial activities. For this reason, the results attained for Romania should be interpreted with precaution. Finally, it was not possible to obtain reliable and representative data concerning financial costs and benefits of packaging waste management for the German and British case studies due to the competitive nature of the recycling schemes in these countries (i.e. the trade secret enforced by the various compliance schemes).

For the case of the UK, the data gathered represents only around 2 percent of the population. Nevertheless, the results attained for the different selective collection strategies are still reported in the next Chapter, even though they are not comparable with the remaining case-studies. For Germany it was impossible to apply the comparison model altogether. But since in this country packaging waste management operations are not an exclusive responsibility of local authorities (there is a dual system: one for mixed waste managed by local authorities and one for separated waste managed by the compliance schemes), the aforementioned research questions have a more trivial response for the German case: packaging waste management (i.e. selective collection flow) is entirely financed by the industry and the EPR principle is strictly respected. Whether or not this system is optimal (i.e. one that minimizes the overall costs of packaging waste management) is still an open question.

Because the economic-financial data gathered represents only around 2 percent of the population for the case of the UK and in Romania most of the packaging waste managed by Eco-Rom Ambalaje comes from the industrial flow, the results are not comparable with the remaining case studies (Belgium, France, Italy and Portugal). The coverage of the economic-financial data gathered for these countries is as follows: 100 percent of the Belgian population, 20 percent of the French population, 100 percent of the Italian population and 100 percent of the Portuguese population.

The environmental analysis was only undertaken for Belgium, Italy and Portugal due to the extensive amount of data required. This analysis includes a life-cycle assessment (LCA) to evaluate the emissions related to the packaging waste collection and treatment and a monetization of those emissions (environmental valuation). After converting the environmental impacts into the same unit (Euros), all costs and benefits arising from the packaging waste management operations (from the perspective of local authorities) were compared. In brief, the methodology applied in the ensuing Chapters can be described or subdivided in four different stages:

1. An economic and financial analysis where the costs of selective collection and sorting are compared to the respective benefits attained by the local authorities;
2. A LCA to estimate and evaluate the environmental impacts associated with packaging waste collection and treatment;
3. An environmental valuation to ascribe monetary values to the quantified impacts;
4. The comparison of all economic and environmental costs and benefits.

Financial Costs and Benefits

All expenditures and revenues relative to the selective collection and sorting of municipal packaging waste carried out by the Belgian, French, Italian, Portuguese, Romanian and British local authorities were considered in the financial analysis. Referring to the year 2010, the data were obtained from the annual account reports of the local authorities, reports and other documentation provided by the compliance companies and surveys sent to the waste management operators. On the expenditure side, the aspects considered were the following:

- The operational and maintenance expenses of selective collection and sorting (the treatment cost of packaging waste rejected during sorting was also considered here);
- The depreciation of assets allocated to these activities.

On the revenue side, all financial benefits attained by the waste management operators due to their selective collection and sorting activities were also accounted for, namely:

- The FSLA (i.e. the values paid by the compliance schemes of each country case study—Fost Plus in Belgium, Eco-Emballage in France, CONAI in Italy, SPV in Portugal and Eco-Rom Ambalaje in Romania);
- Sale of sorted packaging material (attained from direct transactions with recyclers or guarantors in those countries where local authorities own the sorted packaging waste even after receiving the FSLA);
- Other financial revenues (e.g. performance fees or sale of non-packaging material, such as newspapers that enter the selective collection stream);
- Subsidies to investment (the ones allocated to selective collection and sorting assets).

Specific details of each national recycling system have an effect on the inclusion/exclusion of some of these variables. For instance, among the benefits, the sale of packaging material was not considered for the Portuguese case study. For this country the only revenue from the packaging waste taken back is the FSLA (which internalizes the market value of the recyclables). Government grants (subsidies to the investment) were not considered in Romania because the waste management operations in 2010 were mainly performed by private companies that do not receive them. Moreover, most of the packaging waste collected comes from industrial facilities and, therefore, the system does not involve the complexity of managing household packaging waste nor does it require the same technology and infrastructure investments.

One should also bear in mind that the FSLA calculation models vary from country to country. Some systems are more sophisticated and seemingly promote the efficiency of waste management operators or, at least, increased efforts in collecting packaging waste materials separately. Others simply vary the unit fee with the type of packaging material collected. All costs and benefits were calculated based on tons of packaging waste selectively collected (to make comparisons simpler).

Other (Economic) Costs and Benefits

The cost-benefit comparisons offered in this book include two components that often get sidelined in purely financial analyses, one on the benefits side and one on the costs side. First and foremost, the savings (of the local authorities) that derive from the diversion of packaging waste from the refuse collection circuits and other waste treatment/disposal activities (landfilling, incineration, etc.), henceforth called "opportunity costs," were considered as an economic benefit. These opportunity costs were calculated separately according to Equations 1 and 2. The variables and values used to calculate the opportunity costs and the efficiency of the sorting processes are indicated in Table 4.1.

$$\begin{matrix} \text{Costs avoided with} \\ \text{refuse collection} \\ \text{(€/year)} \end{matrix} = \begin{matrix} \text{Quantity of waste} \\ \text{selectively collected} \\ \text{(ton/year)} \end{matrix} \times \begin{matrix} \text{Unit cost of} \\ \text{refuse collection} \\ \text{(€/ton)} \end{matrix} \quad \textbf{(1)}$$

$$\begin{matrix} \text{Costs avoided with} \\ \text{waste treatment} \\ \text{(€/year)} \end{matrix} = \begin{matrix} \text{Quantity of waste} \\ \text{taken back} \\ \text{(ton/year)} \end{matrix} \times \begin{matrix} \text{Unit cost of} \\ \text{treatment} \\ \text{and disposal} \\ \text{(€/ton)} \end{matrix} \quad \textbf{(2)}$$

On the costs side, the return on capital employed (both debt and equity) concerning the investments due to the selective collection and sorting activities were also included in the comparison framework. This component corresponds to the return on capital that was necessary to mobilize for the construction of the new infrastructure and the acquisition of the equipment required for setting up the recycling system. The return on capital employed on the investments made on selective collection and sorting equipment and infrastructure was calculated through Equations 3 and 4 (WACC stands for Weighted Average Cost of Capital). The values used in these calculations are presented in Table 4.1.

$$\begin{matrix} \text{Return on} \\ \text{capital employed} \\ \text{(€/year)} \end{matrix} = \begin{matrix} \text{(Depreciation-} \\ \text{subsidies)} \\ \text{(€)} \end{matrix} \times \begin{matrix} \text{Useful life of} \\ \text{the assets} \\ \text{(-)} \end{matrix} \times \begin{matrix} \text{WACC} \\ \text{(\%)} \end{matrix} \quad \textbf{(3)}$$

$$\begin{matrix} \text{WACC} \\ \text{(\%)} \end{matrix} = \begin{matrix} \text{Cost of} \\ \text{equity} \end{matrix} \times \frac{\text{Equity}}{\text{(1-marginal corporate tax)}} + \text{Cost of debt} \times \text{debt} \quad \textbf{(4)}$$

Table 4.1   Variables used in the economic and financial analysis

Variable	Portugal	France	UK	Romania	Belgium	Italy
Useful life of the assets (years)	9.6	9.6	7.0	9.6	9.6	
Cost of equity (%)	6.0	6.0	7.5	6.0	6.0	
Equity in the capital structure (%)	19.0	19.0	19.0	19.0	19.0	(-)*
Marginal corporate tax (%)	20.3	11.1	28.0	16.0	34.0	
Cost of debt (%)	4.6	4.5	4.5	4.6	4.6	
Unit costs of refuse collection (€/ton)	49	85	99	12	60	191.3
Unit costs of other treatment (€/ton)	54	96	101	15	101	
Efficiency of glass sorting (%)	97			90	100	
Efficiency of paper & cardboard sorting (%)	90	76–99	90–99.5	45	100	90–99.5
Efficiency of other packaging sorting (%)	61				84	

*The value of 14.3€/ton was estimated by "Rapporto Rifiuti 2013" (ISPRA, 2013), taking into account the depreciation costs of the waste bins and collection trucks, the depreciation for relinquished financial assets and others, the cost of accruals and the costs related to the return on invested capital.

As for the case of the above-mentioned opportunity costs (in that case, a benefit), this corresponds to an indirect economic impact (in this case, a cost). Even if local authorities are public (and not-for-profit) entities, the return on capital employed on the assets allocated to selective collection and sorting of packaging waste should be accounted for. Public money is an increasingly scarce resource that should therefore be managed with concerns for economic sustainability (da Cruz et al., 2012). Figure 4.2 shows the several components (direct and indirect) that set up the economic and financial analysis of the packaging waste recycling systems of the various country case studies. The costs and benefits were calculated per ton of packaging waste selectively collected. Evidently, the mix of materials in an aggregated ton varies from country to country.

€/ton collected

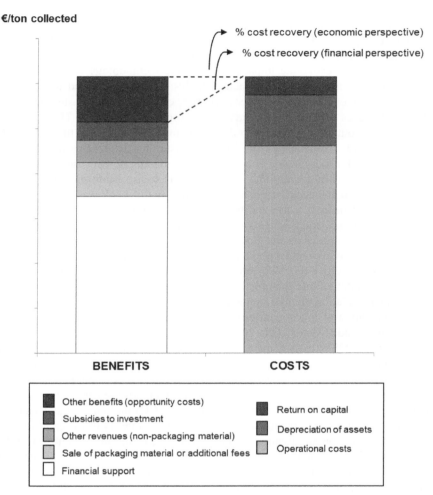

Figure 4.2   The economic-financial benefits and costs of recycling

Source: adapted from EIMPack (2014a)

Environmental Impacts[2]

Introduction

Many human activities produce emissions or other effects that result in environmental impacts. However, some environmental impacts can translate into

---

2   The following scholars contributed with research for this subchapter (in alphabetical order): Marta Cabral, Nuno Ferreira da Cruz, Pedro Simões, Rui Cunha Marques and Sandra Ferreira.

benefits or costs incurred to a third party that is not directly involved in the activity. If there is a gain or loss in welfare for the third party, this is usually referred to as an externality. In general, these externalities may not be fully internalized or translated into economic impacts. LCA is the methodology most commonly used in the literature for environmental analysis. It is a tool used to assess all environmental exchanges (resources, energy, emissions and waste) occurring during all stages of the relevant activities' or product's life-cycle. The necessary steps to carry out a LCA have been described and standardized in the recent ISO 14040 standards. Nonetheless, the LCA of waste management systems (or any other systems for that matter) is not a simple undertaking, because it involves a significant amount of assumptions, variables and extensive information.

The financial and economic analysis reported in this book was complemented with the environmental costs and benefits for Belgium, Italy (only covering the Lombardia Region) and Portugal by means of a LCA with the monetary valuation of the impact categories results. Environmental valuation emerges as an instrument for measuring environmental goods and services and the impacts of environmental degradation, in order to obtain direct and indirect costs and benefits resulting from the qualitative and quantitative changes of these goods and services. The economic calculation of environmental goods has become increasingly important in the evaluation of investment projects, government measures and policies and international trade (Matos et al., 2010).

Regarding MSW management, several studies have been developed to assist policy and decision-makers in the definition and adaptation of the best management strategies to combine the three dimensions of sustainable development: Economy, Environment and Society. In this sense, several methods are used, such as LCA, environmental and financial life-cycle costing (LCC) and cost-benefit analysis (CBA). LCA is used to quantify the environmental impacts of different options for waste collection and treatment, constituting one of the fundamental steps for environmental valuation (assigning monetary value to environmental impacts). Many studies focus on single segments of the waste management supply chain (e.g. collection schemes) or compare different treatment options (e.g. landfilling *versus* incineration). Studies, analyzing the whole management systems, concluded that an integrated approach for MSW management leads to lower environmental impacts. As just stressed above, the analysis of the life-cycle of municipal waste involves a great deal of data and several assumptions must be considered. However, some databases have been developed concerning the quantification of emissions arising from typical management operations. Furthermore, different methods and models can be used in order to facilitate the LCA.

LCC combines a financial cost-benefit analysis (financial LCC) with the economic valuation of environmental impacts (environmental LCC) quantified by LCA. The financial costs and benefits are known as internalities. The most common negative internalities considered in the analyzed studies are the operational and maintenance costs of the treatment facilities as well as the transportation costs. The positive internalities include gate fees and sales of electricity and materials recovered. From a financial perspective, waste collection has consistently proved to be a stage with significant impact on the management system.

The environmental impacts (externalities) do not have an immediate market value. Concerning waste management, the externalities commonly analyzed in the literature are the greenhouse gas emissions, other air, water and soil emissions, resources depletion, energy and materials recovery and disamenities. The monetary value of the externalities can be ascribed through the citizens' (or customers, users, etc.) preferences estimated by direct (expressed preferences) and indirect (revealed preferences) methods. Nevertheless, other methods, that attribute approximate values estimated by experts or measure the relationship between the pollution category and its impact, can be applied.

Several databases have been developed in order to facilitate economic calculations (some of them are specific for waste management operations). Furthermore, since carrying out new primary studies consumes considerable amounts of time and funding , many researchers have adopted the benefit transfer method which consists of using existing valuations and adjusting the values for their current purposes. According to the extant literature, recycling has proved to be the most appropriate treatment option from the environmental standpoint. Beyond the positive externalities arising from energy and material recovery, this strategy promotes an increase in the number of new jobs. Employment is considered a positive externality but the estimation of its monetary value is often ignored since, in theory, unemployment is considered a transitional state between one job and another. However, many European countries have been facing increasingly higher unemployment rates, corresponding to a medium-long term involuntary state. In CBA studies, all (environmental, economic and social) costs and benefits are estimated and compared. This methodology plays a key role in the processes of policy and decision making.

Since for the case of Italy it was only possible to gather the data required for the environmental analysis for a particular region, the Lombardia-specific economic-financial results were also sought. The LCA was performed on data collected from the national environmental authorities and the waste management operators involved in the packaging waste management systems with the support of the SimaPro software and the Ecoinvent 2.2 (2007) and ELCD 2.0 databases.

It is worth stressing once again that though the same system boundary was used in both the economic-financial and environmental analyses (comprising only the activities performed by the waste management operators/local authorities in charge of collecting and sorting the municipal packaging waste) in this book the recycling of the sorted materials was also considered in the environmental perspective.

Life-Cycle Assessment

The LCA was developed using the SimaPro software version 7.3.3 according to the ISO 14040:2006 requirements. The investigation was carried out based on a "traditional" LCA, which evaluates the life-cycle of a product, although, in this case, it only focuses on the end-of-life of a specific product (packaging). In other words, the LCA focuses on packaging waste (from the point packaging becomes waste until the point it ceases to be waste either through disposal or recovery). Due to the great amount of data necessary to carry out the LCA, it was only possible to perform the environmental analysis for the case studies of Portugal, Belgium and Italy (specifically Lombardia).

The main goal of this assessment was to quantify the positive and negative environmental impacts arising from the municipal packaging waste management operations carried out by (or in name of) local authorities in charge of selective collection and sorting. Note that in SimaPro negative values are translated into benefits for the environment whereas positive values represent burdens or costs for the environment. The expansion of the system boundaries technique was adopted (Giugliano et al., 2011). With this approach, the environmental impacts resulting from the waste management operations and the savings in terms of energy and raw materials consumption from the recycling process are taken into account. According to Clift et al. (2000), the system model for a waste LCA can be described as two sub-systems:

1. A foreground system, which includes the waste management activities from collection to disposal/recycling;
2. A background system, i.e. systems that interact with the foreground system supplying energy and materials, including the avoided energy and primary materials production in the recycling process.

The background data was taken from the Ecoinvent 2.2 and ELCD 2.0 databases while the foreground data (related to the main consumptions, i.e., electricity, diesel, lubricants, etc.) were collected directly from the waste management operators and the proper official documentation. The assumptions adopted include the following aspects:

- The secondary materials produced through the recycling of packaging waste replace the corresponding primary materials (i.e. those produced from virgin raw materials). The savings in energy, raw materials and emissions released from the avoided production were also considered in the recycling process;
- The electricity produced from landfill gas (LFG) for the Portuguese case (the landfilling of packaging waste was only considered for the Portuguese case because it is virtually non-existent in Belgium and in the Lombardia region) and from waste incineration (for the three case studies) is supposed to substitute the same amount of electricity produced in each country (considering the different energy sources). This energy corresponds to the real energy mix production in 2010 (average approach). The energy mix of the three countries under study, for the year 2010, is shown in Table 4.2.

Table 4.2   Energy mix in 2010 for Belgium, Italy and Portugal

Energy mix	Belgium (%)	Italy (%)	Portugal (%)
Hydropower	(-)	15.6	29.5
Nuclear	45	(-)	(-)
Coal	2.8	11.9	12.6
Natural gas	29	45.8	20.5
Other fossil fuels	5.1	8.8	0.09
Biomass	3.4	(-)	4.2
Other renewable sources	3.2	4.7	44.2
Imported	12	13.2	5.0

Source: REN (2010), REN (2013), DGEG (2013a), DGEG (2013b), Spitzley and Najdawi (2011), Eurostat (2013a), Eurostat (2013b), Terna (2013)

The functional unit (FU) of the LCA study for the "recycling system" (selective collection flow) is one ton of municipal packaging waste managed by each compliance scheme (Fost Plus in Belgium, CONAI in Italy and SPV in Portugal) in the year 2010 (i.e. one ton of each packaging waste flow selectively collected and sent for sorting). Regarding the "non-recycling system" (undifferentiated flow), the FU is one ton of each packaging material waste (plastic, paper/cardboard, metal and glass) taking into account the respective average MSW compositions in the same reference year. Since all the operations carried out by the local authorities were considered in the economic analysis, those same operations were defined in the system boundary as unit processes in the LCA, as illustrated in Figure 4.1.

As already mentioned, although the transport of waste to recyclers and the recycling process itself were not included in the economic analysis, these processes were assessed in the environmental perspective in order to quantify the impacts (in particular, the expected and pursued net benefits) of the recycling activity. These processes were excluded from the economic analysis because the recycling of the different materials is carried out by the private sector and, therefore, it is not relevant to evaluate the extent to which the EPR principle is being respected regarding the funding of the preparation for recycling activities. At this point, the reader should recall that the major aim of this book is to answer the following question: are the extra-costs arising from the recycling of packaging waste being recovered via the sale of sorted packaging waste materials (i.e. by the market), or are they being supported by the consumer (i.e. by the industry which reflects its costs on the price of the products) or by citizens in general (i.e. through higher waste management fees of local taxes)? A related query is to determine whether the industry is paying for the net financial cost of packaging waste management (i.e. not considering what local authorities save with the diversion of packaging waste from landfills, incinerators, etc.). In addition, it is quite difficult to gather detailed information about the revenues and expenditures of private businesses.

In Belgium, the pre-treatment (the mechanical sorting process upstream of the MBT that separates the recyclable materials present in the refuse waste flow—whenever these circuits feed the plants instead of selective collection) and landfill processes were excluded from the system boundary since organic (mainly food) waste is selectively collected and any municipal packaging waste collected in the refuse collection circuits is sent to incineration. In Belgium, the direct landfilling of waste is banned. In Italy, the organic (food) waste is also selectively collected, so the pre-treatment process was also excluded from the system boundary. However, many MBT facilities in Portugal receive mixed waste and, thus, this process was studied for this country.

In the environmental assessment the long term emissions (over 100 years) were excluded because the objective of the study is to quantify the environmental impacts of various unit processes in a particular year. As for the economic-financial analysis, the avoided impacts from the refuse collection and disposal operations ("opportunity costs") were also considered in this assessment.

Life-cycle inventory (LCI)
The data required to model the unit processes included in the system boundary of each case study were gathered through questionnaires sent to all waste management operators and compliance schemes. Some specific processes included in the software's databases (namely, Ecoinvent 2.2 and ELCD 2.0) were also used with the appropriate adjustments to the case studies and some assumptions were made based on the literature. The various unit processes are briefly described below (see EIMPack, 2013b and EIMPack, 2014a and 2014b, for a more detailed description).

Waste collection   Selective collection is the operation of emptying the respective drop-off containers and transporting the packaging waste to the sorting facilities. This transport entails several environmental impacts, mainly related to air pollution. However, the related construction, maintenance and materials disposal of collection vehicles also comprises emissions and energy and raw materials consumption.

For Portugal and Belgium, selective collection was modelled considering the emissions released mainly by the fuel combustion (Spielmann et al., 2007). The Ecoinvent 2.2 (2007) database was used together with data provided by local authorities (fuel consumption and transport distances). The emissions were calculated according to the Tier 1 methodology from EEA (2012), based on the fuel consumption and specific-fuel emission factors from the literature. In these countries, packaging waste is sent to sorting facilities after collection. The consumption of electricity, diesel and lubricants as well as the separation efficiency were considered in the modelling process.

For practical reasons, a different approach based on the "GERLA Project" was adopted for the Italian case (Lombardia region). The collection model was divided into bring system collection and curbside system collection according to different percentages for each material flow. In the studied region, the selectively collected packaging waste is grouped in a certain location and then delivered to the sorting facility using different vehicles. The distance of this transport was assumed to be 10 km and was modelled using Ecoinvent data sets (50 percent Transport, lorry >32t, EURO3/RER and 50 percent Transport, lorry >32t, EURO4/RER). The data used is reported in more detail in Rigamonti et al. (2013).

Similarly to what is described above for selective collection, refuse collection is the operation of emptying the mixed waste drop-off containers and transporting the undifferentiated waste to the treatment/disposal facilities. This process was modelled based on the same methodology used for modelling the selective collection process for Belgium and Portugal. For these countries, it was assumed that the waste is transported directly to the treatment/disposal facilities. In the Lombardia region, the undifferentiated waste is collected through a curbside system (70.8 percent) or a bring system (29.2 percent), with an average mileage of 15.4 and 7.4 km per ton collected, respectively. The curbside collection system was modelled using Ecoinvent datasets Transport, lorry > 16t, fleet average/RER (40.9 percent) and Transport, van <3.5t/RER (59.1 percent), whereas the bring system collection was modelled using Ecoinvent dataset Transport, lorry >16 t, fleet average/RER. It was assumed that after collection the undifferentiated waste is delivered at an incineration facility located, on average, at a distance of 18.3 km, by means of trucks modelled by Ecoinvent datasets Transport, lorry >32t, EURO3/ RER (50 percent) and Transport, lorry >32t, EURO4/RER (50 percent).

Sorting facilities   This unit process is the (further) separation of the selectively collected packaging waste by material in a sorting station. For Portugal, the sorting processes were modelled for paper/cardboard, plastic, metal and drink packaging (including the landfilling of rejected packaging waste as the final disposal operation). For glass packaging, only separation efficiency was taken into account (because this stream is not sorted). For Belgium, the sorting process was only considered for the PMD flow (including the incineration of rejected waste as disposal operation) since paper/cardboard and glass packaging waste is sent directly to the recyclers/reprocessors. For Italy, only the sorting of ferrous metals and the separation of the multi-material fraction was modelled since this is the operation actually paid by local authorities (at least in 2010). The sorting processes were modelled based on the main consumptions (electricity, diesel, etc.) related to the operation and considering the rejected material (quantities and type of final disposal). The electricity consumption was assumed and the incineration of rejected waste was considered as the final disposal operation. The main data is indicated in Table 4.3.

Table 4.3   Inputs of waste sorting (weighted averages) for the year 2010

Variable	Paper/cardboard waste	Glass waste	Plastic/metal/other packaging waste
Portugal			
Electricity (kWh/ton)	14.57	(-)	53.05
Diesel (L/ton)	1.62	(-)	5.59
Lubricants (L/ton)	0.03	(-)	0.08
Water (m³/ton)	0.11	(-)	0.14
Rejected waste (ton/ton)	0.100	0.030	0.390
Rejected disposal	Landfilling	Landfilling	Landfilling
Belgium			
Electricity (kWh/ton)	(-)	(-)	32.22
Diesel (L/ton)	(-)	(-)	3.52
Lubricants (L/ton)	(-)	(-)	0.04
Rejected waste (ton/ton)	(-)	(-)	0.159
Rejected disposal	Incineration	Incineration	Incineration
Italy			
Electricity consumption —Ferrous metal sorting (kWh/ton)	47.5		
Electricity consumption— Multi-material separation (kWh/ton)	15.9		
Rejected waste (ton/ton)	0.096		
Rejected disposal	Incineration		

Pre-treatment facilities   Pre-treatment corresponds to the several sequential manual and mechanical operations for preparing the undifferentiated waste before composting or anaerobic digestion. This was considered because the green and food waste are usually not selectively collected in Portugal. This process was modelled based on the consumptions related to the use of equipment, such as electricity, diesel and lubricants (10.34 kWh/ton, 0.11 L/ton and 0.04 L/ton, respectively). The consumptions regarding the actual composting operations were excluded because the packaging waste materials are re-directed to recycling in the pre-treatment operation. The packaging materials are not effectively composted and thus do not contribute for compost production.

Incineration facilities   Incineration is defined as the combustion of MSW in controlled facilities. In Belgium and Italy (Lombardia region), incineration was the only disposal operation considered for undifferentiated waste. In Portugal, the disposal (of undifferentiated waste) activity was modelled by combining composting (specifically pre-treatment), incineration and landfilling taking into account the quantities of undifferentiated waste sent for each of these operations in 2010.

For Belgium and Portugal, the data used were collected from the several incineration facilities, the environmental annual reports and the relevant literature. For Italy, the data used is reported in Turconi et al. (2011). The allocation method was adopted because incineration is a multi input-output allocation process where several inputs (different packaging waste materials) and outputs (energy recovery, ash, slag and scrap generation and emissions) coexist. For most inputs (where there is no relation between the inputs and the waste composition) the mass allocation method was applied. Regarding the emissions of specific pollutants, such as nitrogen compounds, they depend on the technology rather than on waste composition, so the mass allocation was also applied (Margallo, 2013). The CO_2 emissions were calculated based on an estimate of the fossil carbon content in the waste incinerated multiplied by the oxidation factor and converting the product (amount of fossil carbon oxidized) to CO_2, according to the Intergovernmental Panel on Climate Change (IPCC, 2006a).

Since the incineration of waste is carried out with energy production, both fossil and biogenic (combustion of biomass materials) emissions were calculated. The contribution of each material for energy production during the process was determined based on the heating value of each material and the total energy produced by the MSW combusted in 2010 (heating value allocation). Following an attributional approach, the electricity produced by the incineration facility substitutes the electricity mix for each country considering the losses of distribution and transmission of the national grid (7.8 percent in Portugal, 4.6 percent in Belgium and 6.2 percent in Italy). This electricity corresponds to the real mix production in 2010 (average approach; see Table 4.2).

Landfill facilities   In Portugal, landfilling is usually the final disposal of rejected waste resulting from the previous unit processes. There are landfills with and without energy recovery (72 percent and 28 percent, respectively). Both processes for the different packaging materials waste were modelled, using the ELCD 2.0 databases and default values assumed by IPCC (2006b). The environmental impacts estimated in this process were considered as avoided impacts (similar to the costs avoided by diverting the packaging waste materials from the landfill or other waste treatment considered in the economic analysis).

The environmental benefits arising from the electrical energy production from LFG combustion were analyzed and accounted as a lost benefit for the landfills with energy recovery. Note that only the paper/cardboard waste contributes to the production of LFG (as a biodegradable material). Therefore, the electrical energy produced per one ton of paper/cardboard packaging waste (although this flow also includes non-packaging paper waste because it is collected in the same blue container) disposed of in these landfills had to be estimated. The first step was, therefore, to estimate the amount of LFG produced by each ton.

To estimate the amount of LFG produced by decomposing one ton of paper/cardboard packaging waste landfilled, the quantity of methane (CH_4) generated was calculated according to the IPCC methodology (IPCC, 2006b). This methodology is based on the First Order Decay (FOD) method which assumes that the degradable organic carbon (DOC) in waste decays slowly throughout a few decades during which CH_4 and carbon dioxide (CO_2) are formed. Therefore, the impacts cannot be immediately evaluated corresponding to a (short term) forecast of 100 years.

Recycling facilities   After the previous operations (excluding incineration and landfilling), the several packaging waste materials are transported to recyclers. The transport to the recyclers was considered and analyzed with the same methodology used for the selective and refuse collection processes. For the recycling processes, the FU was one ton of each packaging material (differentiating the plastic and metal materials) delivered in the recycling facility. Packaging materials recycling allows to partially or totally replace the primary raw materials in the manufacture of new packaging or other products. The "substitution ratio" depends on the quality of the

Table 4.4   Recycling process and avoided product considered for Portugal and Belgium

Packaging material	Recycling process	Avoided product	Substitution ratio
PET	PET granulate	PET granulate	1:1
EPS	Recycled EPS	EPS from virgin materials	1:1
Mixed plastics	Furniture to use outdoor from plastic recycled	Furniture to use outdoor from wood (Plywood)	1:1
Plastic film	LDPE granulates	LDPE granulates from virgin materials	1:1
HDPE	HDPE granulates	HDPE granulates from virgin materials	1:1
Glass	Glass from cullet	Glass from virgin materials	1:1
Paper/cardboard	Corrugated board, from recycling fibers	Sulphate pulp	1:0.83
Aluminum (non-ferrous)	Secondary aluminum from old scrap	Primary aluminum	1:1
Steel (ferrous)	Ferrous scrap	Pig iron	1:1

secondary products compared to the corresponding primary ones. A substitution ratio of 1:1 means that 1 unit of secondary packaging material replaces 1 unit of the corresponding primary material whereas a substitution ratio of 1:<1 means that 1 unit of secondary material replaces less than 1 unit of the corresponding primary material (Rigamonti et al., 2010).

Hence, in the modelling of the recycling processes the avoided materials production was considered assuming a substitution ratio of 1:1. The paper/cardboard packaging waste was the exception with a substitution ratio of 1:0.83, because paper fibers degrade in the recycling process and thus cannot be reused indefinitely (Rigamonti et al., 2009). The plastics recycling process consists, in general, in a mechanical recycling process, in which the plastic waste is shredded and extruded to form recycled granulate to be used in new plastic products. The glass (cullet) is transported to the glass industry and it is used in the kilns together with the raw materials. The metals, separated into ferrous (steel) and non-ferrous (aluminum), are smelted in the corresponding industries. After casting, the aluminum is molded into ingots and the steel is folded into large coils of rolled steel for producing new packaging or other products. The LCI of the primary production and recycling of materials was obtained from Ecoinvent 2.2 (2007) database and the relevant literature. The recycling and avoided processes modelled are indicated in Table 4.4 for Belgium and Portugal and in Table 4.5 for Italy.

Table 4.5   Recycling process and avoided product considered for Italy

Packaging material	Recycling process	Avoided product	Substitution ratio
Ferrous metals	Liquid secondary steel from iron scraps	Liquid primary steel from pig iron	1:1
Aluminum	Secondary aluminum ingots from aluminum scraps	Primary aluminum ingots from bauxite	1:1
Glass	Generic glass container from cullet	Generic glass container from raw materials	1:1
Wood	Particle board from recovered wood	Plywood from virgin wood	1:0.6
Paper	Non-deinked pulp from wastepaper	Virgin thermo-mechanical pulp	1:0.8
Plastics	Granules of recycled PET	Granules of virgin PET	1:0.8
	Granules of recycled HDPE	Granules of virgin HDPE	1:0.8
	Flakes of mix of polyolefin	50% Wood	1:1

Life-cycle impact assessment (LCIA)

As shown in the following sub-chapter, this book uses three different methods for impact valuation. Therefore, the selected impact categories were the ones in common for these three methods, namely:

- Photochemical oxidant formation;
- Eutrophication;
- Climate change;
- Human toxicity;
- Acidification.

These impact categories were selected in SimaPro in order to be subsequently monetized. Three valuation methods were employed because LCA modelling is subjective and involves a high degree of uncertainty and variability. By reporting the results of three different approaches (each with different assumptions embedded) the reader is able to grasp the range within which the "true" values may vary. This methodological option increases the robustness of the results (perhaps at the cost of extra complexity and uneasiness in their interpretation) and demonstrates that one should be careful in drawing sweeping conclusions regarding the monetary values of environmental impacts. As shown in Table 4.6, the LCIA techniques used for quantifying each of these impact categories varies according to the valuation method.

Table 4.6   LCIA methods used for each valuation method

Impact categories	Eco-costs2012	Stepwise2006	Ecovalue08
Climate change	IPCC GWP100a		
Human toxicity	Usetox + interim characteristics		
Photochemical oxidant formation		Impact 2002 + and EDIP 2003	CML 2001
Eutrophication	Recipe midpoint		
Acidification			

Environmental Valuation

Environmental valuation aims to convert different environmental impacts into a common unit in order to simplify the evaluation of total impacts from different projects (Ahlroth and Finnveden, 2011). The environmental impacts can be transformed into monetary values or non-monetary weights, depending on the objective of the study.

In this study, all environmental impacts quantified through LCA were converted into monetary values to compare all (economic and environmental) costs and benefits incurred by the packaging waste recycling systems analyzed from the perspective of local authorities. To accomplish that, the monetization of environmental impacts was carried out based on the benefit transfer method (Eshet et al., 2007). Three monetary valuation databases/methods were used: Eco-costs2012 (Vogtländer et al., 2001, TU Delft, 2013), Stepwise2006 (Weidema, 2013) and Ecovalue08 (Ahlroth and Finnveden, 2011). The two first methods were developed for Europe as a whole while Ecovalue08 was initially developed for a specific European country (Sweden).

Eco-costs2012
The Eco-costs technique is based on the "marginal prevention costs" or, in other words, the costs required to bring back the environmental burden to a sustainable level. The marginal prevention costs in 2012 were calculated based on West European price levels and on the Best Available Technologies Not Entailing Excessive Costs (BATNEC) for The Netherlands. Contrary to the damage costs (where one substance can cause damage in more than one impact category), in the Eco-costs method, one substance must be considered in a single impact category (the one for which it proves to be more relevant or costly). This method was added to the SimaPro software, so the impact categories were directly converted into monetary values, taking into account that the prices refer to the year 2012 (the currency value is Euro). Since the reference year is 2010, the monetary values obtained were converted into Eur2010, assuming the European (EU27) inflation rates between 2010 and 2012 (1 Eur2012 = 0,94535€ in 2010; Eurostat, 2013c).

Stepwise2006
This method converts all impacts into monetary units (Eur2003) or QALYs (Quality Adjusted Life Years), combining the characterization models from the impact assessment methods, the IMPACT2002+ (v. 2.1) and the EDIP2003 methods (Weidema, 2013). The monetization of a QALY is based on the budget constraint, assuming that "the average annual income is the maximum that an average person can pay for an additional life year" (Weidema, 2009: 1591). Thus, the budget constraint is considered to be the potential average annual income, also called the potential annual economic production per capita. This variable was estimated to be about 74.000 EUR2003, corresponding to the willingness to pay (WTP) determined by the ExternE project. This method was added to the SimaPro software, thus the impact categories were directly converted into monetary values taking into account that prices (in EUR2003) referred to the year 2003. Since the reference year is 2010, the monetary values obtained were converted into Euro2010, assuming the European (EU27) inflation rates between 2003 and 2010 (1 EUR2003 = 1,17234€; Eurostat, 2013c).

Ecovalue08

Ahlroth and Finnveden (2011) developed the Ecovalue08 weighting database based on stated preference methods (in particular, contingent valuation). The authors characterized some impact categories using the CML2002 method (Guinée et al., 2002). However, the CML2001 was used instead of the CML2002 method in this study because this was the most recent version available in the SimaPro software. For the impact category "Acidification," the authors used local characterization factors between Europe and Scandinavia (based on the differences in soil conditions). Nonetheless, the current book also uses the CML method for this impact category since the local factors are not applicable to the three country case studies (Belgium, Italy and Portugal). Regarding the monetary valuation, the impact categories were monetized using estimates for the WTP of previous studies (see Ahlroth, 2009; Tol, 2008; Stern, 2006; Methodex, 2007; Espreme, 2008; World Bank, 2009). For some impact categories, the minimum and maximum values were estimated to illustrate the uncertainty involved in these modelling processes. Indeed, Ahlroth and Finnveden (2011) observed significant variations in the damage values for different toxic pollutants and in the values for abiotic resources. This is another indication of the uncertainty related to impacts' modelling and valuation. In this case, the impact categories quantified through LCA had to be multiplied by the weighting factors (estimated by the authors), taking into account the currency conversion (1 SEK = 0,10485€ in 2010; ECB, 2013).

All Costs and Benefits[3]

In the last stage of the methodological approach, all economic and financial (internal) and environmental (external) unit costs and benefits of the packaging waste recycling systems of Portugal, Belgium and Italy in 2010 were added and compared together in a graph, as illustrated in Figure 4.3. Evidently, from a social welfare (and sustainable) perspective, the total benefits should outweigh the total costs.

On the costs side, the negative externalities related to the emissions released in the transport of packaging waste and sorting operations were added to the economic-financial costs incurred in the same operations. As benefits, the avoided emissions due to the recycling of packaging waste (instead of incineration or landfilling) were considered in addition to the financial revenues due to the packaging waste management activities (FSLA and other revenue sources as a result of the selective collection and sorting carried out by local authorities). The environmental results obtained for the "non-recycling system" (composed of refuse collection and other treatment or disposal of packaging waste) correspond to the environmental opportunity costs.

---

3   The following scholars contributed with research for this subchapter (in alphabetical order): Marta Cabral, Nuno Ferreira da Cruz, Pedro Simões, Rui Cunha Marques and Sandra Ferreira.

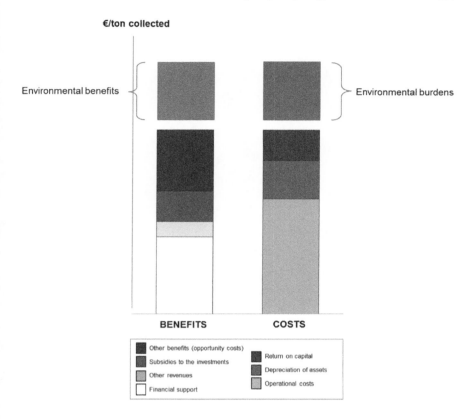

Figure 4.3   Comparison of benefits and costs of recycling
Source: adapted from EIMPack (2014a)

Chapter 5

The Value-For-Money of Recycling

Belgium[1]

Economic and Financial Costs and Benefits

This step of the analysis comprises the comparison between the economic and financial costs and benefits of the selective collection and sorting activities carried out by the Belgian *intercommunales*. The results obtained are presented per ton of packaging waste collected and as shown in Figure 5.1.

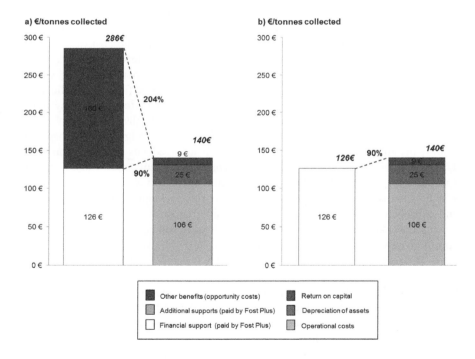

Figure 5.1   Cost coverage in Belgium considering the tons of packaging waste collected in 2010

1   The following scholars contributed with research for this subchapter (in alphabetical order): Marta Cabral, Nuno Ferreira da Cruz, Pedro Simões, Rui Cunha Marques, Sandra Ferreira and Simon De Jaeger.

The Local Authorities benefited 286€ per ton of packaging waste collected in 2010, considering the opportunity costs. In a strictly financial perspective (i.e. not taking into account the opportunity costs) the benefits are only 126€ per ton. In Belgium, the discussions about considering (or not) the opportunity costs in the economic-financial balance may not be as relevant for the level of sustainability of the service as in other countries. In fact, the financial benefits cover practically all the costs of the packaging waste service: about 90 percent of the total costs of the service are covered by the FSLA. Actually, Fost Plus finances 100 percent of the financial costs related to a "standard" level of service. The difference of 10 percent depicted above might be explained by local authorities opting to provide higher collection frequencies or density of collection point (which makes sense economically considering the size of the opportunity costs). In sum, the current (and standard) Belgian recycling system is financially sustainable and has virtually no public money directly involved.

If one separates the costs of selective collection and the costs of sorting of packaging waste, it is concluded that the average cost of selective collection is 97€ per ton of packaging waste collected whereas the cost of sorting is 178€ per ton effectively sent for sorting. Note that in Belgium only the PMD stream is sorted after collection. Globally, the cost of sorting is lower than the cost of selective collection, corresponding to about 46 percent of the complete service cost.

Figure 5.2 shows the costs of the recycling service per packaging waste stream. Not surprisingly, the preparation for recycling costs (selective collection and sorting activities) depend on the material flow considered, since they have different characteristics. The lower service cost of the waste glass (especially when compared to the PMD flow) can be justified by its high weight and density and also by the adopted bring system, which significantly reduces the collection cost. The PMD, in contrast, has a relative low density (a full collection truck contains approximately 3 tons of PMD) and is collected every two weeks at the curbside, which explains the relative high service cost for this packaging flow. Finally, paper and cardboard is also collected at the curbside but only once a month and the density is considerably higher than the PMD flow (a full collection truck contains approximately 9 tons of paper and cardboard).

In Belgium, the implementation of the PPW Directive was a great success not only in terms of the recycling rates achieved, but also in the strict application of the EPR principle. The financial transfers undertaken by Fost Plus (guaranteed by the green dot fees paid by the industry) ensure the sustainability of the system. For this case-study the consideration (or non-consideration) of the opportunity costs in the economic-financial balance does not seem to be an issue. However, it is notable that the opportunity costs (costs with refuse collection and other waste treatments—160€ per ton collected) are higher than the costs of selective collection and sorting, which may also help to explain the high recycling rates attained by this country.

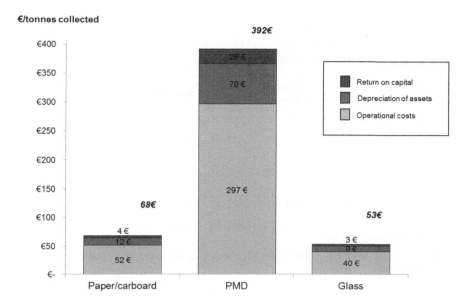

Figure 5.2   Costs of the service per packaging waste stream in Belgium

Environmental Impacts

The environmental impacts of the packaging waste management operations are indicated in Table 5.1 for the selected impact categories. The negative results are considered avoided impacts (which were obtained for incineration due to the energy produced).

The packaging waste selectively collected is routed to sorting. In the sorting process the packaging rejected is incinerated. These packaging waste operations have the objective of preparing the packaging waste for recycling; therefore, this system is hereafter called "Recycling scenario" and represents the packaging waste selectively collected in 2010 in Belgium. The impacts from the "Recycling scenario" are indicated in Table 5.2. If no selective collection was carried out, all packaging waste would be collected in the refuse collection system and sent to final disposal. Therefore, this scenario is hereafter called the "Incineration scenario" (hypothetical scenario where all packaging waste would be collected and treated with the undifferentiated waste flow which, for the case of Belgium, would lead to incineration).

Table 5.1   Environmental impacts incurred by the different packaging waste management operations per ton of packaging waste managed in 2010 in Belgium

Impact category	Unit	Selective collection	Refuse collection	Sorting	Recycling	Incineration
Climate change	kg CO2 eq.	3,77E+02	4,59E+01	9,11E+01	-2,11E+04	1,10E+04
Human toxicity cancer effects	CTUh	8,97E-08	1,02E-08	3,66E-08	-9,14E-07	2,14E-07
Human toxicity non-cancer effects	CTUh	4,99E-09	5,91E-10	5,73E-10	-2,13E-06	-5,96E-10
Ecotoxicity	CTUe	3,99E-01	4,54E-02	2,37E-02	-7,09E+01	-5,03E-02
Photochemical oxidant formation	kg NMVOC	1,74E+00	1,98E-01	1,23E-01	-6,99E+01	1,02E-01
Aquatic eutrophication	kg P eq.	1,07E-03	1,27E-04	4,41E-04	-9,25E-01	9,82E-02
Abiotic depletion	kg Sb eq.	1,03E+00	1,17E-01	1,75E-01	-2,06E+02	-1,13E+00
Acidification	mol H+ eq.	2,64E+00	2,99E-01	2,99E-01	-3,23E+02	-9,91E-01
CED	MJ	2,36E+03	2,68E+02	6,01E+02	-4,61E+04	-7,70E+03

Table 5.2   Total environmental impacts allocated to the "Recycling scenario" in Belgium

Impact category	Unit	Selective collection	Sorting	Recycling	Total
Climate change	kg CO2 eq.	1,05E+08	1,49E+07	-4,58E+08	-3,29E+08
Human toxicity cancer effects	CTUh	2,50E-02	5,97E-03	-2,12E-02	9,94E-03
Human toxicity non-cancer effects	CTUh	1,39E-03	9,35E-05	-5,07E-02	-4,87E-02
Ecotoxicity	CTUe	1,11E+05	3,86E+03	-3,33E+06	-3,20E+06
Photochemical oxidant formation	kg NMVOC	4,84E+05	2,01E+04	-1,85E+06	-1,28E+06
Aquatic eutrophication	kg P eq.	3,00E+02	7,19E+01	-2,22E+04	-2,17E+04
Abiotic depletion	kg Sb eq.	2,88E+05	2,86E+04	-3,82E+06	-3,44E+06
Acidification	mol H+ eq.	7,34E+05	4,88E+04	-1,05E+07	-9,68E+06
CED	MJ	4,26E+08	9,92E+07	-7,86E+09	-7,19E+09

The results of the LCIA for the "Incineration scenario" are indicated in Table 5.3. The negative results obtained for the incineration process are related to the energy production from the packaging waste combustion.

Table 5.3   Total environmental impacts allocated to the "Incineration scenario" in Belgium

Impact category	Unit	Refuse collection	Incineration	Total
Climate change	kg CO2 eq.	5,68E+07	-1,96E+07	3,72E+07
Human toxicity cancer effects	CTUh	1,26E-02	6,77E-02	8,02E-02
Human toxicity non-cancer effects	CTUh	7,31E-04	1,45E-04	8,76E-04
Ecotoxicity	CTUe	5,62E+04	2,40E+03	5,86E+04
Photochemical oxidant formation	kg NMVOC	2,45E+05	5,25E+04	2,98E+05
Aquatic eutrophication	kg P eq.	1,57E+02	7,57E+04	7,59E+04
Abiotic depletion	kg Sb eq.	1,45E+05	3,03E+04	1,76E+05
Acidification	mol H+ eq.	3,70E+05	-4,87E+04	3,22E+05
CED	MJ	3,32E+08	-1,35E+09	-1,02E+09

Figure 5.3 illustrates the contribution of the two scenarios described above for each impact category. The impacts incurred in the "Incineration scenario" are higher than the impacts related to the "Recycling scenario" with exception of the Cumulative energy demand (CED) impact due to the production of energy in the incineration process. Note that the negative figures indicate that some emissions and materials consumption were avoided (i.e. "good" for the environment). Regarding energy, the savings from the production in the incineration process are lower than the savings in energy from the recycling process. As regards human toxicity (cancer effects), emissions from the collection and transport of the packaging waste contribute to the "bad" results.

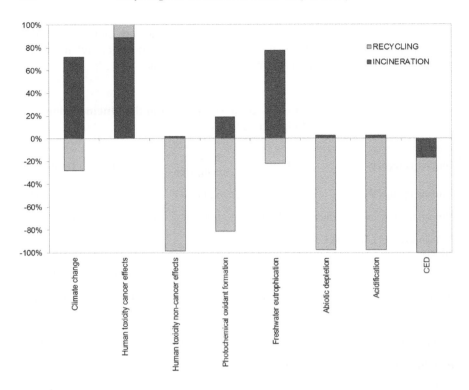

Figure 5.3   LCIA contribution results of the "Recycling scenario" and the "Incineration scenario" in Belgium

Environmental Costs and Benefits

As the results below will show, from the environmental point of view, the "Recycling scenario" proved to be more advantageous than the "Incineration scenario," achieving better results for all environmental impact categories analyzed.

Eco-costs2012
The results for the environmental valuation of the "Recycling scenario" using the Eco-costs2012 method are indicated in Table 5.4. The selective collection activity is responsible for the higher costs related to the analyzed environmental impact categories. The results for the "Incineration Scenario" are expressed in Table 5.5. With this method, the packaging waste incineration achieves good results for the impact categories "Aquatic eutrophication" and "Acidification."

Table 5.4   Environmental valuation for the "Recycling scenario" in Belgium (Eco-costs2012)

Impact category	Selective collection	Sorting	Recycling	Total
Climate change	13.523.416,21€	1.906.609,14€	-72.649.626,97€	-57.219.601,62€
Human toxicity	3.175.492,89€	552.584,71€	-13.655.762,06€	-9.927.684,46€
Photochemical oxidant formation	181.683,62€	18.605,58€	-3.075.937,12€	-2.875.647,92€
Aquatic eutrophication	31.171,86€	2.443,93€	-1.267.813,33€	-1.234.197,54€
Acidification	2.097.505,46€	122.552,72€	-30.916.694,38€	-28.696.636,21€

Table 5.5   Environmental valuation for the "Incineration scenario" in Belgium (Eco-costs2012)

Impact category	Refuse collection	Incineration	Total
Climate change	7.281.468,84€	99.799.169,70€	107.080.638,54€
Human toxicity	1.714.234,27€	2.139.197,13€	3.853.431,39€
Photochemical oxidant formation	91.900,13€	136.360,86€	228.260,98€
Aquatic eutrophication	15.781,17€	-9.338,78€	6.442,40€
Acidification	1.057.740,46€	-146.482,68€	911.257,78€

Stepwise2006

The results for the environmental valuation of the "Recycling scenario" through the Stepwise2006 technique are indicated in Table 5.6. As expected the selective collection activities are responsible for the higher costs related to the environmental impact categories analyzed. With this method, the "Incineration Scenario" (see Table 5.7) achieves a better result for the category "Acidification" due to energy savings.

Ecovalue08

The results for the environmental valuation of the "Recycling scenario" achieved with the Ecovalue08 method are indicated in Table 5.8. Selective collection is responsible for the higher costs related to the analyzed environmental impact categories. In this analysis only the minimum weighting values were used since the results obtained with the maximum values are significantly higher and not comparable to the results obtained for the other methods. The results for the "Incineration scenario" are presented in Table 5.9. The energy production from packaging waste incineration avoids some impact categories, thus achieving better results for the impact category "Acidification." However, considering the other waste management operations, the final results are harmful for the environment.

Table 5.6   Environmental valuation for the "Recycling scenario" in Belgium (Stepwise2006)

Impact category	Selective collection	Sorting	Recycling	Total
Climate change	9.512.466,30€	1.447.035,66€	-46.640.819,00€	-36.491.988,43€
Human toxicity	94.145,85€	78.150,59€	-23.644.505,98€	-23.512.779,70€
Photochemical oxidant formation	913.835,89€	15.672,41€	-2.900.822,68€	-2.019.125,23€
Aquatic eutrophication	3.494,79€	243,51€	-24.976,46€	-21.700,89€
Acidification	30.557,15€	2.082,03€	-457.144,92€	-429.182,17€

Table 5.7   Environmental valuation for the "Incineration scenario" in Belgium (Stepwise2006)

Impact category	Refuse collection	Incineration	Total
Climate change	5.119.744,90€	75.751.464,63€	80.871.209,53€
Human toxicity	49.940,04€	1.132.358,78€	1.182.298,81€
Photochemical oxidant formation	481.631,82€	101.584,17€	583.215,99€
Aquatic eutrophication	1.761,31€	1.625,46€	3.386,77€
Acidification	15.419,91€	-7.627,78€	7.792,14€

Table 5.8   Environmental valuation for the "Recycling scenario" in Belgium (Ecovalue08)

Impact category	Selective collection	Sorting	Recycling	Total
Climate change	1.024.607,69€	156.089,41€	-2.290.691,14€	-1.109.994,03€
Human toxicity	185.844,71€	427,86€	325.226,49€	511.499,07€
Photochemical oxidant formation	41.554,62€	956,71€	-560.562,09€	-518.050,76€
Aquatic eutrophication	1.175.999,20€	65.538,61€	-19.199.805,06€	-17.958.267,25€
Acidification	712.226,61€	49.236,32€	-16.081.968,51€	-15.320.505,58€

Table 5.9   Environmental valuation for the "Incineration scenario" in Belgium (Ecovalue08)

Impact category	Refuse collection	Incineration	Total
Climate change	552.461,73€	8.171.133,31€	8.723.595,05€
Human toxicity	113.049,97€	1.036,05€	114.086,02€
Photochemical oxidant formation	24.306,36€	1.187,07€	25.493,44€
Aquatic eutrophication	654.737,99€	214.435,38€	869.173,37€
Acidification	398.496,07€	-133.992,72€	264.503,35€

Economic and Environmental Balance

The results for the economic and environmental balance are illustrated in Figure 5.4, Figure 5.5 and Figure 5.6 for the methods Eco-costs2012, Stepwise2006

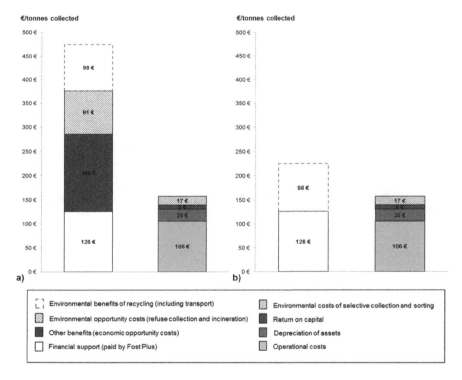

Figure 5.4   Economic and environmental results achieved for Belgium with the Eco-costs2012 method per ton of packaging waste collected: a) with and b) without the economic and environmental opportunity costs

and Ecovalue08, respectively. The results, expressed in tons of packaging waste selectively collected, differ according to the valuation method implemented. As mentioned earlier, the results from the environmental valuation of the several packaging waste management operations were added up to the previously reported economic figures. The financial revenues from waste management operations and the environmental impacts of those operations measured in euros by means of three environmental valuation methods were considered as benefits. The analysis also takes into account the (economic and environmental) opportunity costs of avoiding the incineration of packaging waste. The financial expenses of the packaging waste management operations and also the environmental costs associated with the energy consumption and emissions released were included on the costs side.

Although the recycling of the sorted materials is not an activity performed by the local waste authorities considered in the economic analysis, the environmental (net) benefits achieved with these activities are included in the graphical illustrations above. This approach is acceptable and even conservative (i.e. by

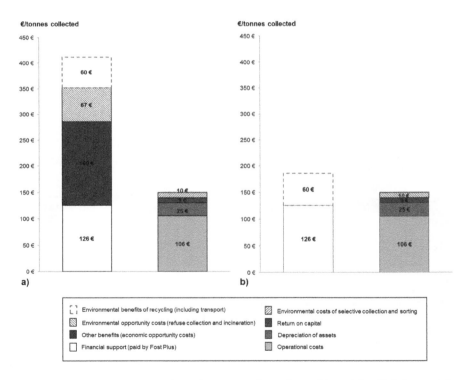

Figure 5.5   Economic and environmental results achieved for Belgium with the Stepwise2006 method per ton of packaging waste collected: a) with and b) without the economic and environmental opportunity costs

possibly underestimating the net benefits) because it is expected that the economic benefits of the recycling operators should, at least, cover their costs (otherwise the business would not be viable). The goal of the activities performed by the local authorities is to prepare the materials for the recycling process and it would not be reasonable to consider only the costs to the environment of the emissions and energy consumption due to the collection and sorting processes. The results of the recycling process included the transport of the materials to the recyclers. The benefits from the recycling of the several sorted materials were, respectively, 98€ (Ecocosts2012), 60€ (Stepwise2006) and 31€ (Ecovalue08) per ton of packaging waste selectively collected.

Considering all the costs and all the benefits, including the opportunity costs, the same overall conclusion is valid for all three valuation methods: the benefits outweigh the costs. Indeed, the benefits, in total, represent 301 percent, 275 percent and 240 percent of the costs considering the methods, Ecocosts2012, Stepwise2006 and Ecovalue08, respectively. However, for Belgium, even if one does not take

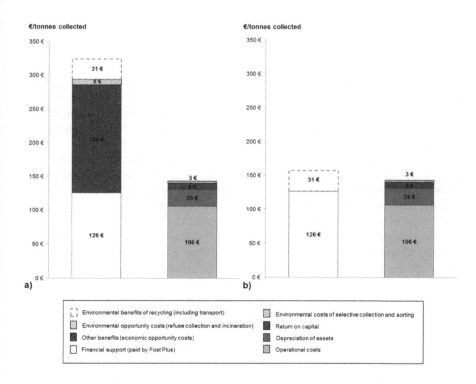

Figure 5.6   **Economic and environmental results achieved for Belgium with the Ecovalue08 method per ton of packaging waste collected: a) with and b) without the economic and environmental opportunity costs**

the economic and environmental opportunity costs into account, the benefits still outweigh the costs but in a smaller proportion, representing 142 percent (Ecocosts2012), 124 percent (Stepwise2006) and 123 percent (Ecovalue08).

France[2]

The balance between the economic and financial costs and benefits of the selective collection and sorting activities undertaken by the 45 selected French local authorities included in the sample is shown in Figure 5.7. In a strictly financial perspective (without including the opportunity costs and without any public money), the benefits represented only 130€ per ton of packaging waste collected in 2010. Conversely, each of these tons entailed a total cost of 232€ per ton. Indeed, the cost recovery is around 135 percent from an economic perspective but only 57 percent if the cost savings due to recycling are not taken into account. Assuming that the financial transfers should follow an economic approach, the FSLA could even be eliminated and the balance would still be positive. However, if the industry was to be 100 percent responsible for the costs associated with the processing of its waste packaging, the FSLA should be about 125 percent higher. In fact, only 56 percent of the packaging waste management cost is being supported by the industry (i.e. considering just the FSLA, sale of packaging material and other revenue). In Figure 5.7 the 57 percent cost coverage refers to all financial revenues, including the subsidies to the investment in selective collection and sorting assets. In a situation of full recovery of service costs by the industry, this (public) money should not be considered.

Unexpectedly, the results show that the depreciation of assets and the return on capital represents a small share in the total costs of the recycling system in France. This might mean that outsourcing and private sector participation in this market is quite relevant for this country. If this is the case, the respective capital costs are embedded in the operational expenditures reported in Figure 5.7.

Concerning the recycling of each stream of packaging waste, there are several distinct characteristics that should be considered when computing unit costs. Although the local authorities did not provide information on the cost per flow on their annual account reports, Eco-Emballages (2010a) reported these values for the selective collection service. Costs are estimated to be of 72€ per ton collected for glass, 167€ per ton collected for paper and cardboard and, finally, 788€ per ton collected for plastic and metals.

Figure 5.8 separates the service costs into the costs of selective collection and the costs of sorting of packaging waste in France. From this graph it can be seen that the global cost of sorting is 142€ per ton effectively sent for sorting (not all packaging

---

2   The following scholars contributed with research for this subchapter (in alphabetical order): Marta Cabral, Nuno Ferreira da Cruz, Pedro Simões, Rui Cunha Marques and Sandra Ferreira.

€/tons collected   €/tons collected

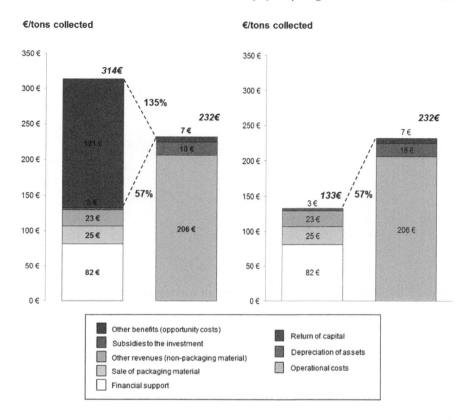

Figure 5.7   Cost coverage in France considering the tons of packaging waste collected in 2010

waste selectively collected is sorted), and the global cost of selective collection is 144€ per ton collected. These results suggest that the preparation for recycling costs of the paper/cardboard and plastics/metals flows are substantially higher when compared to the costs of the glass flow (glass packaging waste is not sorted).

In 2010, the green dot value paid by the industry should cover 60 percent of net benchmark costs for an optimized waste service. The sales of packaging and non-packaging materials, government grants and local taxes should cover the remaining costs of collecting and sorting packaging waste. But although the French financing model implemented that year (it has changed since then) set this cost coverage level, according to our results, the FSLA only covered 35 percent of the costs of collection and sorting of packaging waste (on average and for a sample that encompasses 20 percent of the French population). This suggests that, globally, the actual costs of the service do not correspond to the ones defined as "benchmark costs" (or efficient costs).

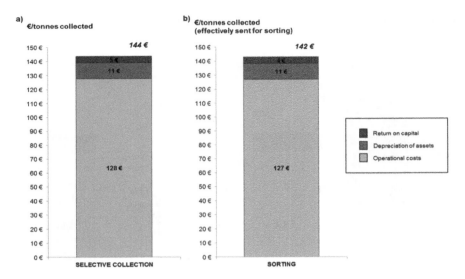

Figure 5.8   Costs of selective collection and sorting in France

The assessment of the opportunity costs in the economic-financial balance of selective collection and sorting of packaging waste seems to be a quite relevant issue for France. The costs of refuse collection and waste treatment avoided with packaging recycling were significant (181€ per ton collected). Adopting this perspective, one might conclude that the financing model of the French "recycling system" was sustainable in 2010.

It should be noted that French local authorities are being encouraged to protect the environment and municipalities to "educate" their citizens so that they can adopt better waste management practices. In this regard, a new agreement (called Barème E) between the Eco-Emballages and local authorities was established to face the new recycling targets (75 percent until the end of 2012) imposed by national legislation ("Grenelle Act"). This national effort intended to adjust the FSLA model in order to encourage a better performance of waste collection and treatment of the public services in the next years.

Italy[3]

Economic and Financial Costs and Benefits

In Italy, the local authorities benefit an average of 250€ per ton of packaging waste selectively collected. Adopting a strictly financial perspective, the benefits are

---

3   The following scholars contributed with research for this subchapter (in alphabetical order): Lucia Rigamonti, Mario Grosso, Marta Cabral, Nuno Ferreira da Cruz, Pedro Simões, Rui Cunha Marques and Sandra Ferreira.

significantly reduced to 58€ per ton. Regarding the cost of selective collection and sorting of packaging waste, it amounts to a total of 121€ per ton collected for the local authority. As can be observed in Figure 5.9, the cost coverage in 2010 was around 207 percent when adopting an economic perspective, but amounts only to 48 percent if cost savings from the avoided disposal (the opportunity costs) are not considered.

Once again, the question about the fairness of the system of financial transfers needs to be raised. Adopting an economic or (strictly) financial approach for the analysis leads to fairly distinct conclusions. Assuming that the financial transfers should follow an economic approach, then the CONAI financial support in 2010 could even be eliminated. However, if the industry was to be 100 percent responsible for the processing of its packaging waste, the financial support should increase by about 116 percent. In fact, only 48 percent of the costs were being supported by the industry in Italy.

The selective collection and transport to the first treatment plant activities represent the largest (84 percent) share of the operational costs incurred by the local authorities. The "operational cost of separation" (10 percent) represents the cost for the separation of the multi-material fraction into the individual materials. The cost share due to sorting is quite small (only about 1 percent) because the

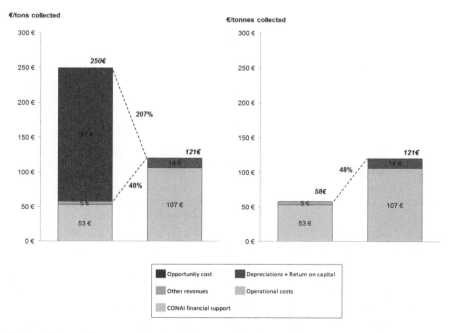

Figure 5.9   Cost coverage in Italy considering the tons of packaging waste collected in 2010

Italian local authorities in 2010 paid only for the sorting of steel. The "operational cost of residues disposal" (5 percent) includes the costs for the disposal of residues arising from the separation of the multi-material fraction and from the sorting of steel collected according to a "heavy" multi-material scheme (i.e. together with glass). In Italy, the global cost of "collection" (selective collection plus transport) is 103€ per ton collected, whereas the global cost of "sorting plus disposal" is 70€ per ton sorted. The cost of "sorting plus disposal" was calculated by dividing the sum of separation, sorting and residues disposal costs by the total amount of multi-material fraction and steel collected in a mono-material way (i.e. the only material for which the local authority pays the separation/sorting operations).

Figure 5.10 shows the operational costs expressed per ton of each collected material. Aluminum is not present because in 2010 it was not collected in a mono-material scheme. As the figure shows, plastics, steel and the multi-material fraction are the most expensive streams. For plastics and steel this is due to the high cost of collection, while for the multi-material fraction the costs are mainly due to the collection (55 percent) and the separation activities (29 percent).

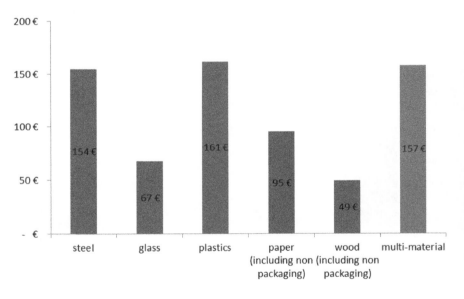

Figure 5.10   Costs of the service per packaging waste stream in Italy

As shown above, the magnitude of the opportunity costs is quite significant in Italy, averaging 191€ per ton (this includes refuse collection, transfer and disposal). They even seem to be larger than the costs involved in selective collection and sorting. This means that the creation of the recycling system had no incremental costs in this country. In fact, it seems that even if in a scenario where the industry would not fund the selective collection and sorting of packaging waste, it would still be worth for Italian local authorities to do it (because, globally, it would reduce their waste management costs).

Environmental Impacts and Respective Valuation

The environmental data for this case study refers to the specific situation of the Lombardia region in order to take advantage of the very detailed evaluation recently carried out within the "GERLA" Project which has provided a valuable and updated set of primary data on the overall waste management scheme (Rigamonti et al., 2013). The LCA was performed with the support of the Simapro software (version 7.3.3).

The results of the environmental assessment of the waste management activities for which the local authorities are responsible are listed in Tables 5.10, 5.11 and 5.12 for the methods Eco-costs2012, Stepwise2006 and Ecovalue08, respectively. Values are expressed per one ton of selectively collected material. Each table reports, first of all, the results of the characterization step and, secondly, the results

Table 5.10 **Environmental assessment of the management of one ton of selectively collected material in the Lombardia region (Eco-costs2012)**

Impact category	Characterization	Monetization
Climate change	24.3 kg CO2 eq.	3.10€
Human toxicity	0.000003 CTUh	2.92€
Photochemical oxidant formation	0.033 kg NMVOC	0.18€
Aquatic eutrophication	0.001 kg P eq.	0.01€
Acidification	0.053 kg SO2 eq.	0.41€

Table 5.11 **Environmental assessment of the management of one ton of selectively collected material in the Lombardia region (Stepwise2006)**

Impact category	Characterization	Monetization
Climate change	24.5 kg CO2 eq.	2.384€
Human toxicity, carcinogens	0.210 kg C2H3Cl eq.	0.067€
Human toxicity, non-carcinogens	0.197 kg C2H3Cl eq.	0.063€
Photochemical ozone, vegetation	240 m²*ppm*hours	0.105€
Aquatic eutrophication	0.008 kg NO3⁻ eq.	0.001€
Acidification	0.649m²	0.006€
Respiratory organics	0.022 pers*ppm*h	0.007€

Table 5.12   Environmental assessment of the management of one ton of selectively collected material in the Lombardia region (Ecovalue08)

Impact category	Characterization	Monetization
Climate change	24.5 kg CO2 eq.	0.26—5.14€
Human toxicity	7.53 kg 1,4-DCB eq.	0.003—9.47€
Photochemical oxidant formation	0.005 kg C2H4 eq.	0.008—0.02€
Aquatic eutrophication	0.013 kg PO_4^{3-} eq.	0.31€
Acidification	0.046 kg SO2 eq.	0.14€

of the monetization step. The figures in these tables represent the "Environmental Operational costs."

Environmental operational costs vary in the range 0.72–15.09€ per ton of selectively collected material. This range represents the result of the Ecovalue08 method. The results of Eco-costs2012 (6.6€ per ton) and of Stepwise2006 (2.6€ per ton) are included in this range. The contribution given by global warming (climate change) is significant for all the analyzed methods (from 34 percent to 91 percent). Other important categories are human toxicity in Eco-costs 2012 (44 percent) and eutrophication (36 percent) and acidification (20 percent) in Ecovalue08 when considering the minimum multiplier in the monetization step.

The results of the "environmental opportunity costs" (avoided management as residual waste of one ton of selectively collected material) are indicated in Tables 5.13, 5.14 and 5.15 for the methods Eco-costs2012, Stepwise2006 and Ecovalue08, respectively. Values are expressed per ton of selectively collected material managed as residual waste. Each table shows the results of the characterization step and the results of the monetization. In these tables negative monetary values represent a cost (benefit avoided), while positive monetary values represent a benefit (costs avoided).

Table 5.13   Environmental assessment of the avoided management of one ton of selectively collected material in the Lombardia region (Eco-costs2012)

Impact category	Characterization	Monetization
Climate change	-172 kg CO2 eq.	-21.92€
Human toxicity	0.000027 CTUh	25.94€
Photochemical oxidant formation	-0.153 kg NMVOC	-0.83€
Aquatic eutrophication	-0.128 kg P eq.	-1.43€
Acidification	-1.191 kg SO2 eq.	-9.29€

Table 5.14   **Environmental assessment of the avoided management of one ton of selectively collected material in the Lombardia region (Stepwise2006)**

Impact category	Characterization	Monetization
Climate change	-170 kg CO2 eq.	-16.513€
Human toxicity, carcinogens	-1.94 kg C2H3Cl eq.	-0.615€
Human toxicity, non-carcinogens	0.503 kg C2H3Cl eq.	0.160€
Photochemical ozone, vegetation	-1313 m^2*ppm*hours	-0.574€
Aquatic eutrophication	-0.016 kg NO3- eq.	-0.002€
Acidification	-21.1 m^2	-0.191€
Respiratory organics	-0.118 pers*ppm*h	-0.035€

Table 5.15   **Environmental assessment of the avoided management of one ton of selectively collected material in the Lombardia region (Ecovalue08)**

Impact category	Characterization	Monetization
Climate change	-170 kg CO2 eq.	-35.59 to -1.78€
Human toxicity	-86.57 kg 1,4-DCB eq.	-108.92 to -0.04€
Photochemical oxidant formation	-0.071 kg C2H4 eq.	-0.30 to -0.10€
Aquatic eutrophication	-0.454 kg PO_4^{3-} eq.	-10.39€
Acidification	-1.37 kg SO2 eq.	-4.30€

For the Lombardia region, all the results are negative in sign, except for human toxicity—cancer in Eco-costs2012 and human toxicity—non-carcinogens in Stepwise2006. A negative sign means that the benefits associated with the avoidance of energy from fossil fuels and primary materials are larger than the burdens associated with the waste collection and combustion. As the total monetized impacts result negative in sign irrespective of the method, they represent an avoided benefit (i.e. a cost). This cost varies between 7.5 and 17.8€ per ton selectively collected instead of being disposed as residual waste (not considering the Ecovalue08—maximum multipliers). The contribution given by global warming is significant for all the analyzed methods (from 11 percent to 291 percent). Other important categories are human toxicity—cancer in Eco-costs2012 (-344 percent), eutrophication (63 percent) and acidification (26 percent) in Ecovalue08 when considering the minimum multiplier in the monetization step.

The results of the environmental assessment of the recovery of the material sorted from one ton of selectively collected material are reported in Tables 5.16, 5.17 and 5.18 for the methods Eco-costs2012, Stepwise2006 and Ecovalue08, respectively. Again, values are expressed per ton of selectively collected material. Each table reports the characterization step and the result of the monetization. This last component represents the contribution "Benefits from recovery."

Table 5.16   Environmental assessment of the recovery activity for one ton of selectively collected material in the Lombardia region (Eco-costs2012)

Impact category	Characterization	Monetization
Climate change	-490 kg CO2 eq.	-62.53€
Human toxicity	0.000066 CTUh	64.27€
Photochemical oxidant formation	-0.341 kg NMVOC	-1.85€
Aquatic eutrophication	-0.261 kg P eq.	-2.92€
Acidification	-2.39 kg SO2 eq.	-18.61€

Table 5.17   Environmental assessment of the recovery activity for one ton of selectively collected material in the Lombardia region (Stepwise2006)

Impact category	Characterization	Monetization
Climate change	-489 kg CO2 eq.	-47.58€
Human toxicity, carcinogens	-38.9 kg C2H3Cl eq.	-12.36€
Human toxicity, non-carcinogens	-3.21 kg C2H3Cl eq.	-1.02€
Photochemical ozone, vegetation	-3522 m^2*ppm*hours	-1.54€
Aquatic eutrophication	-0.413 kg NO3- eq.	-0.05€
Acidification	-26.77 m^2	-0.24€
Respiratory organics	-0.310 pers*ppm*h	-0.09€

Table 5.18   Environmental assessment of the recovery activity for one ton of selectively collected material in the Lombardia region (Ecovalue08)

Impact category	Characterization	Monetization
Climate change	-489 kg CO2 eq.	-102.52 to -5.13€
Human toxicity	-232 kg 1,4-DCB eq.	-292.17 to -0.10€
Photochemical oxidant formation	-0.124 kg C2H4 eq.	-0.52 to -0.18€
Aquatic eutrophication	-0.997 kg PO$_4^{3-}$ eq.	-22.80€
Acidification	-2.56 kg SO2 eq.	-8.04€

All the results are negative in sign, except for human toxicity—cancer in Eco-costs2012. In this case, a negative sign means that the benefits associated with the avoidance of primary materials are larger than the burdens associated with the waste recovery activities. As the total "benefit from recovery" results negative in sign irrespective of the method, it actually represents a benefit. This benefit varies between 21.6 and 62.9€ per ton selectively collected and sent to recovery (not considering the Ecovalue08—maximum multipliers). The contribution given by global warming is once again significant for all the analyzed methods (from 14 percent to 289 percent). Other important categories are human toxicity—cancer in Eco-costs2012 (-297 percent), human toxicity—carcinogens in Stepwise2006 (20 percent), eutrophication (63 percent) and acidification (22 percent) in Ecovalue08 when considering the minimum multiplier in the monetization step.

Economic and Environmental Balance

The overall results of the economic and environmental balance are illustrated in Figures 5.11, 5.12 and 5.13 for the methods Eco-costs2012, Stepwise2006 and Ecovalue08, respectively. They are expressed in Euro 2010 per ton of material selectively collected. Furthermore, unlike Figure 5.9, the economic-financial results in Figures 5.11 to 5.13 also report to the specific case of the Lombardia region.

If one excludes from the analysis the benefits associated with the recovery of packaging waste represented by the dashed line (this activity was not considered in the economic-financial analysis), one can conclude that the overall benefits are still higher than the total costs for all the methods analyzed. In fact the benefits represent 180 percent, 172 percent and 176 percent of the costs for the methods Eco-costs2012, Stepwise2006 and Ecovalue08—minimum multipliers, respectively.

Evidently, when the benefits from the recovery of the sorted materials are taken into account, the benefits are even higher for all the methods analyzed (this would still be true considering the Ecovalue08—maximum values, which were excluded because the extreme differences in the magnitude of the values would be confusing for the reader). In this case, cost coverage ranges between 197 percent and 218 percent for the three methods. The benefits achieved with the recovery are quite similar for the three methods implemented and they vary between 22 and 63€ per ton selectively collected and sent to recovery.

The modifications to the data used in the economic analysis to make it applicable only to the Lombardia region led to a negligible variation in the results. At the national level, the cost coverage was around 207 percent from an economic perspective, but only 48 percent if the cost savings from the avoided disposal are not taken into account. Similarly, for the Lombardia region, the cost coverage is around 202 percent when considering an economic perspective, but only 50 percent if the cost savings due to avoided disposal are not considered.

euro/t selectively collected

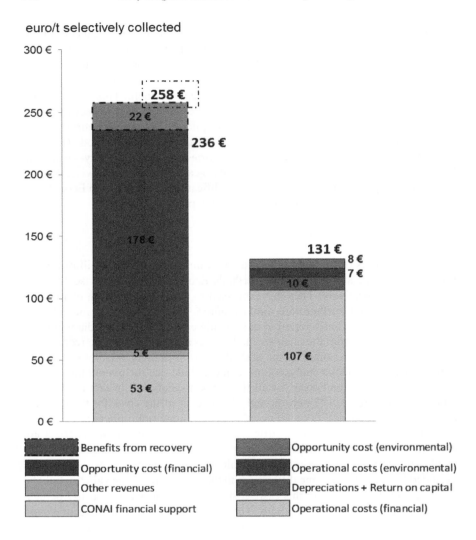

Figure 5.11   Economic and environmental results achieved for the Lombardia region with the Eco-costs2012 method per ton of packaging waste collected: a) with and b) without the economic and environmental opportunity costs

euro/t selectively collected

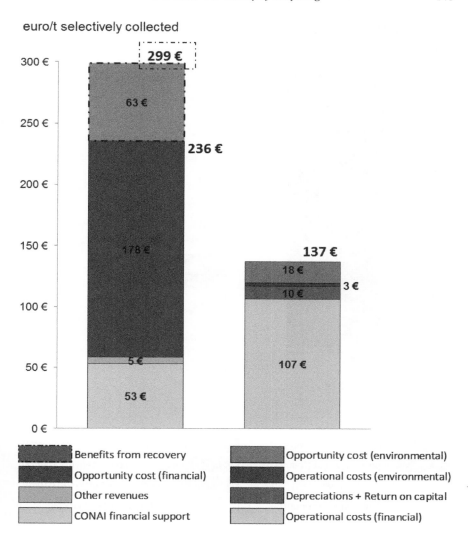

Figure 5.12 Economic and environmental results achieved for Lombardia region with the Stepwise2006 method per ton of packaging waste collected: a) with and b) without the economic and environmental opportunity costs

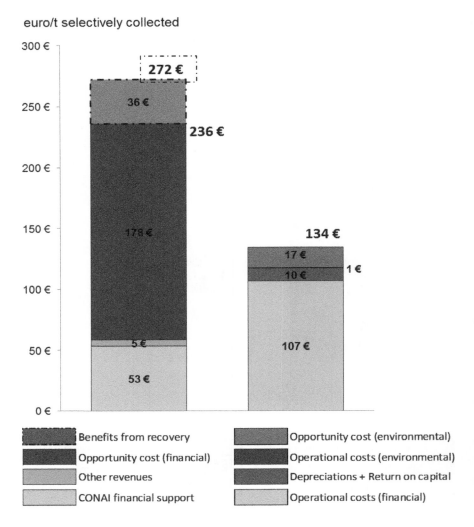

Figure 5.13   Economic and environmental results achieved for Lombardia region with the Ecovalue08 method per ton of packaging waste collected: a) with and b) without the economic and environmental opportunity costs

Portugal[4]

Economic and Financial Costs and Benefits

In Portugal, on average, the local authorities benefit 260€ per ton of packaging waste collected. Adopting a strictly financial perspective, the benefits are significantly reduced to just 158€ per ton. The services of selective collection and sorting of packaging waste represent a cost of 204€ per ton collected for the waste management operators. As for the other country case-studies, the unit costs and benefits were weighted by the tons recovered by each system.

As can easily be observed in Figure 5.14, in 2010, the cost coverage was around 128 percent considering an economic perspective but only 77 percent if the cost savings from recycling are not taken into account. Moreover, the cost coverage is only 68 percent if the subsidies (mainly EU funds) are also not considered in the calculation. Again the (policy) question about the suitability of the financial transfers depends on which perspective should be taken as the norm. If an economic

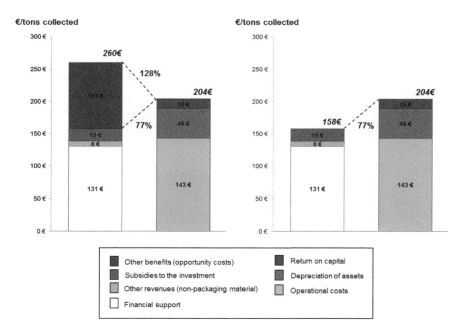

Figure 5.14   Cost coverage in Portugal considering the tons of packaging waste collected in 2010

4   The following scholars contributed with research for this subchapter (in alphabetical order): Marta Cabral, Nuno Ferreira da Cruz, Pedro Simões, Rui Cunha Marques and Sandra Ferreira.

approach was followed, the FSLA should be globally reduced around 43 percent, but if the policy was to make the industry 100 percent accountable for its packaging waste, that is, excluding other benefits and subsidies from the assessment and exempting local authorities from any financial responsibility (like in the German Dual System, MS2 and Perchards, 2009), the FSLA should increase by 35 percent.

There are several characteristics distinguishing the different packaging waste streams and, therefore, their respective management costs. The glass waste selectively collected is not sorted and its high density enables a lower collection frequency which significantly reduces the preparation for recycling costs (when compared to other waste materials). Based on the research by Ambirumo (2009) and on the information collected directly from the local authorities, the average selective collection and sorting unit operational costs for the different streams are estimated as follows: 541€ per ton collected for plastic and metal, 224€ per ton for paper and cardboard and 54€ per ton for glass. The high costs of the "yellow bin" stream (plastic and metal) show that there are no real incentives for the waste management operators to invest in the recovery of these materials and achieve high rates. For this particular stream the sorting activities also involve high operational costs and low efficiencies when compared to the other flows, which increases the weight and relevance of these activities in the cost structure of the local authorities.

Figure 5.15 shows the service costs split into selective collection and sorting. The global cost of sorting is 117€ per ton collected and effectively sent for sorting, whereas the global cost of selective collection is 133€ per ton collected. These results provide further evidence of the higher recycling costs for the plastic and metal flow.

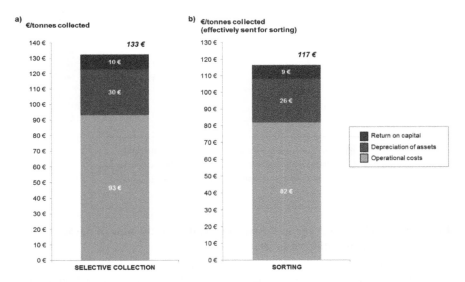

Figure 5.15   Costs of the service per packaging waste stream in Portugal

Apparently, if one was to consider the polluter-pays principle as the main issue in the recycling of packaging waste, it seems that the purely financial approach would apply (even excluding public subsidies). According to a very strict interpretation of this principle, the industry should also pay for the portion of packaging waste that gets landfilled or incinerated (which would then reduce the incentives for selective collection and sorting). However, this approach has several difficulties. First of all, as in other member states, in Portugal, the national law states that municipalities are the competent authorities concerning solid waste management and the local authorities own the infrastructure. Secondly, as hinted above, it would be very difficult to set a framework of incentives if local authorities were paid irrespectively of the packaging waste final destination. Moreover, the costs presented above are not necessarily efficient. That is, there is no evidence that all local authorities are cost-efficient (the same is valid for all other countries analyzed in this book). While the industry can be liable for the recovery of its packaging waste, it is not liable for possible inefficiencies in waste management operations (because the industry does not hold decision-making power regarding these operations).

Despite the possible discussion about the "opportunity costs," the savings (corresponding to the other waste treatment facilities; in particular, the landfill) with the waste recycled and diverted from the other waste treatment facilities are undeniable. The costs of refuse collection and waste treatment are quite expressive (around 100€/ton) and in countries with more limited land resources these costs are even higher. Hence, the question on whether or not saving these costs should be accounted as a benefit of recycling for local authorities is a quite pertinent one with relevance for all EU countries.

Environmental Impacts

The environmental impacts of the packaging waste management operations for the selected impact categories are given in Table 5.19. In the recycling process the transport from the local authorities to the recyclers was taken into account. The negative results are considered avoided impacts (i.e. represent a benefit). The avoided impacts shown in the table below were obtained for incineration and landfilling in some impact categories due to the energy produced. However, for landfilling, only the material paper and cardboard contributes to LFG production. Most environmental impacts from the incineration process are negative (i.e. good for the environment) with the exception of the climate change and aquatic eutrophication impact categories.

In the "recycling system," the packaging waste is selectively collected and sent to sorting. After the sorting process the rejected packaging waste is landfilled. These packaging waste operations correspond to the "Recycling scenario" which represents the packaging waste selectively collected in 2010 in Portugal. The impacts are indicated in Table 5.20. If no selective collection was implemented, the packaging waste would be collected in the refuse collection system and directed

Table 5.19 Environmental impacts incurred by the different packaging waste management operations per ton of packaging waste managed in 2010 in Portugal

Impact category	Unit	Selective collection	Refuse collection	Sorting	Pre-treatment	Recycling	Incineration	Landfill
Climate change	kg CO2 eq.	5,46E+02	6,40E+01	1,27E+02	4,10E+00	-1,71E+04	3,94E+04	6,66E+02
Human toxicity cancer effects	CTUh	1,10E-07	1,11E-08	4,85E-09	2,74E-10	-3,14E-06	-5,73E-08	1,42E-08
Human toxicity non-cancer effects	CTUh	6,62E-09	9,29E-10	1,15E-09	6,63E-11	-2,10E-06	-7,24E-09	2,64E-09
Ecotoxicity	CTUe	4,94E-01	5,19E-02	5,53E-02	1,59E-03	-5,03E+01	-1,35E-01	1,05E-01
Photochemical oxidant formation	kg NMVOC	2,17E+00	2,23E-01	2,62E-01	1,75E-02	-6,45E+01	-7,12E-01	8,45E-01
Aquatic eutrophication	kg P eq.	1,43E-03	2,02E-04	2,07E-02	1,50E-04	-8,29E-01	5,23E-02	3,23E-01
Abiotic depletion	kg Sb eq.	1,28E+00	1,33E-01	5,97E-01	3,55E-02	-1,51E+02	-6,62E+00	1,21E+00
Acidification	mol H+ eq.	4,64E-01	4,76E-02	2,33E-01	9,36E-03	-3,95E+01	-1,30E+00	3,35E-01
Total energy (CED)	MJ	2,91E+03	3,04E+02	1,43E+03	9,63E+01	-4,17E+05	-1,89E+04	2,64E+03

Table 5.20 **Total environmental impacts allocated to the "Recycling scenario" in Portugal**

Impact category	Unit	Selective collection	Sorting	Recycling	Total
Climate change	kg CO2 eq.	7,64E+07	1,75E+07	-2,85E+08	-1,91E+08
Human toxicity cancer effects	CTUh	1,55E-02	5,24E-04	-1,16E-01	-1,00E-01
Human toxicity non-cancer effects	CTUh	9,31E-04	1,20E-04	-3,41E-02	-3,30E-02
Ecotoxicity	CTUe	6,95E+04	6,00E+03	-2,87E+06	-2,79E+06
Photochemical oxidant formation	kg NMVOC	3,05E+05	3,06E+04	-1,87E+06	-1,53E+06
Aquatic eutrophication	kg P eq.	2,01E+02	2,94E+03	-1,15E+04	-8,33E+03
Abiotic depletion	kg Sb eq.	1,80E+05	6,41E+04	-3,60E+06	-3,35E+06
Acidification	mol H+ eq.	6,54E+04	3,37E+04	-1,02E+06	-9,20E+05
Total energy (CED)	MJ	(-)	(-)	(-)	-1,37E+10

Table 5.21 **Total environmental impacts allocated to the "Non-recycling scenario" in Portugal**

Impact category	Unit	Refuse collection	Pre-treatment	Incineration	Landfill	Total
Climate change	kg CO2 eq.	2,87E+07	1,49E+04	6,27E+08	9,07E+07	7,46E+08
Human toxicity cancer effects	CTUh	4,98E-03	9,95E-07	-1,45E-03	1,42E-03	4,95E-03
Human toxicity non-cancer effects	CTUh	4,16E-04	2,41E-07	-1,76E-04	2,41E-04	4,82E-04
Ecotoxicity	CTUe	2,32E+04	5,77E+00	-3,38E+03	1,04E+04	3,03E+04
Photochemical oxidant formation	kg NMVOC	9,99E+04	6,35E+01	-1,33E+04	9,70E+04	1,84E+05
Aquatic eutrophication	kg P eq.	9,06E+01	5,45E-01	1,82E+03	3,23E+04	3,42E+04
Abiotic depletion	kg Sb eq.	5,95E+04	1,29E+02	-1,68E+05	1,18E+05	8,83E+03
Acidification	mol H+ eq.	2,13E+04	3,40E+01	-3,19E+04	3,57E+04	2,52E+04
CED	MJ	(-)	(-)	(-)	(-)	-8,83E+07

to final disposal. The results from the LCIA for this scenario, hereafter called the "Non-recycling scenario," are provided in Table 5.21. The negative (good for the environment) results obtained for the incineration process are related to the energy production from the process.

Figure 5.16 illustrates the contribution of the two scenarios for each impact category in percentage of the sum of the two scenarios. The impacts incurred by the "Non-recycling scenario" are higher than the impacts related to the "Recycling scenario" with exception of the Ecotoxicity impact category due to the influence of the paper recycling industry which is responsible for a high production of liquid effluents, mainly composed of particulate matter, halogenated compounds and phosphates (Celpa, 2010).

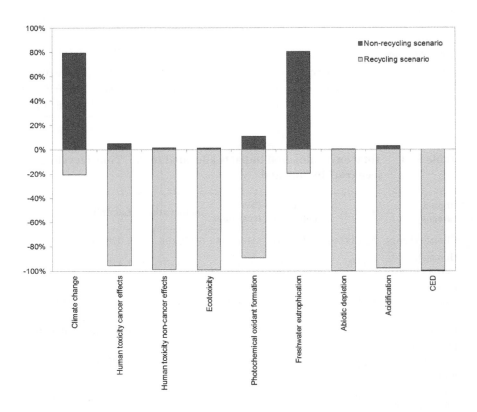

Figure 5.16   LCIA contribution results of the "Recycling scenario" and the "Incineration scenario" in Portugal

Environmental Costs and Benefits

Eco-costs2012

The results for the environmental valuation of the "Recycling scenario" (i.e. actual situation in 2010) using the Eco-costs2012 method are indicated in Table 5.22. The positive values are costs and the negative values represent benefits for the environment. Selective collection is responsible for the higher costs related to the analyzed environmental impact categories. The results for the "Non-recycling scenario" are expressed in Table 5.23. With this method the packaging waste incineration achieves negative results (benefits for the environment) for all the impact categories with exception of the category Climate change.

Table 5.22   Environmental valuation for the "Recycling scenario" in Portugal (Eco-costs2012)

Impact category	Selective collection (€)	Sorting (€)	Recycling (€)	Total (€)
Climate change	9.747.583,00	2.227.194,41	-13.692.708,86	-1.717.931,45
Human toxicity	2.299.962,93	51.219,65	-2.575.884,46	-224.701,88
Photochemical oxidant formation	2.490.876,97	43.467,81	-424.418,17	2.109.926,60
Aquatic eutrophication	19.448,87	75.813,83	-270.391,19	-175.128,49
Acidification	1.299.252,51	231.700,2	-9.787.102,31	-8.256.149,59

Table 5.23   Environmental valuation for the "Incineration scenario" in Portugal (Eco-costs2012)

Impact category	Refuse collection (€)	Pre-treatment (€)	Incineration (€)	Landfill (€)	Total (€)
Climate change	3.657.616,38	1.897,15	80.032.024,55	11.572.469,96	95.264.008,04
Human toxicity	876.362,67	55,25	-54.306,89	192.326,51	1.014.437,55
Photochemical oxidant formation	937.273,94	134,46	-193.526,07	86.119,15	830.001,48
Aquatic eutrophication	6.566,47	8,60	23.256,56	388.349,19	418.180,82
Acidification	421.709,75	505,00	-366.150,99	603.056,86	659.120,61

Stepwise2006

The results of the environmental valuation for the "Recycling scenario" using the Stepwise2006 method are given in Table 5.24. Once again, selective collection is responsible for the higher costs related to the analyzed environmental impact categories. Table 5.25 displays the results for the "Non-recycling scenario."

Table 5.24   Environmental valuation for the "Recycling scenario" in Portugal (Stepwise2006)

Impact category	Selective collection (€)	Sorting (€)	Recycling (€)	Total (€)
Climate change	6.883.585,29	796.899,92	-9.500.923,46	-1.820.438,25
Human toxicity	755.362,93	23.026,11	-5.675.344,99	-4.896.955,94
Photochemical oxidant formation	631.103,01	59.777,14	-298.156,27	392.723,87
Aquatic eutrophication	2.172,95	246,21	-37.819,76	-35.400,60
Acidification	19.044,40	4.555,37	-205.743,12	-182.143,35

Table 5.25   Environmental valuation for the "Incineration scenario" in Portugal (Stepwise2006)

Impact category	Refuse collection (€)	Pre-treatment (€)	Incineration (€)	Landfill (€)	Total (€)
Climate change	2.582.237,25	1.441,32	60.588.869,73	3.294.673,82	66.467.222,12
Human toxicity	286.064,49	46,15	-64.765,53	48.755,15	270.100,26
Photochemical oxidant formation	226.146,73	40,14	23.954,51	329.418,66	579.560,04
Aquatic eutrophication	700,91	0,33	254,98	1.014,00	1.970,21
Acidification	6.224,42	10,62	-10.486,52	10.692,67	6.441,18

Ecovalue08

The results of the environmental valuation for the "Recycling scenario" achieved with the Ecovalue08 method are provided in Table 5.26. The selective collection is responsible for the higher costs related to the analyzed environmental impact categories. In this analysis, only the minimum values of the weights (as they are closer to the other methods employed) were used. The results for the "Non-recycling scenario" are expressed in Table 5.27. The energy production from the packaging waste incineration avoids some impact categories, achieving some negative results for the impact categories Human toxicity, Photochemical oxidant formation and Acidification. However, when considering the other waste management operations, the final results are positive (representing a burden to the environment). The negative values achieved for the incineration process are a result of the avoided impacts from energy production.

Table 5.26   Environmental valuation for the "Recycling scenario" in Portugal (Ecovalue08)

Impact category	Selective collection (€)	Sorting (€)	Recycling (€)	Total (€)
Climate change	742.475,43	178.941,08	-33.037,66	888.378,84
Human toxicity	152.865,38	219,00	291.945,55	445.029,92
Photochemical oxidant formation	32.210,34	8.304,48	71.730,26	112.245,09
Aquatic eutrophication	807.638,32	706.566,57	-2.863.151,89	-1.348.947,00
Acidification	491.793,48	101.958,94	-4.036.919,92	-3.443.167,49

Table 5.27   Environmental valuation for the "Incineration scenario" in Portugal (Ecovalue08)

Impact category	Refuse collection (€)	Pre-treatment (€)	Incineration (€)	Landfill (€)	Total (€)
Climate change	278.524,58	155,42	6.580.240,90	924.303,80	7.783.224,70
Human toxicity	57.527,18	0,78	-1.013,58	156,59	56.670,97
Photochemical oxidant formation	11.826,32	20,39	-30.836,57	25.846,04	6.856,18
Aquatic eutrophication	261.406,33	151,69	317.623,79	3.687.230,83	4.266.412,64
Acidification	160.111,72	227,62	-196.852,81	252.776,50	216.263,03

Economic and Environmental Balance

The results for the economic and environmental balance are illustrated in Figures 5.17, 5.18 and 5.19 for the methods Eco-costs2012, Stepwise2006 and Ecovalue08, respectively. The results are expressed in Euros per ton of packaging waste selectively collected. The benefits (environmental and financial) are higher than the costs for all the methods. In fact, for the Ecovalue08 method the benefits represent 137 percent of the costs. The benefits for the Stepwise2006 method represent 183 percent of the costs. Applying the Eco-costs2012 method the difference is even higher with the benefits achieving 196 percent of the costs. Considering the benefits from the recycling of the sorted materials (not considered in the economic analysis) the cost coverage is about 144 percent, 199 percent and 220 percent for the Evovalue08, Stepwise2006 and Eco-costs2012 methods, respectively.

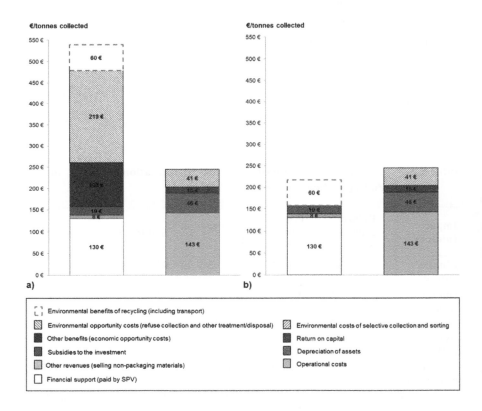

Figure 5.17   Economic and environmental results achieved for Portugal with the Eco-costs2012 method per ton of packaging waste collected: a) with and b) without the economic and environmental opportunity costs

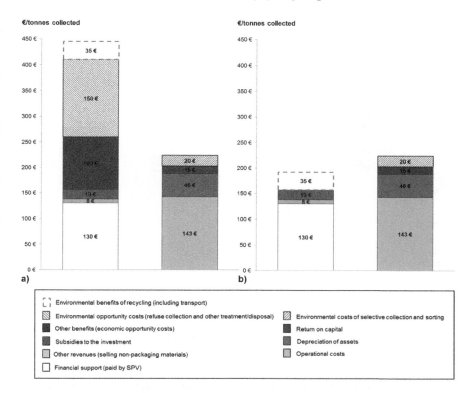

Figure 5.18   **Economic and environmental results achieved for Portugal
with the Stepwise2006 method per ton of packaging
waste collected: a) with and b) without the economic and
environmental opportunity costs**

From the environmental point of view, the "Recycling scenario" proved to
be more advantageous than the "Non-recycling scenario" achieving better results
for most environmental impact categories. The employed environmental valuation
methods are based on different LCIA techniques and different weighting sets for
the several environmental impact categories (which influences the results). The
results of the economic and environmental balance vary significantly according to
the environmental valuation methods adopted. In the economic and environmental
balance achieved with the Ecovalue08 method, the benefits represent 137 percent
of the costs. For the Stepwise2006 method the benefits covered 183 percent of
the costs. For the economic and environmental balance achieved with the Eco-
costs2012 method the benefits amount to 196 percent of the costs.

The systems analyzed in this book comprise only the operations carried
out by the local authorities (waste management operators). However, the goal
of packaging waste selective collection and sorting is to prepare the packaging
waste materials for recycling. It is with the recycling of the sorted materials that

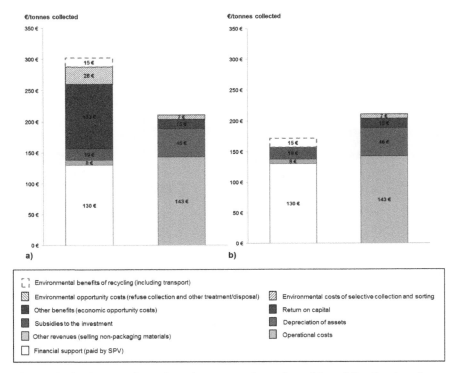

**Figure 5.19   Economic and environmental results achieved for Portugal
with the Ecovalue08 method per ton of packaging waste
collected: a) with and b) without the economic and
environmental opportunity costs**

more benefits for the environment are achieved (through the energy and material
savings). The benefits from recycling represent 15€, 35€ and 60€ per ton of
packaging waste selectively collected (attained for the Ecovalue08, Stepwise2006
and Eco-costs2012 methods, respectively).

Romania[5]

Figure 5.20 shows the balance between the economic-financial costs and benefits of
the selective collection and sorting activities conducted by the waste management
companies that participate in the Eco-Rom Ambalaje system. On average, the waste
management companies benefited 111€ per ton of packaging waste selectively

---

5   The following scholars contributed with research for this subchapter (in alphabetical
order): Marta Cabral, Nuno Ferreira da Cruz, Pedro Simões, Rui Cunha Marques and
Sandra Ferreira.

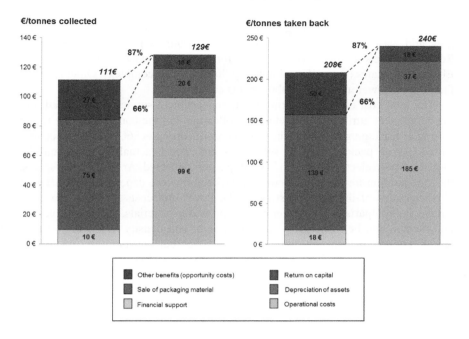

€/tonnes collected

€/tonnes taken back

Other benefits (opportunity costs)	Return on capital
Sale of packaging material	Depreciation of assets
Financial support	Operational costs

Figure 5.20   Cost coverage in Romania considering the tons of packaging waste collected in 2010

collected in 2010. In a strictly financial perspective (i.e. not taking into account the avoided costs) the benefits represent only 84€ per ton. Each ton of packaging waste entering Eco-Rom's recycling system had a total cost of 129€. It should be noted that due to the low efficiency of sorting in the country (on average, 45 percent for paper, plastic and metal packaging waste), the unit costs and benefits mentioned above are nearly the double if one considers tons taken back (i.e. effectively sent to recycling after sorting) instead of tons selectively collected.

As can be observed below, in 2010 the cost coverage was only around 87 percent under an economic perspective and 66 percent if the cost savings from recycling are not taken into account. Under an "economic perspective" (including the opportunity costs) the "bonus payment" should be significantly higher (about 179 percent) so that break-even may be achieved. If the industry was to be fully responsible for the processing of its packaging waste, the increase of the "bonus payment" should be even higher (more 459 percent than the value adopted in 2010).

Apparently, only 66 percent of the costs are being supported by the industry. It was not possible to gather reliable data on the amount of public money that has entered in the recycling system; the selective collection of household packaging waste (usually performed by private companies contracted by local authorities) was not yet widely implemented in the country in 2010. Eco-Rom managed a significant quantity of packaging waste but only about 7 percent came from the household flow. The remaining 93 percent came from the industrial/commercial flow and was funded directly by the industry. This is partly the reason why Romania depicts so low operational costs for the services when compared to other EU member states (the trade and industry flow is not so complex). Other relevant factor is the lower unit cost of labor in this country.

The total cost of the packaging waste management service was divided into the component attributable to selective collection and the component due to the sorting of packaging material. The global cost of sorting is 86€ per ton effectively sorted (not all packaging waste selectively collected is actually sorted), and the global cost of selective collection is 83€ per ton collected. Among other aspects, the "preparation for recycling" costs of packaging waste depend on the different characteristics of the material stream. The lower unit costs of the waste glass stream (in comparison with other packaging waste materials, especially plastics and metals) can be justified by its high weight and density. Glass is collected less frequently, which substantially reduces the fuel consumption. Moreover, glass waste is not sorted nor baled. The unit operational cost for different flows

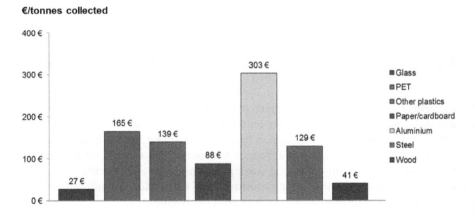

Figure 5.21   Costs of the service per packaging waste stream in Romania

of packaging waste was calculated according to the information provided by the waste management companies. The results are presented in Figure 5.21.

United Kingdom[6]

In order to compute the costs and benefits of collection and sorting activities of household packaging waste, questionnaires were sent to all local authorities operating in the UK (WCA—waste collection authorities; WDA—waste disposal authorities; and unitary authorities). However, very few of these entities filled in the questionnaires correctly. Since it was difficult to gather consistent information (probably due to the high diversity and complexity of collection systems and contracts between the local authorities and the operators of materials recycling facilities), it was not possible perform a global and representative economic analysis of all packaging waste recycling systems in the UK. Therefore, only a few case-studies with different collection systems are analyzed in this chapter.

Case-study I: Curbside Sort Collection System

To calculate the benefits and costs of the curbside sort type collection, a sample of 11 English local authorities, covering 1,032,922 inhabitants (about 2 percent of total population of England) was analyzed for the year 2010. Since packaging waste

€/tonnes collected

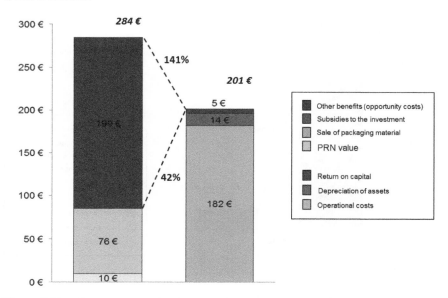

Figure 5.22   Cost coverage for the curbside sort collection case-study (England) considering the tons of packaging waste collected in 2010

6   The following scholars contributed with research for this subchapter (in alphabetical order): Francis Ongondo, Ian Williams, Marta Cabral, Nuno Ferreira da Cruz, Pedro Simões, Rui Cunha Marques and Sandra Ferreira.

collected through the curbside sort system is directly delivered to reprocessors, the local authorities do not have costs with sorting activities. Moreover, most of the surveyed local authorities did not enjoy any subsidies to the investment concerning their recycling system. Considering the information reported by the local authorities and several data from the official documents (mainly from Detini, 2008, WRAP 2008a, 2008b, 2009 and 2011, APSE, 2011), the results obtained for this type of collection are graphically presented in Figure 5.22.

The total cost of curbside sort type collection was 201€ per ton of packaging waste collected. In 2010 the cost coverage was around 141 percent under an economic perspective, since the costs of refuse collection and other treatments (such as incineration and landfill) are rather significant (199€/ton collected). But if those benefits are not considered (as avoided costs) the cost coverage is only 42 percent.

Case-study II: Two Streams Co-mingled Collection System

The benefits and costs of two-streams co-mingled type collection were calculated using a sample of 12 English local authorities, covering 1,198,131 inhabitants (about 2 percent of total population of England) for 2010. Given that packaging waste collected through this type of collection has to be delivered in a materials recycling facility for sorting, the operational costs include the respective gate

€/tonnes collected

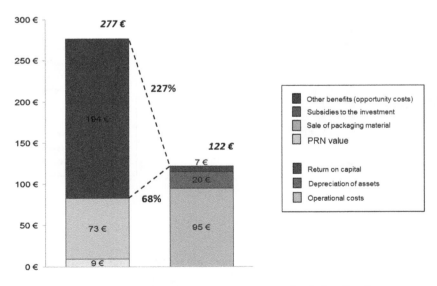

Figure 5.23   Cost coverage for the two-streams co-mingled collection case-study (England) considering the tons of packaging waste collected in 2010

fees and haulage. Although it is assumed that local authorities receive the total revenue from the sale of materials, actually most of them only receive directly an income from the sale of paper/cardboard waste since it is separately collected. Local authorities did not report income from governmental grants/subsidies for packaging waste recycling.

The results obtained are graphically presented in Figure 5.23. The total cost of two streams co-mingled collection was 122€ per ton of packaging waste collected. Adopting an economic approach, the benefits cover all costs. However, in this type of collection opportunity costs are slightly lower since the rejected rates are higher than in curbside sort collection. For the same reason, the revenues from the sale of materials and PRN/PERN value are lower too.

Case-study III: Single Stream Co-mingled Collection System

The benefits and costs of single stream co-mingled type collection were calculated using a sample of seven English local authorities, covering 922,540 inhabitants (nearly 2 percent of the total population of England) for 2010. Most of these local authorities do not receive direct revenues from the sale of materials since all packaging waste materials are collected in the same container and have to be sorted. Hence, operational costs also include the materials recycling facilities gate

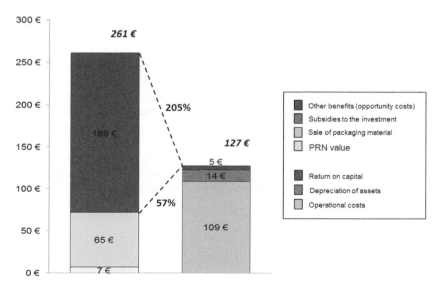

Figure 5.24   Cost coverage for the single-stream co-mingled collection case-study (England) considering the tons of packaging waste collected in 2010

fees and haulage. No governmental grants/subsidies allocated to the recycling system were reported. The results obtained are presented in Figure 5.24.

The total cost of single stream co-mingled collection service was 127€ per ton of packaging waste collected and is not covered by the financial benefits. In this case, the opportunity costs are the lowest since rejected rates are higher than in the other two types of collection.

In a strictly financial approach, all selective collection systems seem to be unbalanced (however, the results are not representative). Nonetheless, if opportunity costs are considered as benefits, this leads to a different conclusion. In fact, the costs of refuse collection and other waste treatments seem to be quite expressive (189€–199€ per ton) and even higher than the costs of co-mingled collection systems.

Summary of Findings

The economic and financial methodology (explained in the previous chapter) was applied to the cases of Belgium, France, Italy, Portugal, Romania and the UK. In France and Romania, the sale of packaging material was considered as a separate component because in these cases local authorities are able to deal directly with the recyclers if they wish to (whereas in the other cases the green dot agency owns the packaging waste once it pays the FSLA). Government grants (subsidies to the investment) were not considered in Romania because the current packaging waste management operations are generally performed by private companies. In fact, in this country most of the packaging waste collected comes from the trade and industry flow, which is significantly less complex (and costly) than the municipal packaging waste flow (industrial packaging waste is usually much better separated at the source and the frequency of collection is optimized). As far as the authors were able to determine, in Belgium and Italy, subsidies to the investment in selective collection and sorting activities were also not relevant. Finally, it should be highlighted that the data collected for the UK is not representative of the national situation.

For a better understanding of the importance of the packaging waste recycling/recovery green dot systems in the analyzed member states, the global values of each economic-financial component are shown in Tables 5.28 to 5.31 (for each country).

Table 5.28   The global and unit economic-financial costs and benefits of the Belgian packaging waste recycling system in 2010

Operation	Global values (in Euros)	Unit values (in Euros per ton)
Operational costs	70,822,631.67	105.97
Depreciations	16,612,716.07	24.86
Return on capital	6,120,474.34	9.16
Total costs (A)	*93,555,822.08*	*139.99*
FSLA	84,256,773.40	126.07
Sale of packaging material	0.00	0.00
Other revenues[a]	0.00	0.00
Subsidies to the investment	0.00	0.00
Opportunity costs[b]	106,721,335.24	159.69
Total economic benefits (B)	*190,978,108.63*	*285.76*
Total financial benefits (C)	*84,256,773.40*	*126.07*
Economic balance (B-A); (B/A)	**97,422,286.52€ (204%)**	**145.77€/ton (204%)**
Financial balance (C-A); (C/A)	**- 9,299,048.68€ (90%)**	**- 13.92€/ton (90%)**

[a] Revenues from selling non-packaging waste;
[b] Costs avoided by diverting waste from refuse collection and other waste treatments, such as incineration.

Table 5.29   The global and unit economic-financial costs and benefits of the French packaging waste recycling system in 2010 (this information refers to 20% of the French population)

Operation	Global values (in Euros)	Unit values (in Euros per ton)
Operational costs	160,081,551.30	206.27
Depreciations	14,326,394.71	18.46
Return on capital	5,649,845.80	7.28
Total costs (A)	*180,057,791.80*	*232.00*
FSLA	63,421,071.28	81.72
Sale of packaging material	19,634,766.32	25.30
Other revenues[a]	17,570,399.58	22.64
Subsidies to the investment	2,421,362.49	3.12
Opportunity costs[b]	140,470,067.30	181.00
Total economic benefits (B)	*243,517,667.00*	*313.78*
Total financial benefits (C)	*103,047,599.70*	*132.78*
Economic balance (B-A); (B/A)	**63,459,875.20€ (135%)**	**81.77€/ton (135%)**
Financial balance (C-A); (C/A)	**- 77,010,192.10€ (57%)**	**- 99.23€/ton (57%)**

[a] Revenues from selling non-packaging waste;
[b] Costs avoided by diverting waste from refuse collection and other waste treatments, such as landfilling.

Table 5.30 **The global and unit economic-financial costs and benefits of the Italian (Lombardia region) packaging waste recycling system in 2010**

Operation	Global values (in Euros)	Unit values (in Euros per ton)
Operational costs	147,251,100.50	106.59
Depreciations Return on capital	14,367,308.80	10.40
Total costs (A)	*161,618,409.30*	*116.99*
FSLA	73,660,087.04	53.32
Sale of packaging material	0.00	0.00
Other revenues[a]	7,031,692.48	5.09
Subsidies to the investment	0.00	0.00
Opportunity costs[b]	245,349,427.20	177.60
Total economic benefits (B)	*324,659,734.72*	*236.01*
Total financial benefits (C)	*80,691,779.52*	*58.41*
Economic balance (B-A); (B/A)	**163,041,325.40€ (202%)**	**119.02€/ton (202%)**
Financial balance (C-A); (C/A)	**- 80,926,629.78€ (50%)**	**- 58.58€/ton (50%)**

[a] Revenues from selling non-packaging waste;
[b] Costs avoided by diverting waste from refuse collection and other waste treatments, such as incineration.

Table 5.31 **The global and unit economic-financial costs and benefits of the Portuguese packaging waste recycling system in 2010**

Operation	Global values (in Euros)	Unit values (in Euros per ton)
Operational costs	64,212,395.53	143.29
Depreciations	20,458,773.96	45.65
Return on capital	6,661,718.64	14.87
Total costs (A)	*91,332,888.13*	*203.81*
FSLA	58,497,228.59	130.54
Sale of packaging material	0.00	0.00
Other revenues[a]	3,560,037.25	7.94
Subsidies to the investment	8,540,485.21	19.06
Opportunity costs[b]	46,112,508.23	102.90
Total economic benefits (B)	*116,710,259.28*	*260.44*
Total financial benefits (C)	*70,597,751.05*	*157.54*
Economic balance (B-A); (B/A)	**25,377,371.15€ (128%)**	**56.63€/ton (128%)**
Financial balance (C-A); (C/A)	**- 20,735,137.08€ (77%)**	**- 46.27€/ton (77%)**

[a] Revenues from selling non-packaging waste;
[b] Costs avoided by diverting waste from refuse collection and other waste treatments, such as landfilling.

Any assertion regarding the suitability of the financial transfers carried out by the compliance schemes depends on the perspective adopted. If one accepts that the savings attained by diverting waste from landfills (and incineration, etc.) should be weighed up as a benefit of the local authorities, then the financial support by the industry could be reduced or even eliminated as shown in Table 5.32.

Table 5.32   Amendments to the FSLA for packaging waste management 100% costs coverage

Approach	Belgium (%)	France (%)	Italy (Lombardia Region) (%)	Portugal (%)
Economic perspective	-100	-100	-100	-43
Financial perspective	+11	+121	+110	+35

However, if the EPR principle was to be strictly followed, perhaps the transfers should increase (see Table 5.32). The costs that are not covered by the industry or by other revenue are covered by public money. Table 5.33 shows the public money (government grants and local taxes or waste management fees) involved as a percentage of the costs. Nevertheless, there is no indication about the cost efficiency of waste management operators (Marques et al., 2012). In fact, it could be the case that operators are "dislocating" mixed waste management costs and reporting inflated recycling system costs in an attempt to get more funding from the industry.

Table 5.33   Percentage of public money used to achieve break-even

Type	Belgium (%)	France (%)	Italy (Lombardia Region) (%)	Portugal (%)
Government Grants	-	1	-	9
Local taxes and/or waste fees	10	~40	50	~20

In most cases it is difficult to ascertain whether operators are declaring "costs" or "prices" regarding selective collection and sorting activities. In Belgium, considering the (significant) avoided costs seems to be quite relevant towards encouraging local authorities to go beyond the "standard requirements" in terms of selective collection. Diverting more packaging waste from the undifferentiated flow may significantly reduce the costs with urban waste management for the municipalities.

Romania was not compared directly with the other cases because in this country the selective collection is not universal. Most of packaging waste was coming from the industry in 2010. Nevertheless, in this country, the total (economic and financial) benefits are lower than the costs. Even considering the opportunity costs (which are considerably lower than in the others countries) the cost coverage is only 87 percent.

For the UK, the economic and financial analysis encompasses the different selective collection systems (the sample covers only a very small portion of the total population). The curbside sort system seems to be more expensive than the other collection systems (two-streams and single co-mingled type collections), arguably due to the wide range of collection characteristics (different vehicles, collection frequency, recycling containers, etc.). However, the financial benefits are also higher than the other types of collection since packaging waste is collected separately by material (impurity rates are very low) and local authorities sell it directly to recyclers/reprocessors. Furthermore, some local authorities reported that their recycling rates have increased substantially after introducing a co-mingled system. Hence, choosing the right collection system is not so obvious, since the service efficiency is contingent upon the local characteristics (WRAP, 2009).

In short, both the magnitude of costs and the cost coverage of packaging waste recycling systems differ widely among countries. For example, in Belgium, the collection frequency (per flow) is around two times per month, while in Portugal this increases to twice per week (mainly due to the differences in terms of average temperature between the two countries). In fact, collection costs vary significantly with the type and frequency of collection. The French or Italian cases, where several packaging waste collection flows coexist, provide a good illustration of this (EIMPack, 2012 and 2013a). Finally, it was possible to confirm that in countries with competitive recycling markets (like Germany and the UK) the financial information is very scarce or not available at all.

Regarding the environmental analysis carried out for Belgium, the Lombardia Region in Italy and Portugal, in general, the results are consistent for the three valuation methods. The 2010 "Recycling scenario" proved to be more environmentally friendly than the "Non-Recycling scenario" for the three case studies. Note that this overall result was due to the inclusion of the recycling activity in the system boundary, since the selective collection and sorting of packaging waste only cause damage to the environment (related to the consumption of fuel and electricity).

Concerning the CO_2 emissions (climate change is the only impact category which can be compared among the three valuation methods for the three countries analyzed), in 2010, the "Recycling scenario" saved between 1.4 and 3.3 Gg of CO_2 eq. in Portugal. Note that the environmental impacts from the "Non-Recycling scenario" actually correspond to the avoided impacts. Considering this, the savings were much higher (between 71.6 and 76.5 Gg of CO_2 eq.). In Belgium, around 51.6 to 56.0 Gg of CO_2 eq. were saved with the packaging waste recycling strategies. Taking into account the avoided emissions with the "Non-Recycling scenario," the savings raise to 135.0 to 139.0 Gg of CO2 eq. In Italy (Lombardia region), the "Non-Recycling scenario" showed good results for the environment in contrast to the other two countries due to the incineration process (there is virtually no landfilling in Lombardia). However, it should be noted that only one region with one incinerator was analyzed in the case of Italy. Globally, about 40.0 Gg of CO2 eq. were saved.

The great difference observed between Portugal and the two other countries was due to the recycling of paper/cardboard. In Portugal, the primary pulp production (replaced by the recycling fibers) generates electricity from byproducts (biomass, black liquor, etc.) of the process. The pulp and paper production is self-sustainable in terms of energy (Dias et al., 2007) with a surplus of energy that is introduced in the National Grid. This surplus of electricity is accounted as a benefit lost with recycling since this activity only consumes energy. In Belgium and Italy, the primary pulp is imported and information about the quantity of electricity generated during the pulp production process is not available. The pulp production process existing in the Ecoinvent 2.2 database of SimaPro was assumed as the avoided product in the paper/cardboard recycling process. The surplus of electricity generated in the avoided product was excluded as a simplification of the problem.

The previous environmental impacts were converted into monetary values with the Ecocosts2012, Stepwise2006 and Ecovalue08 valuation methods for each case study (Belgium, the Lombardia Region and Portugal). The results are presented in Tables 5.34 to 5.36, respectively.

Table 5.34   Total environmental costs and benefits obtained with the Ecocosts2012 method

Country	"Recycling scenario" (€)	"Non-recycling scenario" (€)
Belgium	-99.466.614,39	111.533.776,90
Italy (Lombardia Region)	-20.735.894,72	-10.416.298,88
Portugal	-8.263.984,80	98.185.748,51

Table 5.35   Total environmental costs and benefits obtained with the Stepwise2006 method

Country	"Recycling scenario" (€)	"Non-recycling scenario" (€)
Belgium	-61.570.584,85	82.647.903,24
Italy (Lombardia Region)	-83.233.688,00	-24.548.757,44
Portugal	-6.542.214,27	67.325.293,82

Table 5.36   Total environmental costs and benefits obtained with the Ecovalue08 method

Country	"Recycling scenario" (€)	"Non-recycling scenario" (€)
Belgium	-43,755,172.86	9,996,851.22
Italy (Lombardia Region)	-49,083,700.16	-22,932,435.20
Portugal	-3,346,460.64	12,329,427.52

Despite the differences in magnitude, the overall results are consistent among the case studies. The 2010 "Recycling scenario" proved to be less environmentally costly than the "Non-Recycling scenario" for all case studies. Regarding the "Recycling scenario," the total environmental benefits (negative values) are lower in Portugal than in the other two countries due to the recycling of paper/cardboard material, as it was explained before.

In the Italian case, the environmental results for the "Non-Recycling scenario" were positive (negative sign with SimaPro) in contrast with the other two cases, in particular Belgium (for which this scenario assumes the same operations: refuse collection and incineration). The incineration process is responsible for this contrasting result (since it greatly varies with the combustion efficiency and waste composition).

The environmental results were added to the financial-economic ones and the global balance was calculated for each valuation method and country. On the costs side, the environmental costs related to the emissions released in the transport of packaging waste and sorting operations were considered. As benefits, the avoided emissions due to the recycling of packaging waste (instead of incinerating or landfilling) were taken into account in addition to the financial revenues due to the packaging waste management operations (selective collection and sorting). The economic and environmental results obtained for the "Non-Recycling scenario" (composed by the refuse collection and other waste treatment or disposal) correspond to the economic and environmental opportunity costs, respectively. The environmental component (mainly related to the emissions avoided by diverting packaging waste of the operations mentioned above) is a benefit in Portugal and Belgium; however, in Italy, this represents a cost (as explained above, in the Lombardia region the incineration with energy recovery of the packaging waste selectively collected would be globally positive from an environmental point of view).

The results vary significantly with the valuation method considered since the environmental modelling process is subjective and involves a high degree of uncertainty. Moreover, these methods are based on different LCIA techniques and different weighting sets for the several environmental impact categories. Nevertheless, all (economic and environmental) benefits outweigh all the costs of the packaging waste recycling system in the three countries, even if the environmental benefits of the recycling activity are excluded.

In Portugal, total benefits (including recycling) represent 220 percent, 199 percent and 144 percent of the total costs for the Ecocosts2012, Stepwise2006 and Ecovalue08 methods, respectively. If the economic and environmental opportunity costs are not considered, the cost coverage is lower (89 percent, 86 percent and 82 percent) and the packaging waste recycling system would seem unsustainable. The benefits from the recycling represent 60€, 35€ and 15€ per ton of packaging waste selectively collected in each method (in the same order).

In Belgium, the recycling system seems to be sustainable both from the financial and environmental perspectives. In this case, the benefits cover 142 percent, 124 percent and 115 percent of the costs, according to the Ecocosts2012, Stepwise2006 and Ecovalue08 methods, respectively. Taking into account the opportunity costs, the cost coverage is higher (301 percent, 275 percent and 233 percent). The benefits from the recycling represent 98€, 60€ and 38€ per ton of packaging waste selectively collected in each method (in the same order).

In Italy, the recycling system is sustainable from the economic and environmental perspectives (including the benefits from the recycling). In this case, the benefits cover 197 percent, 218 percent and 202 percent of the costs based on Ecocosts2012, Stepwise2006 and Ecovalue08 methods, respectively. Excluding the opportunity costs, the benefits fall below the costs (65 percent, 102 percent and 80 percent for each valuation method, in the same order). The benefits from the recycling activity are 22€, 63€ and 36€ per ton of packaging waste selectively collected in each method (in the same order).

Chapter 6

Conclusions

Final Remarks

As a result of the implementation of the Waste Hierarchy, recycling, energy recovery and biological processing assumed a crucial role in the waste management systems of all the EU member states. However, it is important to keep in mind that waste recovery is not an end in itself and that policies for waste management should focus on minimizing the overall social costs. This book contributes to an informed discussion around these issues, which should be taken at the EU level and considered at the local and national levels.

The book summarizes the research developed in the EIMPack Project (the Economic Impact of the Packaging and Packaging Waste Directive). EIMPack's objectives included the investigation of how the preparation for recycling costs have been distributed among the multiple stakeholders. Accordingly, the schemes established in seven EU countries (Belgium, France, Germany, Italy, Portugal, Romania and the UK) for the recycling of packaging waste were described and analyzed. The development and large scale changes in EU packaging waste management occurred mainly after the Directive 94/62/EC on PPW entered into force. The analysis of these seven systems had the aim of scrutinizing their different approaches to cope with the same problem: meet the recovery and recycling targets imposed by the PPW Directive.

Local governments are generally in charge of waste management, particularly in countries with Green Dot schemes or similar EPR systems. This leads to the need of establishing a system of financial transfers between the industry and the local authorities (mostly due to the costs involved with selective collection and sorting). The same economic-financial methodology was applied for the cases of Belgium, France, Italy, Portugal, Romania and the UK. The costs and benefits allocated to the activities which prepare waste for recycling (selective collection and sorting) and are carried out by, or on behalf of, local public authorities were compared for all these countries using 2010 data.

In addition to the relevant financial costs and benefits, two economic components were considered. Firstly, the return on capital employed (occasionally disregarded when the investments are undertaken by public entities) was included as an economic cost. Secondly, the savings that arise by diverting the packaging waste from the refuse collection circuits and disposal operations (e.g. incineration or landfilling) was considered an opportunity cost and weighed in as an economic benefit.

To carry out this analysis, the data required was gathered through the waste management operators' annual reports and questionnaires sent directly to local authorities. In Germany, the packaging waste recycling system is entirely supported by the industry and managed by private operators based on a competitive market and, because of this, the necessary detailed data are not available. For the case of the UK, the data gathered represented only around 2 percent of the population. In Romania, most of packaging waste managed by Eco-Rom comes from the trade and industry flow. Hence, results from these two countries are not comparable with the remaining case studies. As shown in Figure 6.1, the results for Belgium, France, Italy and Portugal point out that the industry is not reimbursing the net financial cost of packaging waste management. Note that, unlike in the previous Chapter, to be comparable with the subsequent graph—that also includes the environmental costs and benefits—in Figure 6.1 the values for Italy correspond only to the Lombardia region.

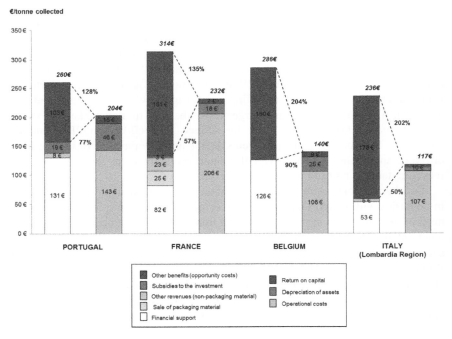

Figure 6.1   Cost coverage of the packaging waste management service per ton selectively collected in 2010 for Portugal, France, Belgium

In fact, if the savings attained by diverting packaging waste from other treatment (e.g. landfilling or incineration) are not considered, it seems that the industry should increase substantially the financial support to local authorities (by 35 percent in Portugal, 121 percent in France, 11 percent in Belgium and 111 percent in Italy—Lombardia region). However, if the avoided costs with other treatment are considered as a benefit for the local authorities, the cost coverage of the systems is as follows: 128 percent in Portugal (i.e. the support could be reduced by 43 percent), 135 percent in France (i.e. the support could be eliminated), 204 percent in Belgium (i.e. the support could be eliminated), and 202 percent in Italy—Lombardia region (i.e. the support could also be eliminated).

The financial and economic analysis was complemented with the environmental costs and benefits for Portugal, Belgium and Italy (Lombardia Region) by means of a LCA with the monetary valuation of the impact categories results. The LCA was performed on data collected from the national environmental authorities and the waste management operators involved in the packaging waste management systems with the support of the SimaPro software and the Ecoinvent 2.2 (2007) and ELCD 2.0 databases. The same system boundary was used in both the economic-financial and the environmental analyses, comprising only the activities performed by the waste management operators (local authorities) in charge of collecting and sorting the municipal packaging waste. However, the recycling of the sorted materials was also considered in the environmental perspective. This operation was not taken into account in the economic analysis because it is not under the responsibility of the local authorities. One should, nevertheless, keep in mind that the benefits for the environment achieved with recycling are the main goal of all the packaging waste recycling systems. It would not make sense to leave these external impacts out of the analysis. Furthermore, it is reasonable to assume that the recycling operation is balanced from the financial point of view, otherwise the private-sector recyclers would not be financially viable and would go bankrupt.

The environmental impact categories were quantified and converted into monetary values by means of three environmental valuation methods: Eco-costs2012, Stepwise2006 and Ecovalue08 (Figure 6.2 presents the results for Eco-costs2012). These methods were selected according to the type of valuation (monetary weighting), the application field (i.e. the common impact categories analyzed), the timeliness of the databases and the target population (Europe). The methods use different LCIA techniques and different weighting sets for the several environmental impact categories analyzed, which has an important impact on the overall results. The magnitude of the results varies significantly with the valuation method and the country analyzed. However, one can argue with some degree of confidence that routing the packaging waste for recycling is less costly for the environment than the alternative disposal operations (the results are consistent across the different countries and methods). The Portuguese and Italian recycling systems proved to be sustainable (i.e. the benefits are higher than the costs) if the environmental and economic opportunity costs are considered. In the Belgian case, considering the opportunity costs seems to be irrelevant in terms of the sustainability of the current recycling system (the benefits cover the costs regardless of the perspective adopted). However, the avoided costs component may assume an important role in promoting the efficiency of the Belgian local authorities and reducing the financial costs and the environmental damage.

€/tonnes collected

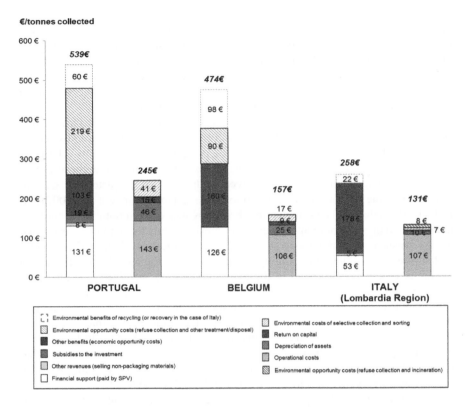

Figure 6.2   Economic and environmental results achieved with the Ecocosts2012 method per ton of packaging waste selectively collected in each country

The current book also sought to examine how the EPR principle, clearly embedded in the PPW Directive, is being operationalized by the several member states. The results presented above show that, in general, the EPR principle does not seem to be strictly respected for most case studies, since there is public money directly (subsidies to the investment) and/or indirectly (paid by citizens through the local taxes) involved in the funding of the recycling systems.

Germany and Belgium are two of the few countries for which the EPR principle seems to be strictly respected although through quite different waste management systems (privately managed and publicly managed, respectively). It should be noted, however, that the implementation of a PAYT scheme is a common feature in these two countries. This represents one of the most relevant features for the success of the recycling systems in these countries. Since citizens have to pay for the collection of municipal solid waste (refuse or undifferentiated waste flow) based on the amount they throw away, there is a true financial incentive for users to separate packaging waste. The citizens' awareness of the environmental problems should always be encouraged by public authorities. Public participation in source separation and awareness about the life-cycle of packaging waste is essential for the efficiency and effectiveness of recycling, particularly in countries like Romania where the selective collection is still quite recent and service coverage is still very low. All the stakeholders involved in the recycling process are important for its success and economic sustainability.

Finally, it should be noted that for all the cases studied (except for Romania) the financial support from the industry has been enough to compensate for the incremental costs of recycling. This means that, in reality, local waste management fees or taxes did not have to increase so that selective collection and sorting could be carried out (because the financial benefits plus the savings attained by diverting packaging waste from the undifferentiated flow compensated for these). However, because the industry is not paying for the full costs of packaging waste management, in most of the cases there is still public money involved in the recycling systems (which seems to contradict the guidelines of the PPW Directive).

Implications for European Policies

The EU policies on PPW had the key objective of protecting the environment by reducing the impact of packaging waste disposal while ensuring the free movement of packaged goods by harmonizing national legislations. To a large extent, this objective has been met. In general, the recovery and recycling rates of all the member states increased significantly after the PPW Directive had been enacted. The question remains, however, of whether the imposed recovery and recycling targets are optimal from a welfare point of view and whether or not EPR recycling systems are the best way of achieving this enhanced environmental protection. Although this book does not provide a definite answer to these concerns, it surely contributes positively to getting closer to it.

Enquiries about optimal recovery and recycling targets, economic incentive systems, financing models, waste management strategies, among others, are extremely complex. The complexity of these themes has its origin in the interdisciplinary nature of the problems and the interconnectedness of the specific components of the packaging waste recycling systems. Technological innovations influence the economic viability of different waste management and recycling activities, environmental impacts constrain the available options, the introduction of economic instruments has an impact on the whole waste management system and on the recycling and packaged goods markets, local conditions (e.g. territory, demography, citizens' awareness and climate) affect the cost structures of waste management operations, and so on.

With so many dynamic and interdependent variables, it is difficult to fully grasp the consequences of new developments in each of them. Therefore, it is also unavoidably challenging to implement a long-term plan and devise a wide-ranging policy that, for example, would be optimal and applicable to all European member states and respective regions. A strategy that is optimal at the EU level (at a given time, given a certain exogenous environment) is likely to be sub-optimal for several or even all individual member-states. It is probably for this reason that such ambitious and wide-ranging recovery and recycling targets as the ones imposed by the PPW Directive can only be found in the EU setting.

Comparing different frameworks and approaches is crucial for EU policy makers and also for other countries that may be thinking about their options regarding the management of packaging waste in an environmentally (and financially!) sound manner. Indeed, by applying the same approach to the Belgian, French, Italian, Portuguese, Romanian and British recycling schemes and plotting the results together, this book provides novel insights with widespread implications.

In general, the sustainability of the recycling schemes depends on the perspective adopted: economic or purely financial. If one adopts an economic approach (i.e. considering the opportunity costs, in other words, the costs avoided with refuse collection and other treatment), the packaging waste management systems display cost coverages above 100 percent. Therefore, according to these results, the financial support coming from the industry to the local authorities could even be reduced and the systems would still be sustainable. However, the full costs of the selective collection and sorting services are not covered by the financial benefits attained by the local authorities. Thus, considering a strictly financial approach, the cost coverage reduces to far below 100 percent and the financial support of the industry should be increased. Ultimately, deciding on which is the "correct" approach is a policy decision.

In principle, if the PPW Directive was to be interpreted to the letter, it appears that the strictly financial approach should be applied. Indeed, it seems that the industry should pay for the full cost of preparation for recycling activities (and, perhaps, even for the management costs associated to the fraction of packaging waste that gets landfilled, incinerated, etc.). However, this raises several operational problems. First and foremost, even in this perspective, the industry should only be required to pay for an efficient selective collection and sorting service. Producers are not responsible for any costs attributable to managerial inefficiency, above-requirement quality of service levels, or any other social concerns that local authorities might have. Since in most EU countries the industry is not legally able/allowed to establish the recycling system itself, it is only bound to pay for the (theoretical) minimum cost of the services. If the industry was required to pay for the full cost of preparation for recycling activities "no matter what" (and, eventually, for the packaging waste that enters the undifferentiated flow), local authorities would have little incentives to operate efficiently.

Considering the environmental results achieved for the Belgian, Italian and Portuguese case studies, it seems that, overall, the PPW Directive had a positive impact in Europe. Environmental damage has indeed been reduced with the imposition of recovery and recycling targets. Moreover, even though this issue was not explored in the book, the establishment of the recycling systems was responsible for the creation of several new jobs and sub-markets. Nevertheless, further investigation should be carried out to find out whether the non-financial benefits achieved were attained at a cost that citizens (and consumers, local authorities, industry...) are willing to pay.

Lessons-learned for Other Countries

It may seem counterintuitive, but "more recycling" and "more recovery" is not always and necessarily beneficial to the general welfare. It is important to examine the optimal rates keeping in mind that these may change from country to country and even from region to region (because the social, economic, demographic, infrastructural, geographic and natural constraints also change). The focus of policy making should be to minimize the social cost of MSW taking into account all the relevant constraints. In Europe, however, the focus was clearly on the enhanced environmental protection and the functioning of the internal market.

All the countries analyzed have a Green Dot company or and equivalent compliance scheme (CONAI in Italy does not administer a Green Dot system) which was created to help producers comply with the PPW Directive (targets and guidelines). Currently, in Belgium, France and Portugal, the Green Dot companies have the total market share for packaging waste management. In fact, these countries have many similarities concerning packaging management. Moreover, most EU local authorities are supported by a financing model based on the quantities of packaging waste taken back through the respective recycling system (there are, once again, exceptions; see the cases of Germany and the UK in Chapter 3). There are also other differences in the compliance schemes existent in each EU member state. Some deal exclusively with the household packaging waste flow (such as Fost Plus in Belgium and Eco-Emballages in France) whereas others also manage the trade and industry flows (such as SPV in Portugal and Eco-Rom in Romania); some hold the large majority of the market share (such as Fost Plus in Belgium and Eco-Emballages in France) whereas others are just a competitor in the recycling market (such as Eco-Rom in Romania and Valpak in the UK).

Nowadays, Belgium is one of the top "recycling countries" in Europe with a recycling rate of around 80 percent in 2010. In this country packaging waste management is under the responsibility of local authorities and the "standard level" service cost is fully covered by the financial support paid by the Green Dot company (Fost Plus). Germany has also achieved high recycling rates, but being a competitive system, it is extremely difficult to know what the costs and benefits of the recycling system actually are. For this reason, it is impossible to discuss which system may be better from a welfare point of view or, in other words, which system minimizes the social costs of packaging waste management.

It could be the case that the German system is very effective (recycling rates are very high), but not very efficient since the related unit costs could be higher than in other countries. Nevertheless, it is clear that the industry (private companies) entirely supports the recycling system. In view of this, it seems that Germany and

Belgium are two of the very few cases for which the EPR principle is respected "to the letter". Moreover, the implementation of a PAYT scheme by these two countries (with high prices for mixed waste bags/containers) represents one of the most relevant features for the success of their recycling system. Because citizens have to pay for the collection of MSW based on the amount they throw away, there is a true financial incentive for users to separate recyclables.

To move up the waste hierarchy, investing in infrastructure and capacity is necessary, but not sufficient. Economic incentives are important to shift the paradigm from disposal to recycling (Watkins et al., 2012). In addition, coordination between the public (national and local authorities, waste management operators) and the private (producers, new markets for composting and recycling) sectors is essential. In Europe the evolution in the waste and recycling sectors was impressive but there is still a long way to go.

After the required investments to set up a system that is capable of complying with the demanding recovery and recycling targets imposed, it is crucial to address other issues. In particular, is important to clarify and improve the operationalization of the EPR principle, encourage the cost efficiency of waste management operators (through fair and robust financing models) and implement actions that promote prevention, reuse and better separation at the source by the citizens.

Future Avenues of Research

As the reader may have gathered from the paragraphs above, the current research topic is far from being exhausted. In fact, the current book performs an investigation on the economic and environmental impacts of a recycling system from the moment a recyclable material is discarded by households up to the moment it is disposed of or, instead, reaches the "doorstep" of the recycling factory (although the environmental assessment includes the actual recycling process). Given the nature of the research questions addressed here, many segments of the life-cycle of packaging (the main recyclable material handled and discarded by households) were outside the scope of this investigation.

Future studies with different objectives could address another segment of the life-cycle of packaging of fast-moving consumer goods, or even try to close the loop. Another challenging objective would be to account for the "social" impacts in addition to the economic and environmental ones scrutinized in this work. The packaging waste recycling topic presents us with a dynamic research agenda that feeds into policy-making. More theoretical and empirical work on the different (social, environmental, economic) costs and benefits of recycling systems is, therefore, expected and desired.

From the results discussed above, it is evident that new research efforts aiming at identifying or devising systems, incentives and policies that minimize the social costs of packaging waste management are required. With the increase of recycling rates, some social costs decrease as a result of: (1) the increase of the positive externalities (e.g. resource conservation) and the financial benefits attained with the sale of recyclables (e.g. sorted material), and (2) the decrease of the negative externalities (e.g. emissions from landfilling or incineration) and the financial costs from disposal operations. But it should be noted that some other social costs show the opposite trend; that is, some social costs increase with the increase of recycling rates as a result of the efforts put on by households and local authorities in preparing, separating and collecting the recyclables. This is why, at a given time, for a given region (with certain socio-economic characteristics, physical conditions, available technology, etc.), there will be theoretical recovery and recycling rates that minimize the social costs.

But in addition to the "one million dollar question" about the optimal recovery and recycling rates, many other topics deserve further attention from the literature. In fact, future developments in waste management and recycling research could be devised around the possible incentives for efficiency (and effectiveness) embedded in the financing contracts firmed between waste management operators and the compliance schemes. Connected to this, more evidence on the existent economic mechanisms and waste management billing models would be useful to policy-makers and practitioners. How can local authorities make a smooth transition from traditionally below-cost tariff systems to sophisticated billing systems with embedded price-signals? What communication strategy should be formulated to avoid rejection and public contestation? How can the political costs of raising the overall bill of waste management services be mitigated? If one wants to devise resilient recycling systems, these are some of the issues that need to be tackled in parallel to more hands-on research focused on technological innovation.

References

Adams, K.T.; Phillips, P.S. and Morris, J.R. (2000). A radical new development for sustainable waste management in the UK: the introduction of local authority Best Value legislation. *Resources, Conservation and Recycling*, Vol. 30, no. 3, pp. 221–44.

Adams, M. (2011). *The Belgian Legislation on Packaging Waste*. Presentation at the Stakeholder event of October 25, 2011—European Commission. Interregional Packaging Commission (IPC), Brussels, Belgium.

Adelphe (2010). *Rapport d'activité. Exercice 2010*. Adelphe S.A., Paris.

ADEME (2010). *Emballages ménagers, Synthèse*. Agence de l'Environnement et de la Maîtrise de l'Energie, Angers.

Agentschap (2011). *Waste Management Research in Romania*. NL Agency, Ministry of Economic Affairs, Agriculture and Innovation, The Hague, The Netherlands.

Ahlroth, S. (2009). Developing a weighting set based on monetary damage estimates. Method and case studies. *Trita_Infra_Fms:*1. Division of environmental strategies research. Royal Institute of Technology, Stockholm, Sweden.

Ahlroth, S. and Finnveden, G. (2011). Ecovalue08 – A new valuation set for environmental systems analysis tools. *Journal of Cleaner Production*, Vol. 19, no. 17, pp. 1994–2003.

Ambirumo (2009). *Estudo de Avaliação da Gestão de RSU Focalizada na Componente da Recolha Selectiva e Triagem de Resíduos de Embalagens*. Ambirumo, Lisboa.

Anderson, S.; M. Browne and J. Allen (1999). Logistics implications of the UK packaging waste regulations. *International Journal of Logistics Research and Applications*, Vol. 2, no. 2, pp. 129–45.

ANPM (2012a). *Raport Anual Privind Starea Mediului în România pe Anul 2010*. Available at: http://www.anpm.ro/upload/48601_6%20Cap%206%20 Managementul%20Deseurilor.2010.pdf

ANPM (2012b). *Situaţia Depozitelor Municipale Conforme- Mai 2010*. Available at: http://www.anpm.ro/upload/3746_Depozite%20municipale%20 conforme%20-%20la%2030.05.2010.pdf.

APSE (2011). *Refuse Collection Performance Information on Cost and Service Quality*. APSE membership resources, briefing 11-07, Manchester, UK. Available from: http://www.apse.org.uk

ARGUS (2001). *European Packaging Waste Management Systems*. ARGUS in association with ACR and Carl Broa/s. Final Report, prepared for DG Environment.

Bailay, I. (1999). Flexibility, harmonization and the single, market in EU environmental policy: The packaging waste Directive. *Journal of Common Market Studies*, Vol. 37, no. 4, pp. 549–71.

Bing, L.; Akintoye, A.; Edwards P.J. and Hardcastle, C. (2005). The allocation of risk in PPP/PFI construction projects in the UK. *International Journal of Project Management*. Vol. 23, no. 1, pp. 25–35.

BMU (2006). *Municipal Solid Waste Management Report.* Available at http://www. Bmu. de/files/pdfs/allgemein/application/pdf/bericht_siedlungsabfallentsorgung _2006_engl.pdf. Federal Ministry for the Environment, Nature Conservation and Nuclear Safety, Berlin.

BMU (2011a). *Evaluierung der Verpackungsverordnung.* Umweltforschungsplan des Bundesministeriums für Umwelt, Naturschutz und Reaktorsicherheit, Berlin.

BMU (2011b). *Planspiel zur Fortentwicklung der Verpackungsverordnung Teilvorhaben 2: Finanzierungsmodelle der Wertstofftonne.* Umweltforschungsplan des Bundesministeriums für Umwelt, Naturschutz und Reaktorsicherheit, Berlin.

Bongaerts, J. and Kemp, R. (2000). *The Implementation and Tecnological Impact of the Packaging and Packaging Waste Directive 94/62/EC in France, Germany and Filand.* MERIT, University of Maastricht, Maastricht, The Netherlands.

Bulkeley, H. and Gregson, N. (2009). Crossing the threshold: municipal waste policy and household waste generation. *Environment and Planning A*, Vol. 41, no. 4, pp. 929–45.

Bundeskartellamt (2011). *Case summary: Coordination of tenders for sales packaging waste collection services by compliance schemes.* Accessed at: http://www.bundeskartellamt.de/wEnglisch/News/2011_10_10_Case_ summary.php.

BVSE (2011). *Vertrags- und Lizenzmengenanteile.* Available online at: http:// www.bvse.de/ 300 / 4445 / Vertrags __ und _ Lizenzmengenanteile _ 2011 Bundesverband Sekundärrohstoffe und Entsorgung e.v., Bonn.

CCC (2009). *A Report Assessing the Impact of Adopting German Waste Collection Practices on the Need for a Recycling Centre in Cambridge Southern Fringe.* Cambridgeshire County Council, Cambridgeshire, UK.

Celpa (2010). *Boletim Estatístico 2010.* Indústria Papeleira Portuguesa. Celpa –Associação da Indústria Papeleira, Portugal.

Cleary, J. (2009). Life cycle assessments of municipal solid waste management systems: A comparative analysis of selected peer-reviewed literature. *Environment International*, Vol. 35, no. 8, pp. 1256–66.

Clift, R.; Doig A. and Finnveden G. (2000). The application of life cycle assessment to integrated solid waste management - Part 1 - Methodology. *Process Safety and Environmental Protection*, Vol. 78, no. B4, pp. 279–87.

COM (2006). *Report from the Commission to the Council and the European Parliament: On the Implementation of Directive 94/62/EC on Packaging and Packaging Waste and its Impact on the Environment, as well as on the*

Functioning of the Internal Market, COM(2006) 767 final. Commission of the European Communities, Brussels, Belgium.

Comieco (2011). *Gestione degli Imballaggi e dei Rifiuti D'imballaggio Cellulosici*. Programma Specifico di Prevenzione 2011. Available at: http://www.comieco. org/.

COPIDEC (2012). *Collecte, Tri et Traitement*. Available at: http://www.copidec.be/

Criekemans, D. (2010). Foreign Policy and Diplomacy of the Belgian Regions: Flanders and Wallonia. Discussion papers in Diplomacy. Ingrid d'Hooghe & Ellen Huijgh editors, Netherlands Institute of International Relations 'Clingendael'.

CSD (2009). *Waste management* (sub-theme 2.4). Belgian Report to the Eighteenth Session of the Commission on Sustainable Development (CSD), Brussels, Belgium.

da Cruz, N., Marques, R.C. and Simões, P. (2012). Economic cost recovery in the recycling of packaging waste: The case of Portugal. *Journal of Cleaner Production* Vol. 37, no. 12, pp. 8–18.

da Cruz, N.; Ferreira, S.; Cabral, M.; Simões, P. and Marques, R.C. (2014b). Packaging waste recycling in Europe: Is the industry paying for it? *Waste Management*, Vol. 34, no. 2, pp. 298–308.

da Cruz, N.; Marques, R.C. (2014). Análise Econômica do sistema da reciclagem em Portugal. *Engenharia Sanitária e Ambiental*. Vol.19, no.3, pp. 335–44.

da Cruz, N.; Marques, RC. and Simões, P. (2014a). Costs and benefits of packaging waste recycling systems. *Resources, Conservation & Recycling*, Vol. 85, no. 4, pp. 1-4.

da Cruz, N.; Simões, P. and Marques, R.C. (2013). The hurdles of local governments with PPP contracts in the waste sector. *Environment and Planning C: Government and Policy*, Vol. 31, no. 2, pp. 292–307.

Defra (2003). *User guide: Producer Responsibility Obligations (Packaging Waste) Regulations 1997 (as amended)*. Published by Department for Environment Food and Rural Affairs (Defra). Available at: http://archive.defra.gov.uk/ environment/waste/ producer /packaging /documents/userguide.pdf.

Defra (2005a). *Hazardous Waste (England and Wales) Regulations 2005 and List of Wastes (England) Regulations 2005*. Department for Environment Food and Rural Affairs (Defra), London, UK.

Defra (2005b). *Guidance for Waste Collection Authorities on the Household Waste Recycling Act 2003*. Department for Environment Food and Rural Affairs, London, UK.

Defra (2007). *Waste Strategy for England 2007*. Department for Environment Food and Rural Affairs, London, UK.

Defra (2009). *Waste Strategy Annual Progress Report 2008/09*. Department for Environment Food and Rural Affairs, London, UK.

Defra (2010). *Review of Schedule 2 of the Controlled Waste Regulations (1992)*. Department for Environment Food and Rural Affairs, London, UK.

Defra (2012). *UK Waste Data. Published by Department of Environment, Food and Rural Affairs* (Defra). Available at: http://www.defra.gov.uk/statistics/environment/waste/ wrfg01-annsector/.

Detini (2008). *Special Feature: Households 10. Department of Enterprise, Trade & Investment (Detini).* LFS Quarterly Supplement: July–September. Available at: http:// http://www.detini.gov.uk

DGEG (2013a). *Renováveis.* Estatísticas rápidas, Dezembro 2010. no. 70. Direcção Geral de Energia e Geologia (DGEG), Portugal.

DGEG (2013b). *Petróleo, Gás Natural e Carvão.* Estatísticas rápidas, Dezembro 2010. no. 68. Direcção Geral de Energia e Geologia (DGEG), Portugal.

Dias, A.C.; Arroja, L. and Capela, I. (2007). Life cycle assessment of printing and writing paper produced in Portugal. *International Journal of Life Cycle Assessment,* Vol. 12, no. 7, pp. 521–8.

Djemaci, B. (2009). *Public waste management services in France. National analysis and case studies of Paris, Rouen, and Besançon.* Working paper CIRIEC no. 2009/02. Centre d'Analyse et de Recherche en Economie. Université de Rouen, Mont Saint Aignan.

ECB (2013). *Euro exchange rates SEK.* Available at: http://www.ecb.europa.eu/stats/exchange/eurofxref/html/eurofxref-graph-sek.en. html [accessed on: December 30, 2013].

Eco-Emballages (2010a). *Annual Report 2009.* Eco-Emballages, Paris.

Eco-Emballages (2010b). *Contrat programme de durée – Barème D (Version actualisée 2010).* Eco-Emballages, Paris.

Eco-Emballages (2011). *Communiqué de presse du 31/05/2011 – Nouveau tariff Point Vert 2012.* Eco-Emballages, Paris.

Eco-Emballages and Adelphe (2011). *Standards par Matériau.* Eco-Emballages and Adelphe, Paris. Available at: http://www.ecoemballages.fr.

Eco-Rom (2011a). *Newsletter no. 3. New Legislation Challenges.* June–August 2011. Eco Rom Ambalaje, Bucharest.

Eco-Rom (2011b). *Annual Report 2010.* Eco-Rom Ambalaje, Bucharest.

EEA (2005). *Effectiveness of Packaging Waste Management Systems in Selected Countries: an EEA Pilot Study.* European Environment Agency, Copenhagen, Denmark.

EEA (2012). *EMEP/EEA Emission Inventory Guidebook 2009, updated May 2012.* European Environment Agency, Denmark.

Eichstadt, T., W. Kahlenborn, B. Simon and M. Kemper (2000). *Packaging Waste: The Euro-Level Policy Making Process.* Ecologic—Centre for International and European Environmental Research, Berlin, Germany.

EIMPack (2012). *The Economics of the Recycling of Packaging Waste: The Case of France.* Economic Impact of the Packaging and Packaging Waste Directive, Instituto Superior Técnico, Lisbon.

EIMPack (2013a). *The Economics of the Recycling of Packaging Waste: The Case of Italy.* Economic Impact of the Packaging and Packaging Waste Directive, Instituto Superior Técnico, Lisbon.

EIMPack (2013b) *Environmental Valuation (Literature Review)*. Economic Impact of the Packaging and Packaging Waste Directive, Instituto Superior Técnico, Lisbon

EIMPack (2014a) *Cost and Benefits of Packaging Waste Recycling. Final Report*. Economic Impact of the Packaging and Packaging Waste Directive, Instituto Superior Técnico, Lisbon.

EIMPack (2014b) *Costs and Benefits of the Recycling of Packaging Waste. The Case of Portugal*. Economic Impact of the Packaging and Packaging Waste Directive, Instituto Superior Técnico, Lisbon.

ENSR (1997). *Environmental, Health & Safety Audit Protocol*. Published by ENSR Corporation in: http://www.stpub.com/pdfs/Sample.pdf

ERM (2005). *Assessment of the Best Practicable Environmental Option for Municipal Solid Waste Arising in North Yorkshire County Council & City of York Council*. Published by ERM in: http://www.northyorks.gov.uk/ CHttpHandler.ashx? Id = 10755&p=0.

ERSAR (2011). *Annual Report on Water and Waste Services in Portugal*. The Water and Waste Services Regulation Authority, Lisbon.

Eshet, T., Baron, M.G. and Shechter M. (2007). Exploring benefit transfer: disamenities of waste transfer stations. *Environmental & Resource Economics*, Vol. 37, no. 3, pp. 521–47.

Espreme (2008). *Estimation of Willingness-to-pay to Reduce Risks of Exposure to Heavy Metals and Cost-benefit Analysis for Reducing Heavy Metals Occurrence in Europe*. External costs. Available at: http://espreme.ier.uni-stuttgart.de [accessed on: October 28, 2008].

Eunomia (2009). *International Review of Waste Management Policy: Annexes to Main Report*. Eunomia Research and Consulting Ltd., Bristol, UK.

Eurostat (2013a). *Imports (by country of origin) – Electricity – Annual Data*. Available at: http://appsso.eurostat.ec.europa.eu/ [accessed on: December 26, 2013].

Eurostat (2013b). *Statistics. Main Tables*. Energy. Available at: http://epp.eurostat.ec. europa.eu/portal/page/portal/energy/data/main_tables [accessed on: December 26, 2013).

Eurostat (2013c). HICP - inflation rate. Annual Average Rate of Change (%). Available at: http://epp.eurostat.ec.europa.eu/tgm/table.do;jsessionid=9ea7d 07d30e7e84a2aa5 0db743a19f49c1b10583cf2d.e34OaN8PchaTby0Lc3aNch uMc3yMe0?tab=table&plugin=1&language=en&pcode=tec00118 [accessed on: December 30, 2013].

FOE (2007). *Landfill Allowance Trading Scheme*. Briefing prepared by Friends of the Earth, London, England.

Fost Plus (2012a). *The Fixed-price Declaration and the Detailed Declaration*. Fost Plus, Brussels, Belgium (accessed on April 12, 2012).

Fost Plus (2012b). *Annual Report 2011 – The Recycling Society in Action*. Fost Plus, Brussels, Belgium.

Giugliano, M.; Cernuschi, S.; Grosso, M. and Rigamonti, R., (2011). Material and energy recovery in integrated waste management system. An evaluation based on life cycle assessment. *Waste Management*, Vol. 31, no. 9–10, pp. 2093–102.

Golding, A. (1999). *Reuse of Primary Packaging - Main report.* European Commission, Brussels, Belgium.

Guinée, J.B.; Gorree, M.; Heijungs, R.; Huppes, G.; Kleijn, R.; De Koning, A.; Van Oers, L.; Sleeswijk, A.W.; Sangwon, S. and Udo de Haes, H.A. (2002). *Handbook on Life-cycle Assessment. Operational Guide to the ISO Standards.* Kluwer Academic Publishers, Dordrecht.

Hansen, W.; Christopher, M. and Verbuecheln, M. (2002). *EU Waste Policy and Challenges for Regional and Local Authorities.* Ecologic – Centre for International and European Environmental Research, Berlin, Germany.

Haris, S. (2004). *Public Private Partnerships: Delivering Better Infrastructure Services.* Inter-American Development Bank, Washington D.C., US.

Hempen, S. (2005). *Status and Trends of the Residual Waste Treatment Options in Germany.* Conference "The future of residual waste management in Europe", 17–18th November, 2005, Luxembourg.

IBGE (2012). *Que Fait-on Avec les Déchets?* Institute Bruxellois pour la Gestion de l'Environnement (IBGE). Available at: http://www.bruxelles-proprete.be/ Content/ html/services/quefaire.asp.

IBGE/BIM (2011). *Obligations Générales Applicables à Tout Type de Déchets.* Institute Bruxellois pour la Gestion de l'Environnement (IBGE), Brussels, Belgium.

IPCC (2006a). *Guidelines for National Greenhouse Gas Inventories.* Chapter 5. Incineration and open burning of waste. Vol. 5, Intergovernmental Panel on Climate Change (IPCC), Geneva, Switzerland.

IPCC (2006b). *Guidelines for National Greenhouse Gas Inventories.* Chapter 3: Solid Waste Disposal. Vol. 5, Intergovernmental Panel on Climate Change (IPCC), Geneva, Switzerland.

ISPRA (2013). *Rapporto Rifiuti Urbani Edizione 2013.* ISPRA (Istituto Superiore per la Protezione e la Ricerca Ambientale). Available at: www.isprambiente. gov.it/.

IVCIE (2011). *Rapport d'Activités 2010* [in French], Brussels, Belgium.

IVCIE (2012). *The Interregional Packaging Commission*, Interregionale Verpakkingscommissie / Commission Interrégionale de l'Emballage (IVCIE). Available at: http://www.ivcie.be/en/page.php?pageId=500.

Jacobsen, H. and Kristoffersen, M. (2002). *Case Studies on Waste Minimisation Practices in Europe.* European Environment Agency, Topic report 2/2002, Copenhagen, Denmark.

Kinnaman, T. (2009). The economics of municipal solid waste management, *Waste Management*, Vol. 29, no. 10, pp. 2615–17.

Lavee, D. (2007). Is municipal solid waste recycling economically efficient? *Environmental Management*, Vol. 40, no. 6, pp. 926–43.

Lavrysen, L. and Misonne, D. (2004). *Producer Responsibility and Integrated Product Policy in Belgium*. Avosetta meeting, Brussels.

Le Bozec, A. (2008) The implementation of PAYT system under the condition of financial balance in France, *Waste Management*, Vol. 28, no. 12, pp. 2786–92.

Letsrecycle.com (2009). *WRAP Collection Report Divides Waste Sector* - letsrecycle.com recycling and waste management news and information.

Margallo, M.; Aldaco, R.; Bala, A.; Fullana, P. and Irabien, A. (2013). *Modeling of Municipal Solid Waste (MSW) Incineration in Spain and Portugal*. The 6th International Conference on Life Cycle Management in Gothenburg, Nebraska, US.

Marques, R.C. and Simões, P. (2008). Does the sunshine regulatory approach work? Governance and regulation model of the urban waste services in Portugal. *Resources Conservation and Recycling*, Vol. 52, no, 8–9, pp. 1040–49.

Marques, R.C.; da Cruz, N.F. and Carvalho, P. (2012). Assessing and exploring (in)efficiency in Portuguese recycling systems using non-parametric methods. *Resources, Conservation & Recycling*. Vol. 67, no. 10, pp. 34–43.

Massaruto, A., De Carli A. and Graffi M. (2011). Material and energy recovery in integrated waste management systems: A life-cycle costing approach. *Waste Management*. Vol. 31, no. 9–10, pp. 2102–11.

Massarutto, A. (2010). Municipal waste management in Italy, *CIRIEC Working paper 2010/01*.

Massarutto, A. (2014). The long and winding road to resource efficiency – An interdisciplinary perspective on extended producer responsibility. *Resources Conservation and Recycling*. Vol. 85, no.4, pp. 11–21.

Matos, A.; Ribeiro, I.; Fernandes, A. and Cabo, P. (2010). *Análise Crítica dos Métodos de Valoração Económica dos Bens e Recursos Ambientais*. VIII Coloquio Ibérico de Estudios Rurales. Cáceres, Spain.

Mazzanti, M. and Zoboli, R. (2008). Waste generation, waste disposal and policy effectiveness: Evidence on decoupling from the European Union. *Resources, Conservation and Recycling*, Vol. 52, no. 10, 1221–34.

MEEDDM (2009). *Annual Report to Parliament on Implementing France's Environment Round Table Commitments*. Ministère de l'Écologie, de l'Énergie, du Développement durable et de la Mer, Paris.

Methodex (2007). *BeTa – Methodex V2-07*. Available at: www.methodex.org/ news. htm.

Morris, J. and Read, A. (2001). The UK landfill tax and the landfill tax credit scheme: operational weaknesses. *Resources, Conservation and Recycling*, Vol. 32, no. 3–4, pp. 375–87.

Morris, J.; Phillips, P. and Read, A. (1998). The UK landfill tax: an analysis of its contribution to sustainable waste management. *Resources, Conservation and Recycling*, Vol. 23, no. 4, pp. 259–70.

MS2 and Perchards (2009). *Product Stewardship in North America and Europe Final Report*. Prepared for Department of the Environment, Water, Heritage and the Arts on behalf of the Waste Policy Taskforce, Turramura, Australia.

Nicolaides and Associates (2010). *Evaluation of the Implementation of the Relevant EC Directives in the Participant Member States, 1st Edition.* P. Nicolaides and Associates Ltd, Nicosia, Cyprus.

NIEA (2010). NIEA Compliance Monitoring Plan for 2011. Available at: http://www.doeni.gov.uk/niea/.

NIEA (2011). *The Producer Responsibility Obligations (Packaging Waste) Regulations (Northern Ireland) 2007.* Published by Northern Ireland Environment Agency (NIEA) in: http://www.doeni.gov.uk/niea/de/index.htm.

ODPM (2002). *Strategic Planning for Sustainable Waste Management: Guidance on Option Development and Appraisal.* Office of the Deputy Prime Minister (ODPM) transferred to the Department for Communities and Local Government (DCLG), London, UK.

ODPM (2004). *Planning for Waste Management Facilities: A Research Study.* Office of the Deputy Prime Minister (ODPM) transferred to the Department for Communities and Local Government (DCLG), London, UK.

Ofgem and EA (2001). *Memorandum of understanding between Gas and Electricity Markets Authority and the Environment Agency Relating to Environmental Issues.* Published by Ofgem and Environment Agency (EA) in: http://www.ofgem.gov.uk/ Sustainability/Environment/Policy/Documents1/150-16july01.pdf.

OVAM (2009). *Activities Report 2009.* Published by Flemish Public Waste Agency (OVAM), Flanders, Belgium.

OVAM (2011). *Tarieven en capaciteiten voor storten en verbranden – Actualisatie tot 2010* [in Dutch], Mechelen, Belgium. Task 5 – Environmental Valuation *References.*

Pagga, U. (1998). Biodegradability and compostability of polymeric materials in the context of the European packaging regulation. *Polymer Degradation and Sfability,* Vol. 59, no. 1–3, pp. 371–6.

Perrin, D. and Barton, J. (2001). Issues associated with transforming household attitudes and opinions into materials recovery: a review of two kerbside recycling schemes. *Resources, Conservation and Recycling,* Vol. 33, no. 1, pp. 61–74.

Phillips, P.S.; Pratt, R.M. and Pike, K. (2001). An analysis of UK waste minimization clubs: key requirements for future cost effective developments. *Waste Management,* Vol. 21, no. 4, pp. 389–404.

Pinckaers, M. (2012). *Belgium – Luxembourg. Food and Agricultural Import Regulations and Standards – Narrative.* FAIRS Country Report prepared by USDA Foreign Agricultural Service, Brussels, Belgium.

Pira and Ecolas (2005). *Study on the Implementation of Directive 94/62/EC on Packaging and Packaging Waste and Options to Strengthen Prevention and Re-use of Packaging - Final report.* Prepared by ECOLAS – Environmental Consultancy & Assistence and Pira International for the EU Environment DG, Brussels, Belgium.

PRO (2008). *PRO EUROPE*. Available at: http://www.pro-e.org/files/08-11PositionPaperMandatory_ Deposit_RBV01.pdf [accessed on June 3, 2011].

PRO-Europe (2010). *Producer Responsibility In Action*. PRO Europe, Brussels, Belgium.

PRO-Europe (2011). *Participation Costs Overview 2011*. PRO Europe, Brussels, Belgium.

Prognos, A.G. (2008). *Endbericht der Abfallmarkt in Deutschland und Perspektiven bis 2020*. Berlin.

R3 and CM (2009). *Evaluating End-of-Life Beverage Container Management Systems for California Final Report*. R3 Consulting Group, Inc. and Clarissa Morawski Principal CM Consulting, Sacramento, California, US.

Read, A. (1999). Making waste work: making UK national solid waste strategy work at the local scale. *Resources, Conservation and Recycling*, Vol. 26, no. 3–4, pp. 259–85.

Reading (2001). *State Of The Environment, Chapter 12 Waste and Recycling*. Published by Reading Borough Council in: http://www.reading.gov.uk/environmentplanning/ General.asp?id=SX9452-A77FAB59

REN (2010). *Dados Técnicos 2010*. Rede Elétrica Nacional (REN), Portugal.

REN (2013). *Estatísticas Mensais Relativas ao Ano 2010*. Available at: www.centrode informacao.ren.pt/PT/InformacaoExploracao/Paginas/EstatisticaMensal.asp [accessed on: February 25, 2013].

Renkow, M. and Rubin, A.R. (1998). Does municipal solid waste composting make economic sense? *Journal of Environmental Management*, Vol. 53, no. 4, pp. 339–47.

REPAB (2010). *Establishment of Waste Network for Sustainable Solid Waste Management Planning and Promotion of Integrated Decision Tools in the Balkan Region (Balkwaste) – Action 2: Assessment of Waste Management Status in Balkan Countries Romania*. Prepared by the REPAB – Regional Environmental Protection Agency of Bacau for Life Program, Bacau, Romania.

Rigamonti L.; Grosso, M. and Giugliano, M. (2009). Life cycle assessment for optimising the level of separated collection in integrated MSW management systems. *Waste Management*, Vol. 29, no. 2, pp. 934–44.

Rigamonti L.; Grosso, M. and Giugliano, M. (2010). Life cycle assessment of sub-units composing a MSW management system. *Journal of Cleaner Production*, Vol. 18, no. 16, pp. 1652–62.

Rigamonti, L.; Falbo, A. and Grosso, M. (2013). Improving integrated waste management at the regional level: The case of Lombardia. *Waste Management and Research*, Vol. 31, no. 9, pp. 946–53.

Schnurer, H. (2002). *German Waste Legislation and Sustainable Development: Development of Waste Legislation in Germany towards a sustainable closed Substance Cycle*. Workshop organized by the Alexander von Humboldt Foundational, the International Institute for Advance Studies (IIAS), in Kyoto, Japan, 29 November–1 December, 2002.

Secretary of State (2010). *The Producer Responsibility Obligations (Packaging Waste) (Amendment) Regulations 2010*. Published by The Stationery Office Limited under the authority and superintendence of Carol Tullo in: http://www. Legislation .gov.uk/ukdsi/2010/9780111503294/pdfs/ukdsi_9780111503294_ en.pdf.

Simões, P. and Marques, R.C. (2012). Influence of regulation on the productivity of waste utilities. What can we learn with the Portuguese experience? *Waste Management*, Vol. 32, no. 6, pp. 1266–75.

Smallbone, T. (2005). How can domestic households become part of the solution to England's recycling problems? *Business Strategy and the Environment*, Vol. 14, no. 2, pp. 110–22.

Spielmann, M.; Dones, R. and Bauer, C. (2007). *Life Cycle Inventories of Transport Services*. Final report ecoinvent v2.0 No. 14. Swiss Centre for Life Cycle Inventories, Dübendorf, Switzerland.

Spitzley, J-B and Najdawi, C. (2011). *Integration of electricity from renewables to the electricity grid and to the electricity market – RES-INTEGRATION*. National report: Belgium (and Flanders & Walloon Regions). Eclareon and Institute for Applied Ecology, Berlin, Germany.

SPV (2010). *Relatório de Actividades e Contas 2009*. Sociedade Ponto Verde, Oeiras. Portugal.

Stern N. (2006). *The Economics of Climate Change – The Stern Review*. Cambridge University Press, United Kingdom.

Terna (2013). *Datistatistici 2010*. Available at: http://www.terna.it/default/ Home/ SISTEMA_ELETTRICO/statistiche/dati_statistici.aspx[accessed on 9/1/2013]

Tol, R.S.J. (2008). The social cost of carbon: trends, outliers and catastrophes. *Economics*, Vol. 2, pp. 2008–25.

TU Delft (2013). *The Model of the Eco-costs / Value Ratio (EVR)*. Delft University of Technology, The Netherlands. Available at: www.ecocostvalue.com [accessed on: July 1, 2013].

Turconi, R.; Butera, S.; Boldrin, A.; Grosso, M.; Rigamonti, L. and Astrup, T. (2011). Life cycle assessment of waste incineration in Denmark and Italy using two LCA models. *Waste Management & Research*, Vol. 30, no. 9, pp. 78–90.

TWB (2011). *Solid Waste Management in Bulgaria, Croatia, Poland, and Romania A Cross-country Analysis of Sector Challenges Towards EU Harmonization*. The World Bank, Washington, US.

UBA (2012). *Anlagen zur Thermischen Abfallbehandlung*. Available at: http:// www.umweltbundesa mt-daten-zur-umwelt.de/umweltdaten/public/theme.do? nodeIdent=2307 [accessed on January 10, 2012].

USEPA (2011). *United States Environmental Protection Agency*. http://www.epa. gov/ wastes/ [accessed on June 24, 2011].

Valpak (2011). *Valpak Packaging Compliance*. Published by Valpak in: http:// www.valpak.co.uk/docs/bottommenu/Packaging_Offer_Document.pdf

Vogel, D.; Toffel, M.; Post, D. and Aragon, N. (2010). *Environmental Federalism in the European Union and the United States,* Harvard Business School, Boston, Massachusetts, US.

Vogtländer, J.G.; Brezet, H.C. and Hendriks, C.F. (2001). The virtual Eco-Costs'99 – a single LCA-based indicator for sustainability and the Eco-Costs – value ratio (EVR) model for economic allocation. A new LCA-based calculation model to determine the sustainability of products and services. *The International Journal of Life Cycle Assessment*, Vol. 6, no. 3, pp. 157–66.

Walls, M. (2006). Extended producer responsibility and product design: economic theory and selected case studies. *Discussion Papers dp-06-08*, Resources For the Future.

Warwickshire Waste Partnership (2006). *Warwickshire's Municipal Waste Management Strategy*. Warwickshire Waste Partnership, Warwickshire County Council, Warwick, UK.

Watkins, E.; Hogg, D.; Mitsios, A.; Mudgal, S.; Neubauer, A.; Reisinger, H.; Troeltsch, J. and Acoleyem, M. (2012) *Use of Economics Instruments and Waste Management Performances*. Available at: http://ec.europa.eu/environment/waste/pdf/final_report10042012.pdf [accessed August 12, 2012].

Wayenberg, E. and De Rynck, F. (2012). *Kingdom of Belgium*. Available at: http://www.cities-localgovernments.org/gold/Upload/country_profile/Belgium.pdf [accessed on April 3, 2012).

Weidema, B.P. (2009). Using the budget constraint to monetarise impact assessment results. *Ecological Economics* Vol. 68, no. 6, pp. 1591–8.

Weidema, B.P. (2013). *Impact Assessment with Option of Full Monetarisation*. Available at: http://www.lca-net.com/projects/Stepwise2006_ia [accessed on: July 1, 2013].

Wilson, C.; Williams, I.D. and Kemp, S. (2011). Compliance with Producer Responsibility Legislation: Experiences from UK Small and Medium-sized Enterprises. *Business Strategy and the Environment*, Vol. 20, no. 5, pp. 310–30.

WMC (2012). *Interview with WMCs Romanian Managers and Solid Waste Experts*, Romania.

WMP1 (2010). *From Guidance WMP1: How to Register as a Producer of Packaging: Guidance Notes, version 2*. Published by Environment Agency (EA) and Scottish Environment Protection Agency (SEPA).

World Bank (2009). *World Development Indicators*. World Bank, Washington DC.

WRAP (2008a). *Kerbside Recycling: Indicative Costs and Performance*. Report published by WRAP (Waste and Resources Action Programme), Banbury, UK.

WRAP (2008b). *Kerbside Recycling: Indicative Costs and Performance*. Technical Annex published by WRAP (Waste and Resources Action Programme), Banbury, UK.

WRAP (2009). *Choosing the Right Recycling Collection System*. Report published by WRAP (Waste and Resources Action Programme), Banbury, UK.

WRAP (2011). *Comparing the Cost of Alternative Waste Treatment Options.* Gate fees Report, 2011. Published by WRAP (Waste and Resources Action Programme), Banbury, UK.

WRAP (2012). *Kerbside Collection of Plastic Bottles Guide.* WRAP (Waste and Resources Action Programme), Banbury, UK.

WYG Environment (2010). *Review of Kerbside Recycling Collection Schemes Operated by Local Authorities.* WYG Group, Lyndhurst, UK.

Index

Agency for Environment and Energy
    Management 34, 37, 40
Austria 7, 19, 21

Belgium 5, 10, 19–23, 25–33, 97, 99–100,
    102, 104, 106–13, 116, 119–30,
    160–67, 169–75
Best Available Technologies Not entailing
    Excessive Costs 115
Best Practicable Environmental Option 85
Brussels' Institute for Environmental
    Management 26–7
Bulgaria 14, 19, 21

Chambers of Industry and Commerce 45
composting 8, 15, 19–20, 98, 110
Consorzio Nazionale Imballagi (Italy's
    National Packaging Consortium)
    18, 54–8, 60, 100, 107, 133, 175
Contributo Ambientale (CONAI
    Environmental Contribution) 57
Controlled Waste Regulations 83
cost-benefit analysis 104–5
Cumulative energy demand 122–3, 146–7
Cyprus 14, 19, 21
Czech Republic 14, 19, 21

degradable organic carbon 112
Denmark 5, 10, 12, 15, 18–19, 21
Department for Environment, Food and
    Rural Affairs 86
Deutsche Gesellschaft für
    Kreislaufwirtschaft und Rohstoffe
    mbH 47
disposal 1, 3–6, 8–9, 15–16, 101, 106,
    108–11, 116, 169, 171, 173, 176–7
disposal plans for municipal waste 36
Duales System Deutschland 45, 47–52

eco-costs 114–15, 124–5, 127, 135–40,
    149, 152, 154, 171
Ecoinvent 105–6, 108–9, 113, 165, 171
Ecovalue 114–16, 125–30, 135–9, 142,
    150–54, 165–7, 171
EIMPack 169
ELCD 2.0 105–6, 108, 111, 171
Empresa Geral de Fomento 66
Environment Agency 84, 86, 90
Environmental Action Programme 3
environmental impacts 4–5, 7–8, 11–12,
    18, 97–9, 103–16, 121–30, 135–42,
    145–54, 164–6, 171, 173, 176
Environmental Protection Agency 9–10
environmental valuation 99, 104–5, 114–16
Estonia 14, 19, 21
European Union 1–23, 169, 173–5
extended producer responsibility 3, 6, 10–11

fee for municipal waste disposal 36
financial support for local authorities 17,
    28, 30–31, 38–41, 55, 58–61, 68,
    70, 100, 116, 120, 130–32, 144,
    160–63
Finland 19, 21
First Order Decay 112
France 12, 19–23, 33–43, 97, 99–100, 102,
    130–32, 160–63, 169–75
functional unit 107

Germany 5, 7, 10, 12, 18–23, 43–54, 99,
    164, 169–70, 172, 175–6
glass 1, 10, 13–15, 22–3, 102, 107,
    109–10, 112–13, 120
Greece 14, 19, 20–21
Green Dot 11–12, 16, 21, 160, 169, 175

Hungary 14, 19, 21

Iceland 19
incineration 1–4, 8–9, 15–16, 20, 98, 101,
    104, 106, 108–12, 116, 121, 163,
    165–6, 169–70, 177
industry 6, 10–11, 16–18, 97, 99, 107, 120
industry flow 1, 7, 16, 20, 98, 160, 163–4,
    169–70, 173–5
Intergovernmental Panel on Climate
    Change 111
intermunicipal cooperation agencies 36
Interregional Packaging Commission 26
Ireland 14, 19, 21
Italy 12, 19–23, 54–63, 97, 99–100, 102,
    104–11, 113, 116, 132–42, 160,
    163–7, 169–71, 175

landfill 1–4, 6, 8–9, 11, 15, 18–20, 101,
    104, 106–12, 116, 163, 165–6,
    169–70, 177
landfill gas 106, 111–12, 145
Latvia 14, 19, 21
life cycle assessment 99, 104–8
life cycle costing 104
life cycle inventory 108–13
life cycle impact assessment 114
lightweight packaging 47–9, 52
Lithuania 14, 19, 21
local authorities 1, 10, 12, 16–18, 97,
    99–102, 105–9, 115–16, 160,
    163–4, 169–71, 174–7
Lombardia 104–6, 108–10, 135–42, 162–6,
    170–71
Luxembourg 19, 21

Malta 14, 19, 21
marginal corporate tax 101–2
mechanical biological treatment 15–16,
    39–40, 46–7, 55, 60–61, 66, 68,
    70, 108
metal 1, 10, 13–15, 22–23, 30, 32, 38, 42,
    46, 49, 52–3, 62, 72–3, 77, 81–2,
    96, 109–13, 130–31
multimaterial 37, 55, 58, 60, 134
municipal solid waste 1, 8, 18, 21–2, 27,
    47, 87, 104, 107, 110–11, 175–6

National Regulatory Authority for
    Municipal Services 76

Netherlands 5, 10, 19, 21
North West Region Waste Management
    Group 88
Northern Ireland Environment Agency 87,
    90, 92

opportunity cost 8, 101–2, 108, 116, 120,
    127–36, 140–42, 145, 152–5,
    159–67, 169, 171, 174
Organisation for Economic Co–operation
    and Development 4
OVAM (Flemish Public Waste Agency)
    26–7

packaged products 6, 16, 25–7, 34, 64,
    67–8, 75, 173
packaging and packaging waste 5–16, 18,
    20, 25, 32–3, 42, 53–4, 58, 61, 64,
    66, 69, 73–5, 84, 91, 95, 97, 120,
    169, 172–5
paper 1, 9–10, 13, 15, 21, 30, 32, 38, 40,
    42, 45–6, 49, 52–3, 55–6, 58, 61,
    67, 76, 79, 89, 95, 107, 109, 111,
    113, 120, 130, 145, 155, 165–6
PAYT 35, 50, 172, 176
PET 28, 71, 75, 79–80, 112–13
photochemical oxidant formation 114,
    122–7, 135–8, 146–50
plastic 1, 9–10, 13, 15, 22–3, 30–33, 37–8,
    40, 45–9, 60–72, 75–82, 85, 89,
    95–6, 107, 109–13, 130, 155–6
PMD 31, 109, 120
Poland 14, 19, 21
Portugal 12, 14, 18–23, 63–6, 69–75,
    97–100, 102, 104, 106–13, 116,
    143–54, 160, 163–7, 169–72, 175
Portuguese Environmental Agency 63–4
prevention 2–3, 6–9, 36, 40, 43–4, 85, 95,
    176
Private Finance Initiative 87
PRO Europe 11, 28
public-private partnership 16, 47, 87

Quality Adjusted Life Year 115

real and complete cost 30
recovery 1–6, 8–11, 13–18, 20–21, 25–8,
    32–9, 43–7, 49, 53–6, 58, 60, 64–6,

70, 74–80, 83–7, 90–91, 105–6, 111, 130, 137–9, 144–5, 160, 166, 169, 173–7
recyclers 17, 29–31, 41, 60, 64, 68, 80, 98, 100, 107, 109, 112, 129, 145, 160, 164, 171
recycling rate 7–8, 10–11, 13–14, 17, 19–23, 26, 32–3, 42–3, 48–9, 53, 61–3, 71–3, 82–3, 91, 94–6, 120, 164, 173–7
Redual GmbH 48
Regulatory Institute for Water and Waste 64
respiratory organics 135, 137–8
Respo Waste 78
retailers 1, 28, 44, 57, 84–5
return on capital 101–2, 130, 161–2, 169
reuse 3, 6–9, 15, 27, 33, 43–4, 46, 64, 85–8, 176
Romania 12, 14, 19–23, 73–82, 97–102, 154–6, 160, 164, 169–75

Scottish Environment Protection Agency 84, 86, 90, 92
SIRAPA – APA's Integrated System of Records 63–4
SIRER – Integrated System of Electronic Record of Waste 63
SIVOM – Multiple Purpose Intermunicipal Association 36
SIVU – Single Purpose Intermunicipal Association 36
Slovakia 14, 19, 21
Slovenia 14, 19, 21
sorting facilities 11, 49, 52, 66, 108–9
Sota Group 78
Spain 19, 21
special fixed reimbursement 30
SPV 64–70, 100, 107, 175

standard cost 30
steel 28, 38, 40–41, 45, 55–60, 67–71, 79, 85, 94, 113, 134
Stepwise 114–15, 125–30, 135–41, 150–54, 165, 167, 171
Sweden 19, 21

Unitary Development Plan 88
United Kingdom 12, 19–23, 82–96, 99, 102, 157, 160, 164, 169–70, 175
United States 9–10

Valorfito 65
Valormed 65
Valpak 90–92, 94, 175
value-for-money 119–67
Veolia Umweltservice Dual GmbH 48
VERDORECA 67
Vfw GmbH 48

Walloon Intermunicipal Companies for Waste Treatment 27
Water and Waste Services Regulation Authority 65
Waste Agency of the Walloon Ministry for Natural Resources and Environment 26
waste collection authorities 87, 157
waste electrical and electronic equipment 6
Waste Framework Directive 1–6, 13, 36, 46, 73, 83–4
waste hierarchy 2, 6–8, 11, 43, 83, 85–6, 95, 169, 176
Weighted Average Cost of Capital 101
willingness to pay 115–16
wood 1, 10, 13–14, 22–3, 32, 42, 46, 53–4, 60–62, 68–73, 75, 79–82, 95, 112–13

Zentek GmbH & Co. KG 48

For Product Safety Concerns and Information please contact our EU
representative GPSR@taylorandfrancis.com Taylor & Francis Verlag GmbH,
Kaufingerstraße 24, 80331 München, Germany

Printed and bound by CPI Group (UK) Ltd, Croydon, CR0 4YY
08/05/2025
01864522-0002